16   INDUSTRIAL ORGANISATION AND LOCATION

CAMBRIDGE GEOGRAPHICAL STUDIES

Industrial organisation and location

PHILIP McDERMOTT
Principal, McDermott Associates, Auckland, New Zealand

MICHAEL TAYLOR
Research Fellow, Australian National University

CAMBRIDGE UNIVERSITY PRESS

Cambridge
London   New York   New Rochelle
Melbourne   Sydney

Published by the Press Syndicate of the University of Cambridge
The Pitt Building, Trumpington Street, Cambridge CB2 1RP
32 East 57th Street, New York, NY 10022, USA
296 Beaconsfield Parade, Middle Park, Melbourne 3206, Australia

© Cambridge University Press 1982

First published 1982

Printed in Great Britain at
The Pitman Press, Bath

Library of Congress catalogue card number: 81–21586

British Library cataloguing in publication data

Taylor, Michael
Industrial organisation and location.—
(Cambridge geographical studies)
1. Industries, Location of—Great Britain
I. Title   II. McDermott, P. J.
338.6′042′0941   HC260.D4

ISBN 0 521 24671 7

Contents

Preface

This book has its origins in work done in industrial geography since the late 1960s. However, rather than being concerned with factories and the factors that influence their location, it is about organisations and their development. This difference marks a shift in industrial geography from concern with manufacturing plants as the basis for geographic variations in economic development to concern with the larger structures of organisations and enterprises which collectively make up the economy, and of which factories are frequently only components.

However, the study described in this volume is only a first step in an attempt to explore some of the elements of a geography of organisations. At the same time it points the way to a more comprehensive approach to spatial development patterns in which the relationships between individual organisations and sets of organisations are made the focus of future research and possibly even policy making.

The present volume can not be divorced from its antecedents. The foundations for the work were laid by two people in two places, David Keeble at the University of Cambridge and Peter Wood at University College London. Both played a large part in advancing the study of industrial geography from a largely deterministic approach to one in which attention has been directed towards the behavioural processes underlying observed patterns of economic activity in space. Both contributed directly as supervisors to the graduate research programmes through which the various ideas brought together in this study were investigated. To them we express our special thanks. We would also like to acknowledge Dr J. H. Johnson for his advice and comments on the use of q-analysis. However, much of the ground work and idea building for this volume took place at the University of Auckland, New Zealand.

Special mention should also be made of the patience of the many businessmen who, through their cooperation with tedious interviews and interminable questionnaires, may have helped to advance geographical research during the past two decades. Thanks are extended especially to the many members of the electronics industry upon whose assistance the empirical research described in this book is based.

The book itself, however, we dedicate to our long-suffering families.

PHILIP McDERMOTT
MICHAEL TAYLOR
Auckland

Part 1 Location, communication and the organisation

1 Introduction

This book seeks to present an old topic in a new light: to pursue the study of industrial geography as a means of investigating *organisations* as well as locations and areas. Industrial geography, and economic geography in general, has tended to view space as a discrete and disembodied variable somehow independent of the organisations that operate within it. As a direct consequence, the subject has tended to overemphasise space. Although founded in *industrial* geography, the present study attempts to temper this preoccupation by elaborating an organisational perspective for the subject which might enhance the explanation of patterns of location and spatial interaction. The present study therefore moves away from a narrowly based industrial geography preoccupied with manufacturing, towards a more broadly based geography of organisations. It attempts to combine principles and concepts developed in organisation theory with the empirical generalisations of geography. The principles of organisation theory, and especially those of the structural contingency model within it, are fundamentally aspatial. Their combination with geography's empiricism might, therefore, add a basic spatial perspective to the approach, improving understanding of the structure, behaviour and integration of formal organisations. Equally, an organisational perspective adds a long-neglected and all but missing conceptual and theoretical dimension to industrial geography which should substantially improve understanding of the operation of organisations in space.

For a long time industrial geography has laboured under an inappropriate conceptualisation of the organisation, one which has, in fact, assumed all participants to have more or less the same goals, aspirations and motives. This conceptualisation has also been largely accepted in the policy-oriented regional economic development field and may well account for some of its shortcomings too. To assume 'economic man' is to assume that all organisations are the same, thereby obviating the need for conceptualisation and examination of individual organisations and their structures. In short, assuming economic man assumes away the organisation. Behavioural challenges to a stance based on economic man are, therefore, confronted with an urgent need to develop for the first time an adequate conceptualisation and specification of organisational structure rather than adopting, as they have, selected aspects of an outmoded classical construct. It is contended here that such a new formulation might be derived, at least in part, from the structural contingency model in organisation theory,

3

elements of which might profitably be incorporated into industrial geography.

However, the introduction of an organisational perspective into industrial geography is more than the replacement of an outmoded conceptualisation with a more thorough conceptualisation of the organisation. The study of economic activity as a whole can be considered as taking place on three different, but not altogether discrete, scales: a *macro scale* dealing with the political economy involving analyses at the societal level; a *meso scale* dealing with the interactions between places (which has been the primary concern of economic geography); and a *micro scale* operating at the level of the individual organisational and the forces within it, which has been primarily the domain of organisation theory. An adequate understanding of the operation of organisations within a spatial framework must integrate elements from all three levels of analysis, although this is a task of considerable magnitude.

Industrial geography has been preoccupied with the meso scale, a middle ground, and has given little attention to more general issues of societal impacts and pressures on organisations, or more specific issues of the internal structuring of organisations and the decision-making processes within these frameworks. This is not to say that there has been no geographic work aimed at clarifying these more general or more specific issues, for this would devalue the contribution of attempts to develop precise decision-making models in industrial geography, on the one hand, and of attempts to introduce societal considerations in work adopting a Marxist stance or dealing with the social responsibility of corporations, on the other.

This book focuses on the micro scale, the more specific level of the individual organisation or enterprise, to expand appreciation in industrial geography of the processes shaping organisational structures and, therefore, influencing their operations in space. These processes might be internally generated or externally imposed but, through the exploration of causal relationships, it might be possible to throw light on the extent to which environmental and technological forces influence the organisation, its structure and the decision-making processes within an explicitly spatial framework. Furthermore, it may also allow some estimation of the extent to which the organisation or enterprise is in at least partial control of its own destiny insofar as it is able to influence the environment within which it operates. Therefore, this volume represents a first attempt to develop an adequate conceptualisation of the organisation in industrial geography and to specify more fully the range of considerations necessary to provide an adequate understanding of the operations of organisations and their component parts in the space economy.

In combining industrial geography with concepts developed in organisation theory, the present study therefore seeks to establish a more broadly based geography of organisations. Three major problems confront this task:

(1) To distil the essential dimensions of organisational structure and

organisation–environment interaction from the structural contingency model.

(2) to determine the general propositions on spatial aspects of organisation–environment interaction that can be gleaned from linkage and information flow studies in industrial geography.

(3) To integrate these conceptual notions and empirical regularities within an *a priori* model to explain the structure, functioning and location of organisations within an explicitly spatial framework.

These three problems are the concern of the first part of this volume. The second part then attempts to test the validity of this model using information from the UK electronics industry. Although this verification exercise deals exclusively with manufacturing organisations, these are used as the basis for experimentation rather than the focus for conclusions. It is important to stress this point, for there is a need in geography to go beyond the traditional preoccupation with manufacturing plants and firms to a fuller treatment of all types of organisation.

In developing a more broadly based geography of organisations within the present study, there are, however, a number of preliminary issues which must be dealt with concerning definitions and general background. The first issue concerns the definition of terms used to distinguish organisations and their component parts. The second concerns the current conceptualisation of the organisation in industrial geography, especially in the regional development literature which the present study seeks to modify. The third issue concerns the selection of the electronics industry as a suitable vehicle for empirical investigation.

Definitions   Industrial geography suffers from a profusion and confusion of terminology with terms such as 'factory', 'establishments', 'firm', 'plant' and 'enterprise', having, through common parlance, been made virtually interchangeable. More properly, these terms should be regarded as defining a hierarchy of units comprising the organisation (Figure 1.1). The smallest unit is the *establishment*, a single locus at which an organisation operates. In the manufacturing situation such a locus might also be referred to as a *plant*, a *branch plant*, a *factory*, or a *works*. In a non-manufacturing situation the establishment can be an *office* or a *warehouse* or, in a more general sense, simply a *centre of operations*. One or more establishments or centres of operations comprise a *firm* or

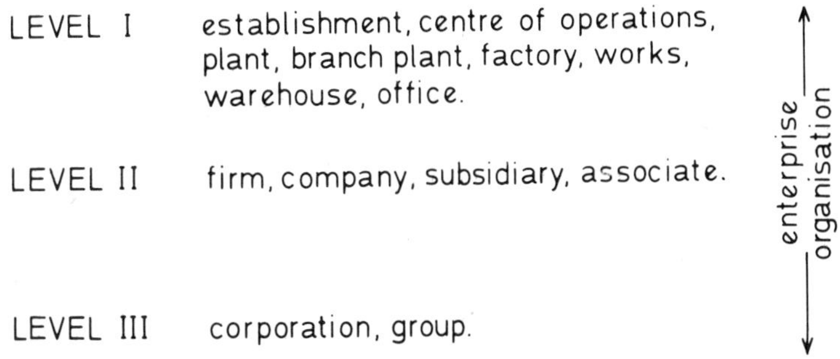

LEVEL I   establishment, centre of operations, plant, branch plant, factory, works, warehouse, office.

LEVEL II   firm, company, subsidiary, associate.

enterprise organisation

LEVEL III   corporation, group.

Figure 1.1 The definition of terms

company. Unfortunately, the term 'firm' has been particularly misused. In a legalistic sense it is a structure designed to meet government regulation, cash flow, and taxation requirements (Stopford and Wells, 1972). However such a designation may have little functional meaning when the firm is only a *subsidiary* of a larger *corporation* or *group*. But, an especially large measure of imprecision has been given to this term from its use in the classical and neoclassical theory of the firm. An essential tenet of this theory is that all organisations operate in a similar fashion to attain a single, profit maximising goal (the dictates of the assumption of economic man). Therefore, all organisations are fundamentally similar, if not the same, and this apparent similarity is further increased by the aspatial nature of the theory itself. Reduced to only one type of organisation, only one label is required to distinguish the decision-making unit, *the firm* – not a battery of unambiguous terms. Within this framework, then, a plant, a company or a corporation can all be called a 'firm' and there is no need to define degrees of autonomy between the levels of the hierarchy. The conflict between this use of the word 'firm' and its use in a legalistic sense is only too plain.

For the purpose of the present study the hierarchic relationship of the terms that are used to distinguish decision-making units can be expressed in diagrammatic form (Figure 1.1), reflecting the discussion above. However, two additional terms are also used: *enterprise* and *organisation*. These are used interchangeably in a generic sense to distinguish relatively autonomous decision-making units. Obviously, there is a major problem involved in measuring autonomy in any precise manner, just as there is a problem in defining ownership and control in the corporate situation (Berle and Means, 1932; Larner, 1966), but here the intention is to use 'enterprise' and 'organisation' to define formal, purposive organisations and production systems. These might be single plants and sites, as in the context of the single plant firm, but they might equally be autonomous subsidiaries or divisions of a corporation or, indeed, the corporation itself.

The organisation and its conceptualisation in industrial geography

The operation of organisations in space has, in the past, been conceived very narrowly in industrial geography with attention directed almost exclusively to the issues of location, the consequences of location decision-making and the patterns of industry distribution that have resulted. In general, industrial geography has not been studied as an end in itself, but as a means to a variety of social and economic ends. For example, the distribution of industrial activity has been investigated to help explain urban, national and even international patterns of economic development and trade flows. At another level, a knowledge of industrial location trends and needs has influenced local infrastructure and service planning and investment. The selective encouragement of economic investment in different areas, particularly within a regional welfare framework, owes much to the observations and generalisations developed in industrial geography. Indeed, the lessons learned from industrial geography and some of the normative principles of location theory have influenced, and are reflected in, the investment decisions of individual organisations, especially those which undertake formal planning. At a more abstract level, models of plant and organisational behaviour in space, which make up industrial location theory, have contributed substantially to the development of multidisciplinary spatial economic theory. Although industrial geography has been largely descriptive and fundamentally preoccupied with pattern, this approach has clearly been fruitful from a variety of points of view.

Attempts to account for the patterns that have been described in industrial geography formerly made recourse to the normative concepts of classical and neoclassical economics. More recently, however, explanation has emphasised the influence that the behaviour of decision-makers may have in shaping these patterns. With the development of this 'behavioural' stance in industrial geography during the past decade, the focus of interest has been widened from the simple description of pattern to embrace all aspects of investment decision-making in firms and organisations. In other words, industrial geography has become more wide-ranging in its examination of spatial behaviour. But, to expand this focus of attention at all adequately, and to raise industrial geography above the level where behaviour is merely described to a level where causal relationships and directions of causality are explored rather than inferred, requires a much fuller and more extensive conceptualisation of the problem under consideration. Indeed, Smith (1971) could not have spelled out this issue more clearly when he complained that industrial geography is long on fact but short on theory.

The need for an organisation-level approach in industrial geography is now acute. Having drawn its conceptualisation in large measure from normative economics, and having rested heavily on the principles of economic man, industrial geography has tended to disregard the individual organisation and treat all decision-making units in much the same manner – as black boxes, capable of a limited number of actions and responses, which are themselves embedded within, and their actions determined by, particular environmental contexts. Notwithstanding the demise of economic man, whose excesses (and contradictions) have been widely debated, the influence of this concept lingers on in the absence of any replacement. Its lingering finds expression in the fact that many studies in industrial geography remain external to the organisation, taking the organisation and its internal processes as given and having no direct bearing upon spatial patterns of production. Nowhere is this stance more apparent than in the cost surface approach to locational explanation in which the organisation is treated as a single plant firm which is no more than a locational 'actor' – one dot in a dot distribution.

Only in behavioural studies of linkages and information flows in geography has any consideration been given to the variable character of organisations, and then only in a very elementary fashion. These studies have started to open the black box of the enterprise using crude and frequently gross variables to describe organisational attributes. But, the absence of a full and adequate conceptual framework to guide the direction of these studies and their choice of variables detracts from the contribution they can make to any understanding of the operation of firms in space. Consequently, the provision of such a conceptual framework in industrial geography and industrial location theory is critical for the future development of these fields of study and their interdisciplinary contribution.

The organisation and regional development

Although regional economic planning has found little of value to policy formation in explanations of location that have relied heavily upon normative economics, a large proportion of the work in industrial geography has, nevertheless, been placed in a regional development context. Constrained by a conceptualisation of the organisation similar to that adopted in more traditional studies of industrial location in geography, diagnoses of regional economic problems have most frequently been grounded in macro-economics. Consequently, the adoption of an organisation-level approach to the study of the spatial aspects of industrial activity would appear to be as urgently required and as potentially important for the formulation of regional development policies and strategies as it is for industrial geography. Indeed, the major significance of policy implications derived from studies adopting an organisation-level approach has already been alluded to in an interregional context (Keeble and McDermott, 1978; Wood, 1978). The adoption of such an approach may also be important for a proper understanding and adequate explanation of the recently raised question of inner city decline in developed countries (Thrift, 1979), for it is possible that the decentralisation of manufacturing from these locations may be not so much a consequence of government policy, but more a coincidental change in the nature of firms and organisations which has led to a dispersal of productive facilities.

The British government has recognised a regional 'problem' since the 1930s (Barlow, 1940), and post-war policy has emphasised the creation of employment opportunities in peripheral areas to redress an apparent imbalance (McCrone, 1968). Major strategies to achieve this aim have included the movement of manufacturing facilities from the south of England and the Midlands to areas designated for assistance (Howard, 1968; Beacham and Osborne, 1970; Keeble, 1971; Manners, 1972), and the encouragement of direct investment in new facilities by external, and frequently foreign, enterprise (Forsyth, 1972; Dicken and Lloyd, 1976). Such strategies find sanction in the belief that regional development differentials are a product of the inefficient spatial allocation of production capacity in comparison with the distribution of both labour and infrastructure (McCrone, 1968). Moreover, policies aimed at achieving spatial equilibrium could be simultaneously directed towards the redress of what was conceived as one of the major underlying causes, namely insufficiently diversified regional economies inherited from 19th century industrialisation (Toothill, 1961; Brown, 1972; Warren, 1972). Explanation of these disparities has also drawn on neoclassical location theory, suggesting that spatial variations in factor costs and accessibility – and therefore in the marginal costs associated with transport – have created competitive disadvantages for industry within the peripheral regions (Cameron and Reid, 1966; Smith, 1971; Brown, 1972).

However, there are contradictions implicit in traditional approaches to the explanation and reduction of regional economic imbalance. Over and above reservations which might be expressed regarding the usefulness of neoclassical location theory (Chisholm, 1971a; Massey, 1974), a diagnosis grounded in *macro-economics* is inconsistent with policy instruments which operate at the level of the *individual organisation*, and intrude directly upon the decision-making process. In Britain, these instruments are based upon selective tax and building subsidies, and capital and employment subsidies, augmented by the disincentive scheme of Industrial Development Certificates applied to more prosperous areas (Chisholm, 1974; Hallett, 1973). Even research into regional policies has, with notable exceptions (Luttrell, 1962; Cameron and Clark, 1966), been concerned mainly with their impact in macro-economic terms (for example, Keeble, 1976; Moore and Rhodes, 1976). Few attempts have been made to gauge the impact of policies on the decision-making in individual companies, that is, the translation of policies designed to correct problems at a macro-level into behaviour at the micro-level (Stewart, 1974; McDermott, 1979). With the exception of work by Green (1974) and Sciberras (1975), this major gulf and research deficiency persists, despite evidence that location decision-making at the firm level does not take place in a manner consistent with the assumptions which underlie macro-economic policies (Townroe, 1969, 1971, 1972; North, 1974; Cooper, 1976).

Although traditional policies may have ameliorated some regional problems in Britain (McCrone, 1972; Donnison, 1974; Keeble, 1974, 1977a), regional economic and social disparities persist (Diamond, 1974; HMSO, 1972). In addition, considerable evidence has accumulated that the importance of some of the 'causes' of these disparities has either been overrated or has diminished (Sant, 1967; Cameron, 1971, 1974; Chisholm and Oeppen, 1973). This has led to the necessary re-evaluation of both problems and policies. Chisholm (1974, 1976) has continued in the macro-economic tradition in his reappraisal of British policy, seeing regional problems as a manifestation of national difficulties, in much the same manner adopted by Lutz (1962) for the interpretation of Italy's regional problems.

At the same time, there has been increased interest in the micro-level of analysis. Of particular concern has been the nature of enterprise and the role it may play in regional economic performance. Attention has been drawn to the major impact that large corporations have on regional performance and development (Parsons, 1972a; Watts, 1972; Evans, 1973; Goddard and Smith, 1978) and to the spatial impact of the reorganisation and rationalisation processes occurring within these firms and organisations (Leigh and North, 1976, 1978; Massey and Meegan, 1976). The spatial impact of a high concentration of branch plants (Townroe, 1975; Sant, 1974) and the implications of high levels of external investment for the further growth of the regional economies (Hamilton, 1976, 273–75) have also been questioned, and doubts have been expressed regarding the employment:capital ratios of establishments which may respond to regional incentives in the form of capital subsidies (Buck and Atkins, 1976). Finally, concern has been expressed about the quality of entrepreneurship and the performance of indigenous enterprise in depressed peripheral economies (Firn, 1974, 1975; Sant, 1974).

These studies mark a growing concern for, and awareness of, the role of individual organisations in shaping differential regional performance. However, having rejected a conceptualisation of the firm and organisation which was consistent with a macro-economic approach to the problem, these studies are left without an appropriate conceptual framework which might lead to their integration. It may be inappropriate to place strong emphasis on cost structures as an integrating device since previous investigations into spatial variations in profitability and productivity have been largely inconclusive (Cameron, 1974; Chisholm, 1976; Parsons, 1972*b*). Instead, attention might more properly be directed towards the nature of the regional environment within which an organisation operates, and which might have bearing upon its structure, behaviour and performance. The network of linkages an organisation establishes within this environment might be conditioned both by the nature of the environment and by its own internal structure. Such an organisation-centred approach coincides with that adopted in the structural contingency models of organisation theory. Should it prove valid as an explanatory framework it could challenge the relevance of regional policies sanctioned by the definition of regional problems at a macro-level.

The UK electronics industry

The electronics industry is an ideal vehicle for investigating the relationships between organisations and their external environments in order to further our understanding of the spatial dimension of enterprise and to assess the policy implications of such an understanding for regional economic planning. Internationally, the electronics industry is a modern growth sector much sought-after both to alleviate regional economic problems and to initiate industrial development. It is also a sector in which inter- and intra-organisational information flows are critical, potentially providing insight into a central concern of the present study. In the United Kingdom context, it has a distinctive distributional pattern and is located not only in the expanding core but also the disadvantaged periphery. Furthermore, the electronics industry has been subject to policy attention in the UK as a means of fostering development in regional areas (McDermott, 1976, 1979; Booz, Allen and Hamilton, 1979).

As a modern, highly scientific and dynamic industry, electronics manufacturing has a record of rapid development based upon occasional major innovations, continuous technological refinement, and progressive extension of market applications. It encompasses a technology which impinges upon a wide range of processes and markets, making the boundaries of the industry somewhat difficult to determine. Electronics manufacturing has its origins in a variety of engineering and electrical activities, while its products are found throughout productive, administrative, distributive, and service sectors. It follows that there is no easy division between electronics and other forms of industry. Boundaries are imposed by the need for consistent terms of reference rather than as a result of any obvious grouping of activities and products.

The British Economic Development Committee for Electronics, a member of the National Economic Development Office (NEDO), recommended adoption of the industry definition proposed by the Electronics Industries Association of the United States (NEDO, 1974):

> The electronics industries are engaged in that branch of science and technology which deals with the study and application of techniques to direct and control the conduction of electricity in a gas, vacuum, liquid or solid state material. Electron tubes and semi-conductors are combined with resistors, capacitors, transformers and similar components in equipments which detect, measure, record, compute and communicate information. (EIA, 1968: 86)

This 'technical' definition emphasises the role of *active* components, which manipulate and direct the flow of electrons and *information* processing. Electronic goods are distinguished from electrical products by the currents they handle, dealing with flows of electrons perhaps millions of times smaller. The flow of electrons is manipulated to produce a series of impulses by which information is registered, transmitted, processed or stored. However, the output (processed information) is usually transformed into usable form by the application of electrical or electro-mechanical devices and processes. Herein lies a major difficulty in distinguishing the limits of the electronics industry as such. While electronics goods depend primarily upon the presence of active components, they are characterised also by a variety of non-electronic components and subassemblies. Conversely, an increasing proportion of electrical and engineering equipment relies for control upon the presence of electronic circuits which programme the sequences to be followed.

Notwithstanding the suitability of this industry as a vehicle for the empirical exercise, it must be stressed that the present study is not simply an examination of the electronics industry. The industry is the subject of experiment as much as a focus for conclusions.

The structure of the study

The task of developing an organisation-level approach in industrial geography and regional economic planning divides the present study into two parts: the elaboration of an explanatory framework; and its testing within the context of the UK electronics industry. In Part I, Chapter 2 attempts to make good the absence of a detailed and thorough conceptualisation of the firm and firm development in industrial geography through a review of organisation theory. Emphasis is placed on the open systems paradigm with particular attention being paid to the contingency model of organisational structure. The three key components of this model, environment, technology and structure, are critically reviewed to identify its strengths and weaknesses as a conceptual foundation for an expanded industrial geography. The relationships between organisations and their environments are examined in

Chapter 3 from an essentially spatial perspective through a review of geographical studies of industrial linkages and information flows. The review highlights the inadequacies of the specification of organisation–environment interactions in industrial geography brought about by the partial specification of interorganisational interaction and the inadequate conceptualisation and specification of organisational structure. The final section of Chapter 3 attempts to integrate the generalisations derived from organisation theory and industrial geography to produce an *a priori* model of organisation–environment interrelationships within an explicitly spatial framework. It also integrates, to a certain extent, the macro, meso and micro scales of analysis, previously distinguished, by charting interconnections and postulating directions of causality between one scale and another.

The empirical study is the second part of the book. Chapter 4 describes the societal environment and environmental domains within which organisations in the UK electronics industry operate, dealing with technological change, the characteristics of different markets, and the role of government and other major institutions within these environments. The internal structure of the sampled organisations is the subject of Chapter 5 together with their performance and development. Chapter 6 deals with the interface between electronics organisations and their environments, and develops a uniform methodology for the measurement and description of interaction fields and communication fields. In Chapter 7, the threads of the empirical investigation are drawn together to establish in a more formal manner the interrelationships between the generalised environmental domain, the more specific task environment, organisation structure and organisational performance. Chapter 8 draws together the findings of the study and explores their implications for industrial geography and regional economic planning.

2 The structural contingency model of organisations

The introduction indicated the sterility lent to industrial geography by inadequate conceptualisation of the nature and behaviour of individual organisations, particularly as this relates to their operation in space. It was also suggested that similar inadequacies of conceptualisation accounted for the limited impact of government policies directed towards the efficient or equitable spatial allocation of industrial investment. This chapter seeks to make good the absence of detailed conceptualisation of the organisation and its development in industrial geography by reviewing closely the field of organisation theory and, in particular, the open systems paradigm as it has evolved in the structural contingency model of organisations.

The firm as a decision-making unit has been more thoroughly conceptualised in organisation theory than in industrial geography and it is contended that the amalgamation of ideas from the structural contingency model (Thompson, 1967; Lawrence and Lorsch, 1967*a*; Kast and Rosenzweig, 1974) with the linkage and information concepts from industrial geography might provide the most profitable avenue for understanding the operations of firms in space. This is not to suggest that some panacea for shortcomings in industrial geography is to be found in the structural contingency model of organisation theory which is not without its own limitations. Indeed, it is the purpose of this chapter to examine the structural contingency model of organisation and to assess what contribution it might make to an improved understanding of the operation of firms in space. Thus, particular attention is paid to the conceptualisation and definition of terms within the structural contingency model.

The structural contingency model

The structural contingency model of organisation hypothesises that environment and technology are related to the structure of complex organisations and will give rise to a range of more or less appropriate organisational forms (Penning, 1975). As such, the model comprises three sets of variables – environment, technology and organisational structure – which interact one with another but with structure most frequently regarded as the dependent set. This contingency approach is a direct derivative of the classical models of management (Weber, 1947; Taylor, 1942) and is closely related to the systems model of management (Harrison, 1978). There is, however, a fundamental difference between the two. While the classical models derive, by and large, from a *closed-system* framework and are concerned with the maintenance of

13

bureaucratic efficiency within the firm, the contingency model springs from an *open-system* framework in which organisational structure is treated as being dependent upon the external constraints and contingencies confronting the firm (Thompson and McEwen, 1958; Katz and Kahn, 1966; Thompson, 1967). Therefore, while the classical models of management attempt to discover the 'one best way' to structure an organisation, the contingency approach envisages a variety of structural forms resulting from different technological and environmental pressures.

The basic characteristics of this open-systems, contingency perspective have been outlined by Katz and Kahn (1966), Thompson (1967) and Haas and Drabeck (1973). They can be conveniently elaborated and examined within the framework of the model of the organisation proposed by Petit (1967) (Figure 2.1) which derives very largely from propositions on the levels of control and responsibility within organisations that were advanced by Parsons (1960).

As an open system involving input, transformation and output, Petit's model treats the organisation as a set of systems within systems, none of which can survive in isolation, but all of which can gain negative entropy

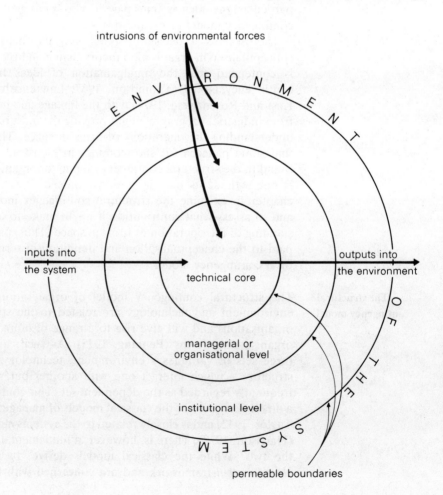

Figure 2.1 Petit's model of firm–environment interaction (after Petit, 1967)

by moving towards states of increased order and organisation. At the centre of the organisation is the technical subsystem, the *core technology*, which produces the goods and services that characterise a particular organisation. This component of the organisation is generally considered to require the greatest degree of stability to perform its task efficiently with the technology that it contains and, therefore, requires the greatest protection possible from the vicissitudes of the external environment. To achieve an approximation of the closed system state that engenders *stability* and *certainty* (Katz and Kahn, 1966), the core technology is buffered by the managerial subsystem within the firm (sometimes called the organisational level) which co-ordinates operations, resolves conflicts within the firm, allocates tasks and formulates policy. The managerial subsystem is, in turn, surrounded by the institutional level of the organisation which deals with those elements of the environment that impinge upon the organisation as a whole, and comprises the *boundary spanning functions* identified by Dill (1958). Beyond and surrounding these subsystems which constitute the firm is the 'environment', a set of systems itself, sometimes referred to as a supra-system. The approach encompassed in Figure 2.1 which defines sets of systems within systems is however not 'reductionistic' but provides a perspective whereby order can be recognised in all subsystems within and around the firm (Bertalanffy, 1968).

Clearly, the different positions of subsystems that make up the organisation reflect variable levels of control and autonomy, with each subsystem having degrees of power over others which may vary over time. An organisation's boundaries also possess an element of imprecision, being ultimately dynamic. Furthermore, paralleling the input–transformation–output sequence in the organisation, is a feedback mechanism whereby subsystems relate one to another and the *environment* intrudes into the organisation. The feedback mechanism converts the organisation into a patterned set of events able to respond to environmental changes and to achieve a reasonable level of self regulation. (Haas and Drabeck, 1973; Katz and Kahn, 1966). These characteristics act to prevent the intrusion of environment into the organisation from completely determining structure. Indeed, the forces of environment can only intrude into the various levels of the organisational system as depicted in Petit's model (Figure 2.1) to the extent that the boundaries between layers are permeable. As Petit (1967) explained:

The technical level has a boundary that does not seal it off entirely from the firms' environment but does have a high degree of closure. The organisational level has less closure and consequently is more susceptible to the intrusion of external elements. The institutional level has a highly permeable boundary and therefore is strongly affected by uncontrollable and unpredictable elements of the environment (p. 346)

Given the relationships between different levels or subsystems within the organisation, and the intrusion of environmental forces into it, organisational subsystems will adapt their behaviour, structure and interrelationships to the internal and external pressure exerted upon them. The mechanisms facilitating this adaptive behaviour have been characterised as the processes of differentiation and integration. *Horizontal differentiation* is thought to lead to the establishment of departments to confront homogeneous sections of the environment. *Vertical differentiation* is thought to establish the appropriate levels and spans of control in the bureaucratic hierarchy of an organisation. *Integration* is reckoned to be essential for the co-ordination of differently structured departments, removing internal tensions and sustaining the performance of the organisation. It is also quite conceivable that similar final structural states could be achieved from different antecedent conditions and via different routes (the so-called equifinality property of open systems). A corollary of this proposition is that under similar external circumstances similar organisational forms will be created, a possibility which is central to the structural contingency paradigm.

It would be wrong to suggest that the structural contingency model of organisations dismisses or replaces classical models of management – far from it. It is perhaps a mark of the partial nature of the paradigm that it still leans upon many of the concepts developed in the closed-system models. For example, it still recognises the organisation as a collection of individuals committed to some goal 'by means of an explicit and stable structure of class, task allocations, roles and relationships' (Starbuck, 1965). However, within the organisation, the derivation of goals and the interrelationships between individuals and groups are dependent not only upon interaction among themselves, but also upon interaction between the focal organisation and other organisations in the environment (Emery and Trist, 1965; Terreberry, 1968). Changes in external relationships may require internal structural shifts, so the structural contingency framework can be seen to create a dynamic framework within which the older, classical concepts of organisation and management, relating to management styles, for example, can be couched.

Nevertheless, the structural contingency model has a number of severe limitations and shortcomings, which stem very largely from the inadequate conceptualisation and specification of key sets of variables, and which, as a consequence, detract from the usefulness of the framework for generating improved understanding of the operation of firms in space. Within the structural contingency framework, as in other behavioural sciences, an open-systems model has been created by little more than grafting simple and naive notions of 'environment' onto existing closed-system management models (Emery and Trist, 1965). Specification of environment has, in fact, amounted to no more than the construction of crude and generalised typologies or sets of circumstances that might be scanned by any particular firm. Furthermore, technology has been treated ambiguously within the model and it has been contended that this set of variables has never been properly integrated into the open-systems framework (Haas and Drabeck, 1973).

To assess the benefits to be obtained from the introduction of structural contingency concepts into industrial geography it is therefore necessary to examine issues relating to environment and technology in some detail. Consequently, the following sections of this chapter will deal with the conceptualisation and specification of first *environment* and then *technology*, and the manner in which they have been reckoned to influence organisational structure.

Environment in the structural contingency model

Specification of the *environment* confronting and surrounding the individual organisation is perhaps the essence of the structural contingency model. Nevertheless, the wide range of studies that have addressed this issue have almost all adopted a highly abstract and generalised stance which, at the same time, is curiously particularised. On the one hand, 'environment' is frequently referred to in highly generalised terms as a supra-system of which the organisation is a component system – a further extension of the systems within systems notion (Thompson, 1967). On the other hand, 'environment' is specified in a very particularised fashion as a host of separate organisations with which a focal organisation may interact and communicate. These counterpart systems include customers, suppliers, competitors and regulators. It is, however, the abstract view of 'environment' which has prevailed when attempts have been made to put the contingency framework into operation. The implicit assumption has been made that an organisation's environment contains so large a number of other organisations and institutions that it acquires an identity of its own, some supra-characteristics, which facilitate generalisation and the drawing up of typologies which are independent of the characteristics of the individual and constituent organisations. In other words, the whole is deemed to be something more than the sum of the parts.

At its broadest, environment can be defined within an open-systems context as *everything* outside the focal organisation. In the terminology of Kast and Rosenzweig (1974), this is the *general* or *societal* environment, an all-embracing notion which has also been referred to as the *macro environment*. Kast and Rosenzweig (1974) identified nine sets of forces operating within this societal environment:

(1) Cultural – the ideologies, values, and norms of a particular society.
(2) Technological – the depth of technological and scientific knowledge in society.
(3) Educational – the general literacy level of a population together with aspects of specialisation and professionalism.
(4) Political – the political climate in a society and the structure of power.
(5) Legal – ranging from constitutional considerations to the impact of specific laws.
(6) Natural resources – the natural endowment of renewable and non-renewable resources.
(7) Demographic – the nature of human resources.
(8) Sociological – class structure and social institutions.
(9) Economic – the general economic framework of a society together with the level of investment.

The comprehensiveness of this specification of environmental forces which influence the operation and structure of individual organisations must be contrasted with the more simplistic notions that have prevailed in industrial geography. Questions of economics have been the almost exclusive concern of industrial location theory, and almost all other elements of the societal environment identified above have been removed through explicit or implicit simplifying assumptions.

However, it would be extremely difficult, if not impossible, to put this broad specification of a societal environment into operation. Any such operationalisation would be of limited empirical value. Of greater significance from a measurement point of view are two aspects of environment, again highly generalised, which were identified by Thompson (1967) in his work which built, in turn, upon earlier studies by Dill (1958), Perrow (1967) and Evan (1966). These are the *domain* and the *task environment* of the organisation. The domain is the group of organisations with which a focal organisation could interact, the points within the societal environment with which that organisation might potentially have contact, given the activity or range of activities it undertakes (Haas and Drabeck, 1973; Thompson, 1967). To establish this domain, however, requires *domain consensus*. Not only does an organisation stake out a sphere of potential operations and impact amongst other organisations, as a result of its charter, but it also needs to be recognised as significant within that sphere by other organisations.

This narrowing of the conceptualisation of environment from the societal environment to the organisational domain has been taken one step further within the structural contingency framework with the development of the concept of the *task environment*, a concept which is potentially more capable of being put into operation. The task environment was defined by Thompson (1967) as the set of organisations with which a focal organisation actually establishes exchange relationships. Such exchanges can be of materials, goods or information and can be considered as fundamental to the survival of the organisation and its decision-making. Dill (1958) categorised the organisations comprising this external task environment as:

(1) customers;
(2) suppliers;
(3) competitors; and
(4) regulators (including government and unions).

Adding a degree of confusion to this straightforward classification is Duncan's (1972) inclusion of technology as a fifth component of the task environment. Dill's categorisation depicts a constellation of other organisations as the task environment; while Duncan removes this tangible quality by adding the more abstract notion of 'technology'. Duncan (1972) also identified technology more closely with the focal organisation by describing the technological component of task environments as acting to (1) meet new technological requirements of an organisation's industry or related industries, and (2) implement new technologies in the industry. This extension of the concept of the task environment must be considered a confusion rather than a clarification, a common tendency amongst studies adopting a structural contingency framework.

In effect, the three components of environment – societal, domain and task environment – represent arbitrary points along a continuum depicting the directness or indirectness with which environmental forces impinge upon the operations of a focal organisation. The relationship is by no means perfect, however, as the impact of a given set of forces or circumstances upon an organisation will be influenced by the amount of relevant information available to it, and the way in which it is monitored; that is, the accuracy of organisational perception.

This environmental continuum also relates to the scale at which environment is considered within the focal organisation. The societal environment, for example, is likely to be delineated by national or cultural considerations, encompassing all potentially relevant systems within a given environment. The domain may be relevant in considering the industry or sector within which an enterprise is active, while the task environment is defined by an organisation's actual contacts at any one point in time.

The aspects of environment identified in the studies outlined above combine to generate very different societal, domain and task environments for individual organisations: different *causal textures* in the terminology of Emery and Trist (1965). Indeed, causal texture should be viewed as the dynamic framework within which interaction between the organisation and its environment takes place. The components that make up any organisation's environment will vary over time as cultural, social and technological changes (changes which appear to be speeding up) proceed at different rates, and this will promote environmental uncertainty (Kast and Rosenzweig, 1974). What is more, as Stinchcombe (1965) has suggested, certain societal conditions are especially conducive to the growth of complex and diverse organisations, these conditions being:

(1) literacy and specialised, advanced schooling;
(2) urbanisation;
(3) a money economy;
(4) political change; and
(5) a density of social life which is also organisationally rich.

The growth of complex organisations, and the birth of new organisations, which might be stimulated by the same conditions, holds the obvious implication that since a dynamic environment usually confronts dynamic organisations the two may or may not be in phase.

However, this detailed conceptualisation of organisational environments in the structural contingency model is only poorly matched, if it is matched at all, by the way in which environments have been measured and calibrated in empirical studies. Indeed, empirical studies adopting the structural contingency approach have completely avoided the complexity of organisational environments by relying upon *a priori* typologies to measure 'environment'. Through this simplification and the arbitrary selection of only the characteristics of organisational environ-

Table 2.1 *Duncan's typology of environments and perceived environmental uncertainty (after Duncan, 1972)*

	Simple	Complex
	Low perceived uncertainty	*Moderately low perceived uncertainty*
Static	Factors and components (1) small in number (2) similar to one another (3) unchanging	Factors and components (1) large in number (2) dissimilar (3) unchanging
	Moderately high perceived uncertainty	*High perceived uncertainty*
Dynamic	Factors and components (1) small in number (2) similar to one another (3) continually changing	Factors and components (1) large in number (2) dissimilar (3) continually changing

ments deemed salient to the researcher, Jurkovich (1974) has argued that environmental typologies are important analytical tools capable of stimulating thinking on the alternative courses of action open to decision-makers. However, before any one typology can lay claim to significant analytical power, agreement needs to be reached on the salient characteristics of organisational environments. There is little evidence that such a consensus has yet been achieved, as indicated by work undertaken in the field to date.

Thompson (1967) identified only two environmental characteristics which he depicted as discrete continua: a *homogeneous/heterogeneous* continuum and a *stable/shifting* continuum. The significance of these dimensions for organisational structure was explained as, 'the more heterogeneous the task environment, the greater the constraints presented to the organisation. The more dynamic the task environment, the greater the contingencies presented to the organisation' (p. 73). Lawrence and Lorsch (1967b) recognised two equivalent continua, but referred to them as environmental *diversity* and environmental *dynamics*. To Duncan (1972), in his study of perceived environmental uncertainty, two continua, labelled *simple/complex* and *static/dynamic*, were identified as the key environmental characteristics (Table 2.1). Hill (1974) added to this confusion of terminology by typifying task environments according to *stability/instability* and *independence/interconnectedness* dichotomies. The independence/interconnectedness variable was held to relate to the degree of dependence upon 'exogenous claimants' – the organisations comprising the task environment, an elaboration which appears to have done little other than to add to the semantic armoury of organisation theory.

The similarity of these approaches for the development of typologies is self-evident, and Table 2.2 attempts to portray the equivalence of terminology used in the four studies. Indeed, this list of terms has been augmented by Harrison (1978) who has seen *complexity* and *rate of*

Table 2.2 *Interchangeability of terminology in selected schemes of environmental classification*

Thompson (1967)	Lawrence & Lorsch (1967)	Duncan (1972)
(1) homogeneous/stable	(1) low diversity/no dynamism	(1) simple/static
(2) homogeneous/shifting	(2) low diversity/high dynamism	(2) simple/dynamic
(3) heterogeneous/stable	(3) high diversity/no dynamism	(3) complex/static
(4) heterogeneous/shifting	(4) high diversity/high dynamism	(4) complex/dynamic

Hill (1974)	Harrison (1978)
(1) interconnected/high stability	(1) simple/rapid rate of change
(2) interconnected/low stability	(2) simple/slow rate of change
(3) independent/high stability	(3) complex/rapid rate of change
(4) independent/low stability	(4) complex/slow rate of change

change as the common themes in schemes of environmental classification.

Emery and Trist (1965) developed perhaps the most cited typology of organisational environments on the basis of a wide range of characteristics, including competition, risk and uncertainty, strategy, and environmental networks. Their approach was, nevertheless, to elaborate only four ideal environmental types (so-called causal textures). These were held to coexist in the 'real world' in different combinations to create a large range of environments within which particular firms might operate. The simplest category in the Emery and Trist typology, the *placid and randomised* environment, is characterised by slow change and minimal instability. Being random, the optimal strategy that an enterprise could adopt to deal with uncertainty in this type of environment was no more than the simple tactic of attempting to do one's best on a purely local basis, much as was postulated in the classical economic model of perfect competition (Harrison, 1978, p. 363). More complicated was the second type of environment, the *placid, clustered* environment in which organisational goals and environmental noxiants ('goods' and 'bads') were postulated as clustered and non-randomly distributed. The organisation under these conditions would need a more adequate knowledge of its environment, with strategy replacing tactics and some specialities developing (*distinctive competence*) to achieve strategic goals. Such an environment has been equated with the economists' conditions of imperfect competition. The *disturbed–reactive* environment constituted the third ideal type. It was thought to contain a number of similar organisations and equates with the economists' situation of oligopoly. Uncertainty and complexity were considered to be extremely high with organisations needing to be flexible to make and meet competitive challenge, which would involve absorption and parasitism for the first time. The most complex and rapidly changing environments in the Emery and Trist typology were labelled *turbulent* and involved 'a gross increase in [the organisation's] area of *relevant uncertainty*' (Emery and Trist, 1965, p. 26). Clearly, this typology is more abstract than those previously cited, its main virtue being the introduction of the notion that environments may be transformed from a predictable to an increasingly unpredictable state. It is virtually impossible to calibrate, however, and therefore adds little more than semantic complexity to the structural contingency framework.

Terreberry (1968) has further extended and elaborated Emery and Trist's abstract typology of organisational environments by attempting to develop a common conceptual framework of the organisation, its transactional interdependencies and the environment, given the historical conditions that:

(1) organisational environments are increasingly turbulent;
(2) organisations are increasingly less autonomous; and
(3) other formal organisations are increasingly important components of organisational environments.

From this conceptual model she drew some tentative hypotheses – a first faltering step towards operationalisation of highly complex conceptualisations of environment.

Jurkovich (1974) has maintained that the sorts of typology so far outlined are all oversimplifications of a complex phenomenon and in his own work he attempted to develop a core typology embracing 64 environmental types (Figure 2.2). He considered there to be four primary environmental factors confronting the organisation: (1) complexity; (2) the routineness or non-routineness of the problem-opportunity state; (3) the presence of organised or unorganised sectors in the environment; and (4) whether the organisations within the environment are directly or indirectly related to the focal organisation. These factors, however, would not be constant and to categorise movement in organisational environments he identified *stability* (stable/unstable) and *rate of change* (low/high) as the key dimensions (Figure 2.2). Bell (1974) proposed a similarly ambitious multivariate typology of organisational environments, but with yet another set of variables including:

(1) dependence/independence of environment;
(2) influential/non-influential environment;
(3) friendly/unfriendly;
(4) demanding/non-demanding;
(5) stable/unstable;
(6) predictable/unpredictable;
(7) homogeneous/heterogeneous.

These studies are amongst the first attempts to develop multivariate typologies of environments which have the capability of calibration. As a result they also demonstrate more clearly the difficulty of achieving consensus as to what constitute salient environmental characteristics.

Movement		General Characteristics															
		Noncomplex						Complex									
		Routine				Nonroutine				Routine				Nonroutine			
		Organised		Un-organised		Organised		Un-organised		Organised		Un-organised		Organised		Un-organised	
		D	I	D	I	D	I	D	I	D	I	D	I	D	I	D	I
Low change rate	Stable																
	Unstable																
High change rate	Stable																
	Unstable																

D = Direct   I = Indirect

Figure 2.2 Jurkovich's core typology of organisational environments (after Jurkovich, 1974)

Indeed, the expansion in typological complexity which they represent could be, in fact, infinite, for Jurkovich also contended that his own typology could be extended to include more variables. He suggested, for example, the inclusion of a tripartite variable for 'friendly', 'unfriendly' and 'neutral' competitors (p. 392).

There is obviously a major measurement problem associated with all the environmental typologies examined in this section. How can degrees of 'friendliness', 'predictability', 'homogeneity', 'stability', 'complexity' or 'directness' be measured? Studies of organisations reported in *Administrative Science Quarterly*, for example, would indicate the range of measurement indices to be almost as great as the number of authors addressing themselves to the issue. Indeed, it was the extreme difficulty of developing measurement instruments which led Hill (1974) to choose what he admitted to be an unambitious bivariate approach to the classification of organisational environments.

More importantly, however, there is a major problem associated with reconciling these *a priori* environmental typologies with the conceptualisation of organisational structure within the structural contingency model. The conceptual framework envisages horizontal differentiation within the organisation producing separate boundary spanning functions (sales, marketing, personnel and purchasing, for instance) which would each confront homogeneous segments of the task environment. Therefore, does the environment defined in any particular typology refer to just one of these homogeneous segments relating to a specific boundary spanning function, or does it refer to the task environment of the organisation as a whole? In either case we are left with a nonsense exacerbated by the fact that different organisations will display different degrees of horizontal differentiation largely depending upon their size. If, on the one hand, a particular typology refers to the environment of only a single boundary spanning function, there arises a problem of aggregation to derive the task environment for the organisation as a whole. If, on the other hand, reference is made to the task environment for the organisation as a whole, a problem may arise in subdividing it into homogeneous segments.

It can be suggested that, notwithstanding this background of semantic confusion, lack of agreement on salient environmental characteristics, and ambiguity in the way in which environmental typologies can be related to organisational structure, the progressive elaboration and extension of these typologies represents an approach which would ultimately lead to the specification of individual linkages and business contacts within environmental networks. In short, the structural contingency theory of organisations would seem set to identify the individual organisations that comprise organisational environments, along with the nature of the connections between them and the focal organisation. The extension of this approach, which has seen a movement from abstract views based on a few continua towards overspecified typologies based on a multitude of continua, may lead to the stance developing in industrial geography, where individual linkages have been the subject of study. Within industrial geography only customers, suppliers, and sources of information flows have been recognised as counterparts in the environment. However, by inference rather than practice, structural contingency models embrace all organisations whose activities impinge upon the focal organisation, whether this involves formal exchanges or not. It would seem that while organisation theory has expended great effort on conceptualising 'environment' it has done little to operationalise the concepts in any useful or meaningful way. In contrast, linkage and information flow studies in geography have gone a long way in addressing the problems of measuring organisation–environment interactions at a highly disaggregated level but within a partially and only poorly developed conceptual framework (Chapter 3).

Despite the problems associated with the development of satisfactory specification of the environments confronting organisations, the structural contingency approach has handled the internal structural implications of organisation–environment interactions much more thoroughly than have studies in industrial geography. In the following section, therefore, the impact of environment on firm structure will be examined as revealed in a series of empirical studies.

Basic to the structural contingency model is the proposition that organisations identify homogeneous segments of their task environments and establish boundary spanning structures which cut across the managerial and institutional levels of the Petit model (Figure 2.1). This is the process of differentiation in organisations (Lawrence and Lorsch, 1967*a*) which can assume two forms. *Vertical* differentiation establishes the hierarchy and the number of levels within an organisation, while *horizontal* differentiation creates, for administrative purposes, an appropriate division of an organisation's activities into separate departments. The bases for horizontal differentiation have been suggested as threefold:

(1) functional (distinguishing manufacturing, marketing, engineering, and research and development, for example);
(2) product-based (especially in large complex organisations); and
(3) locational (important for large-scale multinational concerns) (Dale, 1952; Newman *et al.*, 1972).

Together, horizontal and vertical differentiation have been reckoned to establish the formal structure of an organisation. Based on observation of 1500 component organisations and the 53 larger government agencies to which they belonged, Blau (1970) has gone so far as to attempt a formal theory of differentiation within organisations. To achieve this end he derived a small number of general propositions on differentiation that matched empirical regularities. These main propositions, plus the nine others that were subsequently derived, are presented in Table 2.3.

Within the structural contingency model management structure and the number of boundary spanning subsystems in a firm are held to be dependent upon the nature of the environment, regardless of the various qualities this environment has been ascribed in different typologies. Separate boundary spanning structures might encompass sales, marketing, production, personnel, research, transport and so on. Not all will be of equal importance and Thompson (1973) has attached a special measure of importance to the *output* tasks that are essential to the functioning of any organisation, stating that:

Because disposition of its product is imperative for any complex purposive organisation, the transaction structure is crucial. It may dictate or place significant constraints on (*a*) the acquisition of necessary inputs by the organisation, (*b*) the internal arrangement for allocation and co-ordination of resources and activities, and (*c*) the political and "institutional" requirements of the organisation. The pivotal nature of the output relationship thus claims the attention not only of those in output roles but also those at the several administrative levels. (pp. 231–2)

In a landmark study, Burns and Stalker (1961) related management structure to environmental conditions in the English and Scottish electronics industry. They distinguished two end-points of a continuum of managerial styles through which the structure of an organisation might be aligned with its environment. These extremes were identified as *mechanistic* and *organic* styles. The mechanistic style of control was

Table 2.3 *The propositions and subpropositions advanced by Blau (1970) as a formal theory of differentiation in organisations*

Proposition 1	Proposition 2
The increasing size of organisations generates structural differentiation along various dimensions at decelerating rates.	Structural differentiation enlarges the administrative component in organisations.
1.1 As the size of organisations increases, its marginal influence on differentiation decreases.	2.1 The large size of an organisation indirectly raises the administrative ratio (the ratio of administrative personnel to other personnel) through the structural differentiation it generates.
1.2 The larger the size of an organisation, the larger the size of its structural components of all kinds.	2.2 The direct effects of large organisational size lowering the administrative ratio exceed the indirect effects of size which lower the ratio owing to the structural differentiation that large size generates.
1.3 The proportionate size of the average structural component decreases with increases in organisational size.	2.3 (conjectured). The differentiation of large organisations into sub-units stems the decline in the economy of scale in management with increasing size.
1.4 The larger the organisation, the wider the span of supervisory control.	
1.5 Organisations exhibit an economy of scale in management.	
1.6 The economy of scale in administrative overheads declines with increasing organisational size.	

thought to be most suited to the demands of a stable, relatively unchanging environment – Emery and Trist's (1965) 'placid and randomised' environment or Thompson's (1967) homogeneous and stable environment (Table 2.2). Confronted with such an environment, Thompson (1967) saw the organisation as a whole as having few functional divisions or departments, and those it did have would be very similar one to another. Departments would depend on formal or even written rules for both internal operation and environmental interaction since all possible eventualities would be predictable and routine procedures could be established to deal with any situations that might arise. Internal administration would function simply through the imposition of sets of rules. The mechanistic form of management can be equated with the classical bureaucratic model of management with many levels in the managerial hierarchy and many short spans of control (Figure 2.3). In

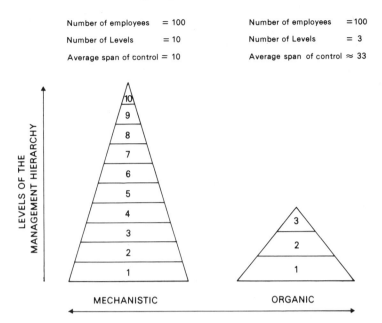

Figure 2.3 Hierarchic
levels and spans of control
in organic and mechanistic
organisational structures
(adapted from Duncan,
1978)

contrast stands the organic style of management with few levels in the
managerial hierarchy and wide spans of managerial control, an arrangement which has been held to be conducive to communication within a
management team and appropriate to 'changing conditions which give
rise constantly to problems and unforeseen requirements for action
which cannot be broken down or distributed automatically' (Burns and
Stalker, 1961, p. 121). In general, therefore, the greater the *stability* or
instability of the environment, the more likely is the management
structure to take on respectively a *mechanistic* or *organic* form.

Research establishments are examples of organisation facing grossly
unstable task environments and, therefore, those most likely to develop
extreme forms of organic management. In the organic organisation any
hierarchy is likely to emerge as a result of interpersonal relations rather
than through rank based upon length of membership, for example. It is
precisely this situation which Allen (1977) has most fully explored for
the management of research, invention and innovation. By analysing
contact networks between individuals in research departments he was
able to identify key reference personnel (Allen and Cohen, 1969) and
therefore, the elements of a managerial hierarchy arrived at by consensus, and one which, as a result, possessed the capacity for reasonably
rapid change.

The organisational characteristics associated with each of the polar
styles of management, either organic or mechanistic, have been summarised by Hower and Lorsch (1967) in their study of organisational
inputs. This summary is presented in Table 2.4. In this comparison of
polar management systems, the organic and mechanistic styles are
shown to differ in eleven important respects relating to management
form, internal communication, authority and decision-making. All
these variables underscore the increased rigidity and formalisation

Table 2.4 *Comparative characteristics of organic and mechanistic management systems* (after Hower and Lorsch, 1967)

	Types of management system	
Organisational characteristics	Organic	Mechanistic
(1) Span of control	wide	narrow
(2) Number of levels of authority	few	many
(3) Time span over which an employee can commit resources	long	short
(4) Degree of centralisation of decision making	low	high
(5) Quantity of formal rules	low	high
(6) Specificity of job goals	low	high
(7) Specificity of required activities	low	high
(8) Content of communication	advice and information	instructions and decisions
(9) Knowledge-based authority	high	low
(10) Position-based authority	low	high
(11) Opportunity for task-related interpersonal contact	high	low

which accompanies progression towards the mechanistic extreme of the management continuum.

Despite the preponderance of conceptual treatises, a number of studies have attempted to verify, through analyses of empirical data, the hypotheses that have been developed concerning the impact of environment on organisational structure. Prominent amongst these studies is the work of Lawrence and Lorsch (1967*a*) which deserves examination in some detail.

The postulated segmentation of an organisation into subgroups dealing with aspects of the organisation's task environment was seen by Lawrence and Lorsch to require both internal *differentiation* and *integration*. Differentiation referred not to segmentation of the system alone, as has previously been described, but also to differences in attitudes and behaviour, depending upon the extent to which each subgroup or department in an enterprise develops specific attributes in response to its relevant segment of the environment. Integration, on the other hand, was taken to refer to the state of collaboration between these subgroups. For the purposes of the study, four dimensions of differentiation were identified:

(1) orientation to particular goals – the extent to which a department is focused on its task;
(2) time orientation – the time perspective within which questions are viewed in different departments, from long-term to short-term perspectives;
(3) interpersonal orientation within departments from a 'getting the job done' arrangement to one which seeks to maintain peer relationships;

(4) formality of the structure of subgroups – from the organic to the mechanistic in the terms used by Burns and Stalker.

In the first instance, the analysis drew on information for six plastics manufacturing organisations operating within what was established to be a diverse and dynamic environment. Within each firm four functional departments were recognised – sales, production, applied research and fundamental research – each of which faced a particular segment of the organisational environment. From existing literature *a priori* hypotheses on each of the four dimensions of differentiation were developed.

It was anticipated that the research departments would have the least formal *structure*, since they faced the most uncertain tasks, while the production departments would fall at the other extreme. Tasks would be routine and greater control exercised in the face of greater certainty. The sales department, it was conjectured, would be placed between these two extremes on the structural formality dimension. *A priori*, it was suggested that environmental uncertainty would create task-oriented interpersonal orientation, while environmental certainty would lead to a de-emphasising of social relationships and an emphasising of attitudes of 'getting the job done'. For the *orientation* aspect of differentiation, Lawrence and Lorsch contended that in a sales department there would be rapid feedback from the environment and, therefore, a short-term focus of interest. Research scientists and engineers, it was contended, would have long-range concerns related to the length of time required for problem solving and the development of new products. Finally, concerning *goal orientation*, Lawrence and Lorsch maintained that efficient managers would focus on specialised tasks, with sales personnel being concerned primarily with customer problems, competition, and the market place in general, and manufacturing personnel being primarily interested in cost reduction, process efficiency, raw materials sources and labour markets, for example. More diffuse goals were held to be a sign of inefficiency.

By and large, the relationship hypothesised by Lawrence and Lorsch were found to hold true for the plastics industry, and the research findings for three of their four dimensions of differentiation are shown diagrammatically in Figure 2.4. For goal orientation, however, the research laboratories ran counter to the hypothesised trend, having far less focus than was anticipated. Lawrence and Lorsch also found that in the diverse and dynamic environment of the plastics industry, the more effective organisations, judged in terms of product innovation and

Figure 2.4 Dimensions of differentiation for four functional departments of enterprise in the plastics industry (from Lawrence and Lorsch, 1967)

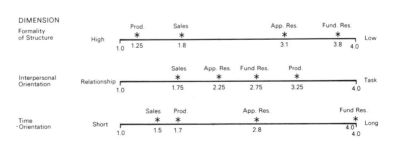

Table 2.5 *Indices of required differentiation between pairs of depart-ments in organisations facing different environments* (from Lawrence and Lorsch, 1967, Table IV–4, p. 95)

| | Industries | | |
Departments	Plastics	Food	Containers
Sales/research	12	3	9
Sales/production	5	10	5
Research/production	15	13	5

growth of profits and sales, possessed higher states of both differen-tiation and integration between departments than the less effective organisations. Integration between departments was achieved through a group or department of integrators which, to be effective in conflict resolution, had to develop goal, time and interpersonal orientations midway between those of the departments they were linking, together with a similarly intermediate departmental structure.

Lawrence and Lorsch extended their work to cover organisations of two other industries operating in other types of environment – the standardised container industry operating in a relatively certain environ-ment, and the packaged foods industry operating in an environment intermediate in certainty to those of the container and plastics indus-tries. In terms of the index employed by Lawrence and Lorsch, the degree of differentiation of departments in each industry required by the exigencies of the environments they confront is shown in Table 2.5. The conclusion reached by these authors was that 'in a more diverse and dynamic field, such as the plastics industry, effective organisations have to be highly integrated and highly differentiated. In a more stable and less diverse environment, like the container industry, effective organisations have to be less differentiated, but they must still achieve a high degree of integration' (Lawrence and Lorsch, 1967*a*, p. 108).

Basic integrating devices in all organisations were shown in this study to be the managerial hierarchy, rules, procedures and the 'paper' system, while organisations faced by more diverse environments de-veloped specific integrative devices, including personnel fulfilling in-tegrating roles, integrating departments, and cross-functional teams. To be effective, however, integrators were found to need relatively high standing in the organisation and they were shown to be more effective when they employed open and confronting approaches to conflict resolution.

Much subsequent work on the impact of environment on organisa-tional structure refers back to this landmark study by Lawrence and Lorsch (1967*a*) and a large number of studies add significant embellish-ments to the foundation they laid. Amongst these embellishments on the impact of environment on firm structure five can be singled out:

(1) the impact of environmental change as opposed to diversity;

(2) the significance of environmental uncertainty with respect to routine and non-routine decision-making;
(3) the impact of time;
(4) the degree of control exerted over the environment by the firm itself; and
(5) the significance of perceived, as opposed to 'real world', environments.

Gabarro's (1973) concern was with environmental change which he explored in the context of two school systems (rather than individual schools) comprising territorially dispersed schoolhouses and centralised support groups. Apart from extending Lawrence and Lorsch's findings to embrace service organisations, he showed that differentiation occurs in organisations operating in changing environments which are not particularly diverse. Environmental change was seen to require both long-term and short-term changes. Coping in the interests of short-term viability gains the ascendancy over longer-term issues unless these are recognised explicitly. Consequently, differentiation in organisations is needed to deal effectively with the long-term and short-term implications of environmental change.

Duncan (1973) attempted to identify the relationships between three sets of variables – structural modification in decision units, uncertainty and organisational effectiveness – in a study of 22 decision units in six organisations (three manufacturing and three R and D organisations). Having judged organisational effectiveness through goal attainment, integration and structural adaptation, his work tended to confirm the contingency theory as proposed by Lawrence and Lorsch (1967a). However, he also showed that, under conditions of high environmental uncertainty, a decision unit may need to adopt very different organisational structures and forms of differentiation to deal with the distinctive information gathering and processing requirements of routine, as opposed to non-routine, decision-making if it is to remain effective. Low environmental uncertainty, by way of contrast, was seen to obviate this need for differentiation in relation to routine and non-routine decision-making.

Hirsch (1975) adopted a somewhat different stance on environment. In going beyond the individual organisation's task environment to the industry environment or, more properly, the organisational domain, in the pharmaceutical and record manufacturing industries, he recognised 'complex levels of institutional processes still largely unexplored by students of organisations' (p. 327). What is more, by using an historical approach he recognised a time perspective in a field usually explored only through cross-sectional studies. The conclusions reached by Hirsch in his study of 53 managers in the two industries again complement those of Lawrence and Lorsch, but also show organisational effectiveness – which he defined in terms of profitability – to be related to an organisation's ability to exert control over relevant parts of its own external environment. The significance of this finding is that it counterbalances the environmental determinism which is found in many studies adopting the contingency framework.

Further elaborating the impact of the organisation on the environment, Pfeffer (1972*a*) has considered the board of directors as an instrument capable of acting in this fashion. From a study of 80 corporations, he was able to show that board size and composition are not random, but rational responses to external environmental conditions. Corporations use their boards to co-opt or partially absorb important external organisations with which they are interdependent – the organisations of their task environment. Not all organisations possess the power to co-opt, however, and they may have external directors *imposed* upon them. Co-option, furthermore, is but one among a number of strategies that organisations can employ to manage their environments and Pfeffer, in a second study (1972*b*), has identified these other strategies as the use of long-term contracts, illegal collaboration, joint ventures, the use of the power of the state, and finally, merger, the ultimate strategy to reduce environmental uncertainty and interdependence.

Considerations of time in relation to the impact of environment on the organisation have been explored conceptually by Goodman (1973) using an elaboration of Emery and Trist's (1965) typology. The conclusion reached in this study was that:

A rich knowledge of the immediate environment leads to short-run effectiveness (tactical brilliance) but it may also lead to long-term ineffectiveness. It does this by shortening the organisational time horizon (strategic myopia). This effect tends to create long-term effectiveness when there is a mismatch between the present environment and the future environment. Conversely, lessening the richness with which the immediate environment is known, lengthens the actual time horizon. This increases the ability to cope with present/future environmental mismatch but at some risk to the present. (p. 225)

Most of the work undertaken on organisational environments has concerned *actual environments* (Dill, 1958; Burns and Stalker, 1961; Lawrence and Lorsch, 1967*a*; Thompson, 1967; and Hirsch, 1975 for example). However, the decision-maker may not react to the 'real' stimuli and constraints imposed by the environment. Environmental impingement may be indirect through the perception of the decision-makers, and this fundamental point has been explored by Negandhi and Reimann (1973) using a sample of 30 manufacturing firms in India. Compared with the United States, the industrial environment of India was suggested as being very much more stable, with predictable and controllable technological and market change. Nevertheless, it was found that organisations in India did not view their environment uniformly and their concern for environmental agents (customers, suppliers, stockholders, government and so on) represented many different dimensions; some with a long-term perspective, others with a short-term perspective. The findings of the study showed that firms having greater concern for the long-term roles of the agents in their task environments had organic management structures. They also tended to adopt consultative decision-making practices. In contrast, firms that had a short-term perspective of their task environments tended to have centralised, bureaucratic organisational structures. Negandhi and Reimann (1973) also showed that the more decentralised firms in the Indian context were also the most effective in both behavioural and economic terms, notwithstanding the relatively stable task environment in India. This finding was felt to be at odds with the findings of Lawrence and Lorsch who had previously suggested that centralised structures were most effective in stable environments and that decentralised structures in such environments were dysfunctional. This apparent conflict of findings highlights the critical importance of managerial perception of the meaning of environmental information, a point that has also been made by Dill (1958).

Not all studies lend support to the contingency theory outlined. A study by Douglass (1976) of 46 US-owned subsidiaries and Danish-owned firms operating in Denmark falls into this category. Judging the performance of firms on increases in sales and net profits over a five-year period he showed high performance to be associated with reduced organisation/environment interaction (men, money, materials and information flows, goods, customers, suppliers, competitors, labour, stockholders and other institution interrelationships). Although he postulated no causal relationships in his study, Douglass' findings imply that effectiveness is directly associated with closure of the organisational system, almost a contradiction of the Lawrence and Lorsch proposition that high performance firms, through strong differentiation and organic management structures, tend to be attuned and open to their environments. Presumably the difference reflects the nature of the environment. In a more stable environment (or period) closure could facilitate internal development.

It is clear, however, that there is a large measure of consensus on the impact of environment on organisational structure, notwithstanding the problems that have surrounded the specification of environment in the structural contingency model. The fundamental relationship would appear to be that, while unstable, complex environments generate organic structures within effective organisations, stable and simple environments favour mechanistic structures. Significant caveats have also been attached to this proposition reflecting concern for perception, time, determinism and a number of neglected environmental conditions. However, organisational structure has also been seen to be significantly affected, if not determined, by technological as well as environmental constraints. The next sections of this chapter deal with the conceptualisation of technology within the structural contingency framework and the impact that technology has been thought to have on organisational structure. It should be remembered, however, that it is artificial, though convenient, to consider the forces of environment and technology as discrete sets for, in reality, there is an extensive degree of overlap between them.

Technology in the structural contingency model

Much of the discussion of environment in organisation theory has maintained that *technology* is a fundamental dimension of environment which remains external to the focal organisation. This tenet is nowhere better exemplified than in the classic study of Lawrence and Lorsch (1967*a*) who interpreted the findings of Woodward (1965) and Burns and Stalker (1961) on the relationships between organisational structure and technology to mean that 'differing technical and economic conditions outside the firm necessitated different organisational conditions within' (p. 15). Quite plainly, technology to these authors is an exogenous force embedded within the societal environment which influences the firm in a potentially deterministic fashion. On this basis it is reasonable to suggest that, as part of the exogenous environment, technology impinges upon the focal organisation as information either on new technologies themselves or on the consequences of adoption and adaptation of such technologies by competitors, suppliers and customers.

Lawrence and Lorsch's definition of technology as an exogenous variable is related to Simon's (1957) philosophical proposition that technology is 'the stock of all human knowledge' and relates to man's problem solving ability. This set of ideas was well expressed by Bell (1974) who held that:

every society has a technological base of skills, tools and knowledge that its members and formal organisations use to provide for their needs. . . . The structures or organisations within a society, then, are highly dependent on the levels of technology existing in that society. (p. 265)

It conflicts, however, with a 'nuts and bolts' definition of technology of the sort employed by Penning (1975) who defined technology as pertaining to, 'the internal operations of the organisation, that is the means that the organisation uses to convert inputs into outputs' (p. 394). Such a mechanical definition of technology treats technological pressure on firm structure as internal to the organisation. Indeed, this is exactly the stance adopted by Woodward (1965) when she used the definition of technology as the tools and machines needed to perform a given task, and as the ideas expressing the goals of the task and the rationale of the methods employed (Duncan, 1978).

These two approaches place technology in an ambiguous position in the contingency model of organisational structure, an ambiguity which can again be illustrated in relation to Petit's model of the organisation (Figure 2.1). The 'environmental knowledge' definition implies that technology influences an organisation from the outside, impinging firstly at the institutional level and then, with progressively less force, inwards towards the core technology. The contrasting 'nuts and bolts' definition of technology implies that technology is an internal force, influencing organisational structure from within, and operating in an outward direction.

The consequences of ambiguity in the role of technology in the contingency model of organisational structure are well illustrated by the definition of technology adopted in the Lawrence and Lorsch (1967*a*) study. These authors appear to have misinterpreted the findings of Woodward's (1965) study, which employed an internalised 'nuts and bolts' definition of technology, by using her findings to indicate the significance of technology as an exogenous environmental force. However, this misinterpretation of technology marries perfectly with their own definition of environment which was extended to include the equipment used *within* the focal organisation:

> Contrary to conventional usage, we have chosen to conceive of the physical machinery, the non-human aspect of production, as part of the environment. Production executives must draw information from this equipment's performance and analyse it in terms of costs, yields and quality, just as they must draw information from outside the physical boundaries of the firm about newly available equipment and alternative processes. (p. 23)

A caveat of this nature about technology contorts any definition of environment. It conflicts directly with the ideas of internal and external organisational environments proposed by Duncan (1972) and effectively turns the firm inside out. Given that a 'nuts and bolts' definition of technology implies internal pressures within the firm to generate an organisational structure appropriate for its 'fulfilment', and that an environmental knowledge definition of technology implies external pressures acting to create an organisational structure capable of ameliorating them, it is not surprising that Penning (1975) saw confusion in the integration of technology and environment within the structural contingency framework. However, he did make the important point that both technology and environment relate to uncertainty. Environment can be described in terms of stability, differentiation, complexity, resourcefulness and competitiveness, all of which are variables characterised by uncertainty. Technology, too, can be defined in terms of uncertainty, particularly in relation to problem solving and search behaviour, so that *uncertainty* might be proposed as the integrating concept.

Recourse to uncertainty is, nevertheless, hardly an adequate solution to the ambiguity surrounding the role of technology in the structural contingency model. This ambiguity may well be a product of semantic confusion which the introduction of 'uncertainty' may only compound rather than reconcile. Indeed, from a survey of the literature, we are left, in the end, with Haas and Drabeck's (1973) inconclusive and largely unhelpful comment that:

> Technology has not been successfully integrated into any of the frameworks within this [open-system] model [of organisations]. Thompson has made some minimal effort in this direction, but it remains greatly lacking. Others have ignored it in any analytical sense. They write about inputs, throughputs, and outputs, but take us no further. (p. 92)

In reality, both definitions of technology contain an element of truth, related to the directness of the impingement of technology on the organisation. The 'environmental knowledge' notion of technology is really no more than a more indirect cousin of the 'nuts and bolts' notion. More satisfactory is the contention that technology constitutes not one but two sets of forces operating upon the organisation through the uncertainty and information that it generates. The first is an *internal* set created by the technical equipment embodied within the organisation. These forces define the current transformation processes within a firm which constitute the antecedent conditions for decision-making and foster inertia in enterprise behaviour. The second is an *external* set referring to technological changes developed or adopted by other organisations. These may change the focal organisation's relationships with the external environment in a manner not of its own choosing. Nevertheless, this distinction between the two ways technology may impinge on organisational structure has not been made clear in organisation theory and attempts to treat it as a single force have led to considerable ambiguity and imprecision.

It may be necessary, therefore, to reappraise the significance of technology within the structural contingency model to incorporate internal and external technological pressures in a more explicit fashion. There would appear to be three aspects to the impact of technology on the organisation:

(1) the technological charter of the firm and the susceptibility of the management team to adopt new technologies either to preserve the existing charter or to move away from it;
(2) the technical personnel of the firm – including the research activities of the firm creating internal pressures for change;
(3) the technical information available to the firm from exogenous information sources.

None of these three aspects is rigid or independent, but while (1) and (2) are internal to the firm, (3) is external. At any given point in time a firm has a certain technical set-up which reflects the technological charter of the firm and its perception of its own technological competence, an aspect of domain consensus. Technical personnel can be regarded as boundary spanning not only as they receive information from outside, but also as they generate and transmit it. Thus, exogenous technical information is not just information from some generalised external environment but information from other organisations – competing, controlling or complementary. Furthermore, if some external source of innovation and technical information is particularly significant to the firm it might well be internalised by appropriation of the relevant personnel. In short, technology can shift from being an external force to being an internal force with very different implications for firm structure.

Nevertheless, studies that have sought to explore the impact of technology on organisation structure have, for the most part, sidestepped this conceptual issue. They have tended to remain partial in their treatments by adopting only the 'nuts and bolts' definition of technology and contenting themselves with analyses of internal pressures on structure. It is to these studies that we turn in the next section.

Technology and organisational structure

Even ignoring the ambiguity which surrounds the concept of technology in studies which have adopted a contingency approach to organisational structure, there is no general agreement as to the significance of the impact of 'nuts and bolts' technology (the existing equipment within a firm) on the form an organisation will assume. This lack of agreement stems primarily from the failure of many studies to appreciate the importance of environment in shaping structure. Some studies (Woodward, 1965; Perrow, 1967; Zwerman, 1970) have, in fact, concluded that technology is the primary determinant of the structure of the firm while others have been less dogmatic and have recognised that it is by no means as powerful a force (Pugh *et al.*, 1968; Hickson, Pugh and Pheysey, 1969; Child and Mansfield, 1972; Blau *et al.*, 1976). Indeed, it has been suggested that size is an even more important determinant of firm structure than technology (Blau and Schoenherr, 1971).

There is, however, no reason to suggest that either stance is appropriate or realistic. Neither technology nor structure are unidimensional variables, but sets of variables which, in all probability, are far from discrete. Moreover, Stanfield (1976) has contended that the variable role ascribed to technology in shaping organisational structure may in itself be a consequence of the inadequate specification of technology in the model. Consequently, no unequivocal statements can be made on the role of technology in shaping organisational structure. This suggests that, as with the impact of environment on structure, the contingency models advanced by organisation theorists have not adequately specified technology, although they have developed significant partial insights.

Building once more upon the propositions concerning managerial structure advanced by Burns and Stalker from their study of firms in Scotland and England (1961) it has been contended that while *organic systems* of management accompany the operation of highly complex technologies within organisations, *mechanistic systems* of management accompany the use of routine technologies. Woodward's (1965) study of industry in South Essex was amongst the first to ascribe such a major role to technology in shaping organisational structure. The very foundation of the study was, in fact, a technological continuum, drawn from a grouping into eleven categories of the production systems of a sample of firms (Figure 2.5), with the continuum ranging from unit and small batch production at one extreme, through large batch and mass production to process production at the other.

Woodward (1965) identified two types of relationships between this technological continuum and the organisational characteristics of her sample, direct relationships and peaked relationships, in which the greatest similarity was between the extremes of the continuum. These two forms of relationship are demonstrated in Table 2.6, and they led Woodward to conclude that there 'is a tendency for organic management systems to predominate in the production categories at the extremes of the technical scale while the mechanistic system predominated in the middle ranges' (p. 64). She was certainly aware that other variables could influence organisational structure but maintained that

Table 2.6 *Relationships between technology and organisational characteristics* (derived from Woodward (1965) Chapter 4)

Direct relationship	Unit	Batch	Process
Levels of management (median)	3	4	6
Executive span of control (median)	4	7	10
% management committee	12	32	80
% wages to total costs	26–50	26–50	12–25
Ratio of managers and supervisors to non-supervisory	1:23	1:16	1:8
Ratio of staff to industrial workers	1:9	1:4	1:1
Ratio of direct to indirect labour	1:8	1:6	1:2

Similarities at extremes	Unit	Batch	Process
Span of control of frontline supervisors	21–30	41–50	11–20
More skilled than unskilled labour	Yes	No	Yes
Formality of organisation	Lower	Higher	Lower
Interpersonal relations	Better	Worse	Better
Pressure and stress	Lower	Higher	Lower

'there are prescribed and functional relationships between structure and technical demands' (p. 51).

Woodward's results have been replicated in other studies including those by Zwerman (1970) and Hall (1962). Harrison (1978) has maintained that they demonstrate the technological determinacy of organisational structure with the essential implication that routine and less complicated technologies lead to the greater bureaucratisation of organisations and intensified centralisation.

While Harvey (1968) has supported this technological determinacy stance, in his study of 43 Canadian industrial organisations he questioned the technological continuum use by Woodward. It was his contention that the 'unit-production/mass-production/process-production' continuum could be envisaged as measuring *increasing*

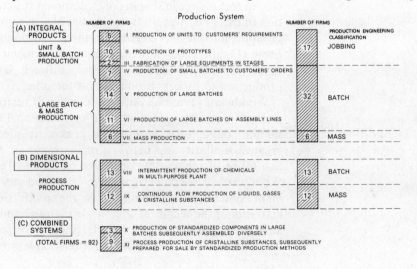

Figure 2.5 Woodward's technological continuum (from Woodward, 1965, p. 39)

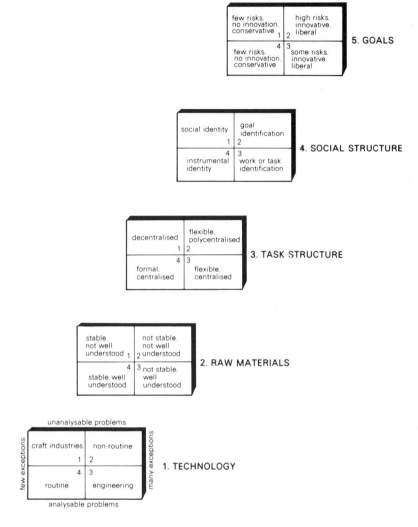

Figure 2.6 Facets of the impact of technology upon organisational structure (after Perrow, 1967)

technical simplicity, not increasing technical complexity as was Woodward's contention. He proposed for his own study a very different continuum on which to measure technology, one distinguishing technological 'diffuseness' from technological 'specificity', and he put this notion into operation in terms of the number of product changes in a firm in a ten year period. When there had been eight or fewer product changes the firm was considered technically *specific*, 20 to 43 changes and the firm was considered technically *intermediate* and 72 to 145 product changes and the firm was technically *diffuse*. This newly defined continuum was then compared with selected organisational variables (subunit specialisation, levels of authority, the ratio of managers and supervisors to total personnel and programme specification) yielding results which tended to confirm propositions concerning the technological determinacy of organisational structure. However, Harvey's study is most significant for its demonstration of the fact that it is possible to measure 'technology' in many different ways, with the choice in this instance of a diffuseness/specificity variable having been purely arbitrary.

Perrow (1967) contended that technology could be measured and conceptualised on two principal variables when technology was defined as work done on raw materials. The two variables were (1) the number of exceptions that must be handled in transforming raw materials to output, and (2) the extent to which search is directed towards analysable or unanalysable problems. Perrow found it convenient to dichotomise these variables for illustrative purposes, and upon this foundation constructed a particularly thorough conceptualisation of the impact of technology on organisational structure. The five facets of this conceptualisation are presented diagrammatically in Figure 2.6.

The raw materials upon which the technology of a transformation process had to operate were similarly characterised on two continua, 'well understood/not well understood' and 'uniform and stable/non-uniform and unstable'. The task structures of managements were also seen to equate with the four categories distinguished for technology and raw materials. In this context two dimensions of managerial task structures were identified. The first was *control*, which was, in turn, subdivided into *discretion* and *power*. The second was *co-ordination*, which related either to the programmed interaction of tasks through rules (*planning*) or negotiated alterations to tasks (*feedback*). Perrow also distinguished three task areas within management – (1) design and planning, (2) technical control and support, and (3) the supervision of production and marketing – but pursued his exploration of the impact of technology on task structures only for the last two types, for which he provided some 'global organisational characterisations of structure' (Perrow, 1967, p. 199). At this point, Perrow's conceptual framework (Figure 2.6) closely resembles the structural types identified by Burns and Stalker (1961). However, through and within his scheme he also related technology to the social structure of organisations and organisational goals (Figure 2.6).

It was made plain in Perrow's work that technology did not make the same impact at all levels within the firm. For much of this analysis he was preoccupied with what happened at the technical and supervisory levels of the firm and not at the design and planning levels. He did, nevertheless, maintain that at the design and planning level of the firm there were many more inputs received from the environment and thus 'its tasks and technologies are derived from both internal and external stimuli' (Perrow, 1967, p. 101). In terms of Petit's model of the organisation as a composite system (Figure 2.1), technology can be envisaged as an internal force decreasing in intensity towards the outer layers of the organisation in precisely the opposite fashion to the impingement of environment.

With the addition of this caveat concerning the intrusion of environment into the organisation, Perrow's (1967) approach can not be labelled technological determinacy. There are, nevertheless, a number of other writers, most notably those involved in the Aston studies, who would more strenuously question the impact of technology on organisational structure. Mohr, for example, (1971) analysed data from 144 work groups in thirteen local health departments in the USA, extending previous analyses from the industrial to the tertiary sector. He postulated from earlier studies that technology was a primary determinant of structure and, for the purposes of measurement, defined technology as the uniformity, complexity and susceptibility to analysis of tasks and materials. Structure was measured as the extent of participation in supervisory styles. He concluded from this work that there was little support for the proposition that technology determines structure stating that 'technology may be related to structure, but not as a magical package' (p. 454). The way in which variables purporting to measure structure and technology should be specified and used was also seriously questioned. The problem was seen as multivariate, complex and problematic, rather than random or 'ironbound' to use Mohr's term.

In the Aston studies (Hickson, Pugh and Pheysey, 1969; Pugh *et al.*, 1969) only operations technology was considered, 'the sequence of physical techniques used upon the workflow of the organisation' (Pugh *et al.*, 1969, p. 102). Hickson, Pugh and Pheysey (1969) remarked that, when their studies were considered, there were no adequate measures of operations technology, and although they recognised four subconcepts of operations technology, they also specified seven additional variables that could have been included but which were extremely difficult to operationalise. As a result, they too looked at only a subset of technological variables. For their analysis of 46 Midlands organisations they created the composite variable '*workflow integration*' to describe technology.

These authors restated the finding of Pugh *et al.* (1969) that technology has a diffuse relationship with structure and frequently takes second place to other variables, especially organisational size. They also concluded that the smaller the organisation, the more the impact of technology would be felt throughout its structure. In larger organisations, the impact of technology would be felt most strongly at the lower levels of the management hierarchy, while being almost undetectable at the remoter upper levels of the bureaucratic hierarchy. Plainly, these findings give empirical support to the outward dissemination of technological influence in much the manner suggested hypothetically by Perrow (1967), but with the important qualification that the degree of impact relates to organisational size.

Many other authors have added to this debate (Aldrich, 1972; Hage and Aiken, 1969; Khandwalla, 1974; Freeman, 1973; Child and Mansfield, 1972; and Blau *et al.*, 1976 for example) but there appears to have been no reconciliation of differing points of view. There would seem to be almost as many ways of specifying technology and structure as there are authors writing on the topic. There is only general agreement on the fact that these two aspects of organisations are multidimensional, with Hickson, Pugh and Pheysey (1969) having remarked upon the major problems involved in measuring some of these dimensions. In all probability the conflict amongst studies of the impact of technology on organisational structure is illusory. It would appear that as the specification of technology and structure has become more complex and comprehensive, so the significance of technology as a structural determinant has been progressively devalued. Stanfield (1976) has been particularly critical in his comments on this subject. Identifying the problem as multidimensional, he has maintained that while some variables obviously relate to structure and others obviously relate to organisation, there is a grey area between the two sets in which a variable taken to measure technology by one author could be taken to measure structure by another. Stanfield has also bemoaned the fact that few authors specify the variable sets they employ and, though using only a subset of all possible variables, assume their conclusions to relate to the whole issue of the relationship between technology and structure. It is his contention that researchers should make their conclusions specific to the variables they employ as was the case in Freeman's (1973) study of 41 manufacturing firms in Southern California.

From the foregoing discussion it is clear that specification of the impact of technology on organisational structure is by no means clear and suffers the same problems of measurement that impede specification of the impact of environment on the organisation. It is indisputable, nevertheless, that technology has some impact on organisation structure, the only debate concerning the extent. Nevertheless, what debate there has been has only been related to the impact of 'nuts and bolts' technology as a set of internal forces influencing organisation structure. This is but part of the wider issue concerning technology as a set of external and internal forces influencing the structure of organisations. External technology – technology as societal knowledge – is most obviously part of any environmental impact. The failure of poorly specified studies to recognise this twofold impact of technology on the organisation may, in fact, account for the technological determinism they display.

Concluding discussion   This chapter has examined some of the principal dimensions of the contingency model of organisations and organisational structure, looking in detail at the manner in which forces of environment and technology intrude into, and impinge upon, the operation and structure of the firm. The discussion has also sought to explore some of the debate which surrounds empirical studies cast within the contingency framework, although it can not be contended that the literature on the subject has been treated exhaustively. The level of debate illustrated notwithstanding, the contingency view of organisation is a very marked improvement over the simple, naive notions of firms and organisations in the linkage and location studies of industrial geography.

In summary form the contingency views of organisation and management have been particularly well presented by Kast and Rosenzweig (1974) and their conceptual model is reproduced as Table 2.7. In this table, the key dimensions of the systems comprising the organisation are identified and their characteristics are listed for the end members of an organisational continuum – from a closed, stable and mechanistic system of management at one extreme to an open, adaptive and organic

Table 2.7 *A summary of contingency views of organisation and management* (from Kast and Rosenzweig, 1974)

Systems and their key dimensions	Characteristics of organisational systems	
	Closed/stable/mechanistic	Open/adaptive/organic
Environmental suprasystem:		
General nature	Placid	Turbulent
Predictability	Certain, determinate	Uncertain, indeterminate
Boundary relationships	Relatively closed. Limited to few participants (sales, purchasing, etc.). Fixed and well defined	Relatively open. Many participants have external relationships. Varied and not clearly defined
Overall organisational system:		
Goal structure	Organisation as a single-goal maximiser	Organisation as a searching, adapting, learning system which continually adjusts its multiple goals and aspirations
Decision-making processes	Programmable, computational	Non-programmable, judgmental
Organisation emphasis	On performance	On problem solving
Goals and Values:		
Organisational goals in general	Efficient performance, stability, maintenance	Effective problem solving, innovation, growth
Pervasive values	Efficiency, predictability, security, risk aversion	Effectiveness, adaptability, responsiveness, risk taking
Goal set	Single, clear-cut	Multiple, determined by necessity to satisfy a variety of constraints
Involvement in goal-setting process	Managerial hierarchy primarily (top down)	Widespread participation (bottom up as well as top down)
Technical system:		
General nature of tasks	Repetitive, routine	Varied, non-routine
Input to transformation process	Homogeneous	Heterogeneous
Output of transformation process	Standardised, fixed	Non-standardised, variable
Methods	Programmed	Non-programmed, heuristic
Structural system:		
Organisational formal formalisation	High	Low
Procedures and rules	Many and specific. Usually formal and written	Few and general. Usually informal and unwritten
Authority structure	Concentrated, hierarchic	Dispersed, network
Psychosocial system:		
Status structure	Clearly delineated by formal hierarchy	More diffuse, Based upon expertise and professional norms
Role definitions	Specific and fixed	General and dynamic. Change with tasks

Table 2.7 (*contd*)

Systems and their key dimensions	Characteristics of organisational systems	
	Closed/stable/mechanistic	Open/adaptive/organic
Psychological system (contd)		
Motivational factors	Emphasis on extrinsic rewards, security, and lower-level need satisfaction. Theory X view	Emphasis on intrinsic rewards, esteem, and self-actualisation. Theory Y view
Leadership style	Autocratic, task-oriented, desire for certainty	Democratic, relationship-oriented, tolerance for ambiguity
Power system	Power concentration	Power equalisation
Managerial system:		
General nature	Hierarchial structure of control, authority, and communications; combination of independent, static components	A network structure of control, authority, and communications; co-alignment of interdependent, dynamic components
Decision-making techniques	Autocratic, programmed, computational	Participative, non-programmed, judgmental
Planning process	Repetitive, fixed and specific	Changing, flexible and general
Control structure	Hierarchic, specific, short-term, external control of participants	Reciprocal, general, long-term, self-control of participants
Means of conflict resolution	Resolved by superior (refer to 'book')	Resolved by group ('situational ethics')
	Compromise and smoothing	Confrontation
	Keep below the surface	Bring out in open

system at the other. These extremes are simplifications of reality, which is less clear-cut, distinctive and discernible. Indeed, even the existence of the postulated continuum can not be proved. It is possible that management types could form discrete sets without any form of interlinking or interrelation.

Despite the general appeal of the structural contingency model for industrial geography, this chapter has highlighted a number of important limitations and shortcomings which detract from the contribution it might make to improved understanding of the operation of firms in space. Six areas of concern can be singled out in this respect:

(1) the general disregard for space within the model;
(2) the inadequate conceptualisation and specification of the organisational environment;
(3) the ambiguity which surrounds the nature of technological forces within the model together with the contradictory evidence on the importance of internal technological forces for shaping organisational structure;
(4) the manner in which performance has been specified for the identification of 'effective' organisations;
(5) the significance of managerial perception for organisational adaptation to conditions of the task environment; and
(6) the role of time.

The structural contingency model is essentially aspatial. None of the three basic elements of the model, i.e. environment, technology or firm structure, are recognised as possessing significant spatial dimensions or even as transmitting or receiving spatially variable forces. Such a disregard for space has not been total, however, as space has been seen as one of the forces promoting the differentiation of firm structure in multilocation firms and multinationals, for example. Nevertheless, this situation contrasts strongly with the situation in industrial geography where spatial aspects of environment, technology and, more recently, firm structure, have received extensive attention. However, in industrial geography, space has been raised to the status of the primary and, all too frequently, the only focus of concern. In other words, total disregard for space in the structural contingency model is matched by spatial fetishism in industrial geography, with the consequence that both subject areas may benefit from a fusion of ideas.

Within the structural contingency framework, environment has been conceived in extremely simple terms as a set of anonymous forces impinging upon the firm from the outside, and intruding into it to varying degrees depending upon the permeability of boundary layers between subsystems of the total organisational system. Empirical research has treated environment much more simply and has concentrated upon the development of typologies to overcome the obvious complexity of the vast array of potential forces shaping organisational structures. As Mohr (1971) has pointed out, however, crude categorisations produce little theoretical profit, and the failure of the contingency approach to particularise the environment of organisations in any meaningful and operational fashion is a major limitation. As Thompson (1967) has pointed out, 'theoretical development and empirical investigation hinge on the adequacy of concepts' (p. 163). This state of affairs, it was conjectured, has arisen from grafting open-system concepts onto closed-system models of organisation to create the contingency models.

The ambiguous role of technology in shaping organisational structure was identified as arising from the various definitions that have been attached to 'technology'. Empirical studies have emphasised, implicitly or explicitly, the technology as machinery definition, and have tended to select only subsets of variables depicting technology and structure. Empirical and conceptual shortcomings seem to have led to the production of apparently conflicting results between these studies. However, the two definitions of technology and their impact on organisational structure may be reconcilable in the manner portrayed in Figure 2.7, when technology as information is seen as no more than a very particular subset of all environmental information. In Figure 2.7, the organisation is proposed as a composite system, and the departmentalised boundary spanning structures are seen to be affected from below, and with diminishing vigour, by technology as machinery – the current technology of transformation employed in the firm. Technology as information – future, potential and competing technologies – is seen to intrude from the environment into the organisation also with diminishing vigour. There is also interaction between boundary spanning

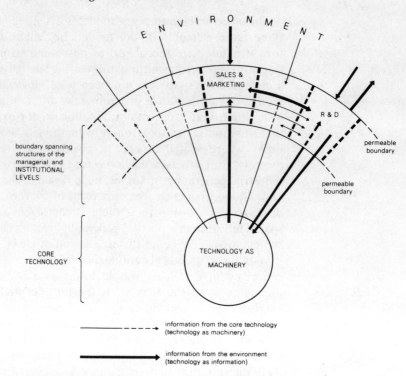

Figure 2.7 The impact of
technology-as-machinery
and
technology-as-information
upon organisational
structure

structures, the sales and marketing and research functions having been illustrated in Figure 2.7. But the research department holds a special position in these interchanges since it can be the avenue whereby environmental technology can reach the core technology. It is also the area within the firm which can generate new technology and transmit such technical information not only to its own core technology but also to the environment in general.

Central to the structural contingency model is the issue of organisational performance, for it is the better performing organisations which are held to be the most 'effective' and in tune with the forces of environment and technology. Unfortunately, as with the specification of environment and technology, performance has also been measured in a variety of ways. In most studies it has been measured as profitability or growth in profits or sales. Duncan (1972), however, measured performance as goal attainment, integration and structural adaptation, variables which in other studies have been used as indices of structure. Lawrence and Lorsch (1967*a*) measured it not only in terms of profits and sales, but also as production innovation, which was precisely the measure used by Harvey (1968) to calibrate technology. In other words, the inter-changeability of variables, which was identified by Stanfield (1976) as a primary source of analytical confusion in relating technology to structure, may be a deep-seated malaise in the structural contingency framework. The variables that can be used to measure all components of the model – environment, technology, structural form and perform-ance – are overlapping sets. No real empirical advances can therefore be expected until agreement is reached on what variables constitute each set.

Two further limitations of the structural contingency model stem from errors of omission rather than from problems of conceptualisation and specification. The first concerns managerial perception, the second, time. Negandhi and Reimann (1973) raised the question of whether it is a real or a perceived environment which impinges upon the organisation. It is doubtful that firms ever react to an objective reality but rather to third and fourth hand perceptions of reality derived from, and moulded by, the organisations of their task environments. Yet, this topic has hardly been addressed and certainly not incorporated into the structural contingency model. Not only does perception influence organisation/environment interactions, it is also extremely relevant to the issue of integration and differentiation within organisations. Steele (1972), for example, has pointed to the importance for firm operations of what he called 'organisational overlearning' – the inappropriate use in one circumstance of information and actions pertinent to another. This, for example, might affect interdepartmental relations within a firm, especially when the stance the environment requires of separate boundary spanning structures is the antithesis of that required for departmental integration. It is clear that managerial perception and the distortion of information flows need to be built explicitly into the structural contingency model.

Related to the issue of perception is the issue of time, for Steele (1972) has maintained that time introduces the most subtle elements of 'overlearning' into organisational decision-making. Time renders all information obsolete and inappropriate to the task on which it is ultimately employed. In addition to this problem of information distortion, time and the dynamics of postulated processes have never been adequately incorporated into the contingency model. The different time scales on which different departments in a firm may operate have been recognised only insofar as these might impede departmental integration. There is, however, an implicit assumption in the model that, in the most effective organisations, structure responds immediately to changing environmental and technological conditions. This assumption is integral to most empirical studies, and can be ascribed to the simplistic manner in which notions of environment have been grafted onto closed system models in organisation theory. By inferring instant organisational response, environmental and technological conditions at one point in time, 't', can be compared with organisational structure at that time. It is equally possible, however, that the structure of an organisation at time 't' may relate to environmental and technological forces at time $t - 1$ or even $t - 2$. Any lagged response of this nature, which might affect the separate departments of a firm differently, holds important consequences for the empirical studies that have related environment and technology to organisational structure, especially when the forces involved are themselves changing rapidly. In short, the contingency framework has not adequately considered the antecedent conditions that influence decision-making in firms. These conditions introduce rigidities into organisational responses, and are almost certain to have a systematic, rather than random, impact on decision-making. Failure to take them into account may lead to the identification of spurious relationships in simple cross-sectional analyses. Nevertheless, although the open-system framework of the structural contingency model holds potential for the exploration of dynamic aspects of organisational structure, it must also be recognised that the introduction of dynamic elements into this model adds a massive element of complexity to a framework already suffering the difficulties of specification.

Notwithstanding the extensive list of the conceptual and operational limitations and shortcomings of the contingency approach to organisational structure, the situation in this subject must be contrasted with that in industrial geography where virtually no conceptual framework can be identified and where the triumph of the *ad hoc* is all but complete. The advantages of the contingency approach lie in its relatively detailed and more adequate conceptualisation of the structural reactions of firms to external and internal pressures. This conceptualisation might be profitably transferred to industrial geography to improve understanding of the operation of firms in space. However, it is first necessary to establish precisely what generalisations can be extracted from studies in industrial geography on the structural and explicitly spatial dimensions of the interaction between organisations and their environments. This is the subject of the next chapter.

3 The organisation and its external linkages

The present chapter examines the relationship between firms and their external environments as this has been revealed in studies of material linkages and information flows, primarily in industrial geography. The structural contingency model of organisation was suggested in Chapter 2 as being characterised by ambiguity and shortcomings in its treatment of organisation–environment interactions, despite its thorough conceptualisation of organisation structure. Environment within the model has been proposed as a set of external forces shaping the internal structure of the organisation given the implicit assumptions of rationality in decision-making and the pursuit of efficiency as an organisational goal. Technology and technological change have been identified as part of these environmental forces although technology, when considered only as the equipment and machinery operated within the firm, has also been treated as a set of forces which might shape bureaucratic structure from within. Most frequently, however, advocates of the structural contingency model have reduced the myriad of variables depicting the forces of complex and dynamic environments to no more than a few, and frequently only two, dichotomised variables. These variables have been used to define categories of environment in simplistic, *a priori* typologies, with the result that environment has been grossly oversimplified.

The linkage approach to organisation–environment interaction stands in contrast with the structural contingency model. Although it complements traditional industrial geography, it adds little to our knowledge of organisations. Industrial geography has traditionally emphasised organisation–environment interactions in an effort to identify the forces influencing location decision-making. It has also recognised, and perhaps overemphasised, the spatial dimension of environment which has not been incorporated, explicitly or implicitly, into the structural contingency model. Nevertheless, a fundamental weakness of industrial geography has been its partial approach, for it has tended, in the past, to recognise some, but not all, the types of business contact that make up communications networks. Material linkages – the flows of goods and services between plants and firms – have been emphasised to the detriment of information flows. What is more, these material linkages have been considered usually in terms of direct monetary costs, largely as a result of the conceptualisation of the decision-making unit, in the tradition of 'economic man'. Indeed, linkages in neoclassical economic geography have been regarded as individual locational forces which 'pull' plants, firms or organisations to particular sites where either

49

costs are minimised or profits maximised (Smith, 1966, 1971). To some extent, however, the linkage approach, as it has more recently been developed within a behavioural framework (Keeble, 1977b), has widened this narrow and outmoded specification of business contacts and organisation–environment interactions.

Industrial linkages can be conceived as all the external contacts of an organisation or its component parts, which collectively define the space within which it operates. Indeed, it has been maintained that linkage patterns are 'a measure of spatial behaviour demonstrating the role of other places in the operation of commercial enterprises. Their significance . . . lies in the definition which they provide of the effective space within which establishments operate' (Taylor, 1971, p. 296). This suggests a degree of congruence between the linkage approach in industrial geography and the structural contingency model of organisation theory for, as the typologies of environment in organisation theory become progressively more elaborate and particularised, they must eventually become so complex as to define the characteristics of individual linkages and business contacts. Nevertheless, a subtle difference of emphasis remains between the two approaches. Industrial linkage studies have recognised only the current and *direct* contacts of an organisation which constitute the 'necessary set of conditions for the survival and future development of firms' (Taylor, 1970, p. 52). These define only the organisation's task environment. Contributing in part to overwhelming measurement problems, organisation theory, in contrast, has recognised both the *direct* and *indirect* impingement of other enterprises on the activities and operations of a focal organisation – the impact of not only the task environment but also the impact of the domain and societal environments.

To elaborate the contribution of a linkage approach to the understanding of organisation–environment interrelationships, which is necessary for the reconstitution of industrial geography as a more broadly based geography of organisations, four topics are examined in the remaining sections of this chapter. The first of these concerns the specification of material linkages in classical and neoclassical location theories. The maximising and simplifying assumptions on which these theories have been built have severely constrained this specification and, despite their relaxation in behavioural location theories, some of the processes associated with these assumptions, especially the significance of external economies of scale in agglomeration, remain completely unquestioned and are frequently restated. The second topic is the more recent conceptualisation of the organisation in behavioural terms, particularly in decision-making models, and the extended specification of linkage which has been associated with this development. The third and fourth topics concern the relationship between organisational structure on the one hand and material linkages and information flows respectively on the other. They include the dynamics of linkage patterns and managerial perception as a behavioural filter affecting information flows. Finally, this chapter presents a model of organisation–environment interaction which seeks to integrate concepts derived from the contingency model of organisational structure with generalisations gleaned from the linkage approach in industrial geography.

Linkage, location and profit maximising concepts of the organisation

Studies in industrial geography have tended to adopt either inappropriate or inadequate conceptualisations of the organisation around which to build theoretical explanations of the spatial aspects of investment decision-making. The behavioural linkage approach to the operation of firms and enterprises in space has clear normative precedents in the traditional location theories developed in economics. Both Weberian and Löschian location theories, for example, can be interpreted as partial equilibrium, linkage-based models for locational explanation (Smith, 1971; Bater and Walker, 1970). However, by adopting the conventions of normative economics, these 'least cost' and 'interdependence' schools of locational explanation (Friedrich, 1929; Lösch, 1954; Greenhut, 1956), have depended upon unrealistic notions of the organisation and have failed to specify organisations' *relevant* linkage systems. All organisations have been treated as undifferentiated, omnisciently rational maximisers in search of a single goal – maximum profit. The entrepreneur as the operator of the enterprise – with the two being indistinguishable one from the other – was thought to be in possession of all the relevant information upon which to base decisions and, what is more, to be perfectly capable of employing these data to minimise costs or maximise profits. Given these conventions from normative economics, the firm was transformed from a variable into a constant in decision-making models. As Simon (1957) has pointed out, nothing needs to be known of the structure or internal functioning of an organisation under these circumstances and, from the point of view of, say, decision theory, it is of absolutely no consequence whether the enterprise is run by an owner–operator or a team of salaried managers.

Linkages within this framework were envisaged simply as the channels whereby spatially variable costs and revenue accrue, which the organisation seeks to minimise or maximise respectively. Consequently, linkages have come to be regarded as locational forces in themselves, capable of drawing an enterprise from one location to another. Such a model also assumes that factors of production, including capital, are perfectly mobile or susceptible to spatial substitution. The quite separate concepts of interorganisation linkage on the one hand and factor costs on the other, have therefore become intimately intertwined within the literature to the extent that some authors continue to see them as synonymous one with another (see, for example, Gilmour, 1974).

To operationalise models within this partial equilibrium framework, the linkage sets have been simplified arbitrarily to include only those business contacts traditionally considered to be of locational significance, i.e. those which incur 'significant' transfer costs. Thus, Weber (Friedrich, 1929) considered only inputs from a range of materials sources and output to a single point market as business contacts of consequence to spatial investment decision-making, although later this framework was broadened to incorporate substitution between transport costs, labour costs and the external economies of scale claimed for industrial agglomerations. While perhaps appropriate in its context, this framework has since proven both simplistic and restrictive. It was made scarcely more flexible or appealing by Smith's (1970) contention that extension of the list of organisations' business contacts that might be thought to influence investment decision-making simply converted Weber's location triangle into an '*n*'-cornered locational figure. Lösch (1954) too, saw costs and revenue as the sole considerations for investment decision-making by adopting all the conventions of 'economic man'. His concern, however, was with demand and emphasised the output linkages of firms, reflecting perhaps a shift in the relativity of spatial forces in the environment over the half century which separated his work from that of Weber, but unfortunately depended upon gross simplifying assumptions to accommodate the cost complexities of input linkages.

Many other studies have adopted this particular conceptualisation of the manufacturing organisation as being run by 'economic man', together with the implication that only the cost characteristics of inter-firm linkages are important for location decision-making. Attempting to explore the locational significance of internal economies of scale within this traditional framework, Hoover (1937) reduced his problem to a trade-off between costs which do or do not increase in proportion to increases in plant size (Stigler, 1958). This same approach has since been reiterated by Isard (1956) updated by Cigno (1971) and given a linear programming expression by Stollsteimer (1963). Moses (1958) was more comprehensive in his treatment of the impact of economies of scale on location decisions by dealing with both input and output linkages, but again within a profit maximising framework. Optimal location became a matter of trading off production costs for the transfer costs on output, and in these circumstances it was shown that optimal plant size, profits and market area are determined simultaneously.

The concept of external economies of scale, however, is a complete artifact of normative economic theory, and is based upon the assumed response of decision-makers to a set of locational forces said to characterise concentrations of economic activity. Weber (Friedrich, 1929), Florence (1948) and Hoover (1948), for example, sought a cost rational explanation for agglomeration and industrial 'swarming', which was consistent with profit maximisation as a firm goal. They identified the juxtaposition of firms in related sectors and hypothesised that the small, autonomous and specialised enterprises found in these locations functioned in the same manner as the separate departments of large, integrated firms. Their locational interdependence was seen as a conscious response to the advantages of proximity, with local linkages yielding pecuniary rewards. The rewards were *immobile external economies* which were thought to be inappropriable in their entirety by any one organisation within the agglomeration or industrial complex. However, there is no evidence to support the existence of these economies, other than theorising and conjecture based on the principles of multiples, massed reserves and bulk transactions. The evidence most frequently derives from wholly circular reasoning which leans upon the existence of local interorganisation linkages. Gilmour (1974), for example, has maintained that it is:

. . . only through the study of linkages between firms and industries that the presence of external economies of scale can be detected; and if, for example, it can be demonstrated that linkages confined within an agglomeration are of greater relative importance than those extending beyond the agglomeration, there would be reason to suspect that external economies of scale, expressing themselves in transactions, exert an important locational attraction. (p. 338)

This is doubtful logic. Because local linkages have been hypothesised as avenues through which external economies might accrue, there are no grounds whatsoever to maintain that external economies exist because local linkages have been found. It is weight of paper, rather than analytical evidence, which supports the existence of immobile external economies and, to the present day, they remain enshrined as major locational forces (Todd, 1978; Czamanski, 1976; Streit, 1969) despite the frequent debunking of the 'economic man' concept, and despite the obvious historical observation that pools of skills, labour, services and infrastructure tend to follow, rather than precede, the initial concentration of basic economic activity. Certainly, evidence based upon observations at the level of the plant and firm suggests that agglomeration and localised linkages are manifestations of attempts by decision-makers to reduce risk and uncertainty in their operations, rather than part of a search for maximum profits which translates into spatial concentration at the macro-level. By definition, localised linkages must follow from location and may be counted as advantages developed subsequent to location, perhaps even contributing a degree of inertia (Pred, 1976), but by no means determining it.

Thus, elaborating upon work on the ironfoundry industry involving firms in the West Midlands and East Lancashire conurbations, Taylor (1973) compared actual linkage patterns revealed in survey data with simulated patterns generated in a simple interaction model. The aim of the model was to reproduce linkage patterns that might arise under conditions of cost rationality in decision-making. This set of analyses showed local linkage in both conurbations to be stronger than expected. It showed the producers of engineering castings to be the most strongly locally linked for sales, with the weakest local linkage being exhibited by producers of automobile castings. The last of these findings was surprising since the vehicle industry has been held to head the West Midlands industrial complex (Florence, 1948; West Midlands Group, 1948; Wood, 1966) and therefore producers of castings for that industry would have been expected to be strongly locally linked. This research also showed that strong local linkage did not endow East Lancashire ironfoundries with improved survival qualities and, when this finding was added to the fact that the highest death rate of foundry firms in the West Midlands conurbation occurred amongst the types of firm exhibiting the greatest degree of local involvement, the conclusion was drawn that agglomeration may not yield pecuniary external economies at all. Only behavioural advantages in the form of reduced perceived risk and uncertainty may have been derived by participating firms. In short, business was not suggested as being cheaper to conduct in agglomeration, simply easier, and possibly even more expensive (Taylor, 1969).

Also in line with a profit maximising approach, many industrial location studies undertaken in the 1950s and 1960s sought to identify *location factors* which accounted for the presence of firms and establishments in particular cities and regions. Such studies have been summarised by Krumme (1969) and Turner (1971) and their methodological shortcomings have been the subject of considerable discussion (Vernon, 1957; Krumme, 1969; Taylor, 1971). However they did serve as the normative forerunners of more structured studies of industrial location decision-making. Empirical studies of location factors were generally placed within the framework of cost rational decision-making in line with the 'economic man' conceptualisation of the firm. Managerial 'deviation' was accommodated simply through provision of a catch-all 'personal factors' category (Katona and Morgan, 1952; Colberg and Greenhut, 1962) and little or no account was taken of the effects of variations in motivation, perception, information availability, search procedures or rationality. Even personal factors were treated as imposing costs which were traded off against marginal returns in alternative, less personally-attractive locations (Greenhut, 1956; Carrier and Schriver, 1968).

Linkage, location and the behavioural concept of the organisation

Since the mid 1960s there has been a progressive shift in studies of industrial location away from the economic determinism imposed by the adoption of maximising principles. Commonly, the focal organisation has been reconceptualised as an open system which receives, processes and transmits information and materials to the organisations of its operational environment. It is assumed to be controlled or operated by a coalition of 'boundedly rational' individuals making 'satisficing decisions' in order to cope with the uncertain and dynamic environments which confront them (Pred, 1967; Simon, 1960; Dicken, 1971). This development led Wood (1969) to maintain that Weber's work was no longer an adequate starting point for studies of industrial location. It also led to the exploration and development of a number of decision-making models which severely modified the economic maximisation principles accepted as the basis for industrial location decisions in many earlier studies.

Pred (1967, 1969) was amongst the forerunners in this field, and proposed the *quantity of information* and the *ability to use information* as the basic parameters of decision-making underlying industrial location patterns. These variables were used to create a behavioural matrix in which each element represented a given mix of knowledge and rationality. Firms could be mapped conceptually into the matrix and the derived distribution compared with their spatial pattern for one point in time (cf. Smith, 1971, Chapter 12). While in practical terms this framework contributed little to resolution of the location problem (Chisholm, 1975), it isolated important elements of location decision-making. Pred viewed the organisation as responding through its spatial behaviour to the perceived rather than the objective environment. He also introduced an approach structured from the point of view of behaviour rather than from the perspective of a deterministic economic environment.

Like Pred, Dicken (1971) drew upon 'various behavioural sciences' to develop a conceptual framework within which decisions with a 'spatial expression' could be placed. Within this framework emphasis was placed on the importance of process, the ongoing relationship between organisation and environment, the role of information feedback, and the mediating effect of managerial perception in decision-making. In addition, Dicken suggested that aspects of internal structure (for example, departmentalisation or economies of scale) might affect the ability of an organisation to collect and process external information, thereby beginning to specify some of the processes which underlie Pred's matrix.

However, only a few studies have applied a structured, process-dependent framework to an empirical investigation of location decision-making. Townroe's (1971) use of the sequential decision model developed by Friend and Jessop (1969) led to the identification of pressure upon space as a result of external circumstances as the major precondition for site and location decision-making. A decision to expand or contract could lead to a relocation or branch plant strategy and, eventually, to the choice of a new site. Data from 59 companies in the West Midlands and the North East of England led Townroe to conclude that the outcome of the decision sequence was ultimately a function of the specific context within which it was taken. Context was associated with the degree of uncertainty involved in the decision process, and the major sources of this uncertainty were identified as:

(1) concurrent decisions;
(2) the risks implicit in technical change; and
(3) imperfect knowledge of the market place.

Thus, the attributes, or perceived attributes, of alternative sites (traditional location factors) were held to be less relevant to location decisions than the nature of the industrial and organisational environment within which they are made, a contention which is clearly in sympathy with the structural contingency model elaborated in Chapter 2.

Stafford's (1974) content analysis of industrial location decisions in Ohio tends to support Townroe's process-based framework. Stafford isolated shifts, or anticipated shifts, in organisations' relationships with their environments as a common element in their location decisions. He stressed the limited number of alternative sites considered as a consequence of the particular organisational and spatial context within which decisions were made. He also outlined the 'hierarchical' nature of spatial search, which works down quickly from a comparison of a few locations to the choice of a particular site at one location, and stressed the importance of ratification by senior management at the end of the search. Stafford concluded that the location decision is an ordered 'strategic' decision (cf. Chamberlain, 1968) by which the firm adapts to shifts in the environment (Alchian, 1950; Tiebout, 1957).

Rees (1974), extended the notion of the 'strategic location decision', and claimed that firm growth could be conceptualised as a series of such decisions, in which different location strategies were a manifestation of ongoing internal structural change. Similarly, North (1974) attempted to identify the spatial ramifications of the impact of all forms of impetus for change within the organisation. He conceived of location decisions as encompassing on-site expansion, branch plant establishment, merger, take-over, relocation, and closure. From a survey of 100 British plastics establishments it appeared that:

(1) transfer or relocation decisions were made most typically by rapidly-growing, small-scale, youthful firms;
(2) extensions on-site were most commonly made by long-established, medium- or large-scale, capital intensive firms;
(3) branch and take-over decisions were made by successful medium- or large-scale firms; and
(4) closures tended to occur most frequently amongst old public firms with poor profitability or growth records. (North, 1974, p. 243)

Given the strategic role that has been ascribed to the location decision in organisational growth, it is perhaps surprising that the search and selection stages of the decision process are highly constrained. However, from a survey of 98 firms in the North West and West Midlands, Cooper concluded that:

The decision maker . . . does not have access to a complete set of alternatives, does not know all the consequences of even those alternatives that can be identified, does not have a preference ranking that would indicate the best solution . . . and, finally, may not be able to select, for various reasons, the alternative leading to the preferred set of consequences. (Cooper, 1976, p. 96)

Townroe, too, has remarked that 'the limited perception of key individuals of both the situation facing the company and the possibilities open to it will narrow both the criteria used and the range of alternatives considered' (1971, p. 125), and similar points have been made by both Stafford (1972, p. 213) and North (1974). These empirical results imply that the location decision is strategic only in so far as its outcome may involve substantial capital commitment by the company. In itself, though, the location decision is perhaps no more than a consequence of a prior strategic decision. As a means to an already prescribed end it is therefore by no means inconsistent that the spatial allocation of investment should be decided with some haste, using only limited search procedures and meeting minimum, rather than maximum, criteria (Green, 1974).

While studies of the location decision have placed this spatial aspect of organisations' investment decision-making in a wider industrial context, they have also emphasised the influence of organisational structure and external relationships on the location decisions and spatial adjustments that have been made. They have also drawn attention to the uniqueness of decisions, but have remained inconclusive on the questions of why some regions are preferred as locations over others, and why geographic concentration is such a prominent characteristic of space economies. Indeed, such studies have drawn attention to the indeterminate nature of the location decision without resolving it. As a result they have failed to replace or even modify the profit maximising framework of classical economics upon which the explanation of agglomeration is founded.

The explicitly spatial dimension within the behavioural approach to economic geography has been conceptualised mainly in studies of industrial linkage. However, an important distinction must be drawn between two types of linkage study in industrial geography. *Macro-level* studies have dealt with spatial linkage at the sectoral level within an input–output framework, while *micro-level* studies have been concerned with the separate business contacts of individual firms and industrial establishments. The macro-level approach is typified by the work of Karaska (1969), Martin (1966), Chinitz (1961), Streit (1969), Richter (1969), Roepke *et al.* (1974), Lever (1972), Czamanski (1971, 1974, 1976), Hoare (1975) and Todd (1978) for example. Studies of this type are related closely to the normative economic approach. They seek to explain industrial location patterns in terms of minimising the costs involved in flows or goods and materials by the juxtaposition of functionally linked activities. They are, in fact, little more than complex versions of the approach to location adopted by Florence (1948) and usually identify immobile external economies as prime locational determinants. In these macro-linkage studies, flows within the space economy are measured as aggregate monetary transfers for the inputs and outputs of industrial sectors, with the result that the findings are largely inappropriate to the task of relating spatial linkage patterns to organisational structure. Therefore, macro-linkage studies have not been considered in the present study.

More in line with the changing conceptualisation of the organisation which has occurred in industrial geography is the micro-level linkage approach which has tended to extend the range of linkages and business contacts thought to be pertinent to investment decision-making. Linkages have come to be recognised not simply as the avenues whereby costs accrue to the organisation but, through their overall spatial distribution, to define the 'effective' space within which the organisation operates. This does not exclude costs as important elements of individual linkages, but it is a retreat from the positivist stance adopted in most macro-level linkage studies. Different types of operational space have been identified from micro-level linkage studies, including *action spaces* defined by material linkages, *information spaces* defined by the information flows of a firm and *decision spaces* reflecting spatial bias in the filtered information upon which organisations might base decisions (Taylor and Wood, 1973; McDermott, 1974; Taylor, 1975).

In the early normative studies of industrial location, only tangible, material inputs and outputs were regarded as linkages, conforming with Florence's (1948) definition of linkages as the flows of semi-finished goods and components between manufacturing plants and industries.

Unfortunately, the significance of linkages in the locational context has been confused and obscured in a number of these studies. To Estall and Buchanan, for example (1966, p. 94), 'linkage' occurred only through 'the grouping together in space of a number of separate plants each specialising in a limited contribution to the final products of the area', implying that a localised business transaction is a linkage while one involving the separation of consumer and supplier by a distance greater than some arbitrary yet unspecified distance is not.

Townroe (1969) extended the list of linkages relevant to location decision-making to include servicing linkages for both plant maintenance and the supply of financial and commercial information. In all, he identified four broad categories of linkage:

(*a*) Process: the movement of goods between different firms as stages in the manufacturing process (including subcontracting).
(*b*) Service: the supply of machinery and equipment and of ancillary parts such as tools and dies, as well as repair and maintenance requirements when supplied by separate firms.
(*c*) Marketing: ties with other organisations that aid in the selling and distribution of goods (e.g. packers, printers, wholesalers, agents and transportation concerns).
(*d*) Financial and Commercial: ties with financial and advisory services such as banks, insurance companies and stockbrokers.

Wood (1969) advanced a more comprehensive typology of linkage in which he drew the fundamental distinction between material and information linkages but endowed them with somewhat ill-defined locational qualities. Nevertheless, Wood's distinction between 'simple' and 'complex' patterns of linkage is important as the first statement that organisations' linkages need to be viewed collectively and in relation to organisational structure, rather than individually and only as locational determinants.

Although information flows have been added to the list of linkages which an organisation or enterprise may possess, and greater attention has been paid to them, empirical emphasis has remained on material and sales linkages (Hoare, 1975). Few studies have considered the locational significance of information flows, with the work of Pred (1966, 1973), Goddard (1971, 1973), Thorngren (1970) and Törnqvist (1968, 1973) being the exceptions in this respect. What is more, only one recent study has attempted to integrate the study of material linkages and information flows (Gysberts, 1974). However, if costs are to be displaced as the only characteristics of firms' linkages significant for decision-making, and their information content added, then the whole range of linkage characteristics needs to be more fully specified. This task was first attempted by Le Heron and Schmidt (1976), relying heavily upon the work of Steed (1968, 1971), Townroe (1972) and Moore (1972, 1973). Building on this foundation, Taylor (1978) distinguished nine characteristics for any one linkage, all of which were believed to be important to a greater or lesser extent for defining the nature of organisation–environment interactions:

(1) the *value* of any particular contact;
(2) the *volume* or magnitude of the contact;
(3) the *frequency* or regularity with which a type of contact occurs;
(4) the *type of goods, service or information* involved in the transaction;
(5) the form or *mode* of interchange;
(6) the *type of counterpart* organisation involved (customer, supplier or transport agent for example);
(7) the *formality* or *legal status* of the linkage (from casual to contractual with draw-off arrangements to ownership of the counterpart);
(8) the *time budget* within which to make programmed or non-programmed decisions on any transaction (highly constrained to unconstrained); and
(9) the *spatial dimension* or locational framework within which decision-making takes place (from Euclidean space to some hierarchic space or space defined by some other mental metric).

To add to the complexity of this typology it should be noted that, at the organisation level, linkage characteristics might be most realistically conceived in relative or ordinal rather than absolute terms. However, this is a complex specification of linkage which has not been matched by what has been put into operation. Most linkage studies have concerned themselves simply with the value, volume, type of goods and spatial characteristics of linkages, and the implications of a wider typology for locational explanation have yet to be explored.

The more systematic approach to decision-making in industrial geography has dealt increasingly with organisational structure as well as with the role and character of interfirm linkage. Table 3.1 illustrates the way in which aspects of organisational structure have been treated in a range of studies beginning with Keeble's pioneering work in the late 1960s. Only generalised organisational characteristics have been identified in these studies, and eight are recognised in the table; type of product or service produced, ownership, management type, plant status, productivity, internal organisation and process (including scale of production). It is here that a fundamental weakness of linkage studies is revealed. From organisation theory, 'structure' refers to the definition of subsystems within the enterprise and the allocation of tasks to achieve some collective goal. A structure, therefore, encompasses the set of relationships between tasks and subsystems bringing order to the organisation's operations. None of the studies listed in Table 3.1 treats organisation and structure in these terms. At most, they employ crudely dichotomised variables depicting gross *attributes* of organisations. Little or no effort has been put into interpreting the selected indices in terms of organisational structures, notwithstanding evidence which shows that at least in large corporations, internal structure has considerable locational and operational significance (Parsons, 1972a; Rees, 1972; Stopford and Wells, 1972).

Employment has been the most commonly used index of size, although turnover and output have been used by Moseley and Townroe (1973) and Le Heron and Schmidt (1976) respectively (Table 3.1). Type

Table 3.1 *Organisational attributes distinguished in selected linkage studies*

Author / Attribute	Keeble (1969)	Taylor & Wood (1973) Taylor (1974) Taylor (1978)	Moseley & Townroe (1973)	Lever (1974)	Britton (1974, 1976)	Schmidt (1975), Le Heron & Schmidt (1976)	Stewart (1976)	Walker (1977)	Hoare (1978)
Size (including growth)	(1) Employment	(1) Total employment† (2) Foundry employment	(1) Employment in parent and migrant plant (2) Turnover in parent and migrant plant (3) Growth/no growth turnover (4) Growth/no growth employment	(1) 2 employment classes	(only to satisfy sample)	(1) Employment	(1) 3 employment classes	(1) Absolute employment growth (2) Relative employment growth	(1) Absolute employment growth (2) Relative employment growth
Type of product or service	(1) Industry sector	(1) Type of production† (2) Product speciality† (3) Casting as % output	(1) Metal and engineering/engineering only	(1) 6 industry groups	(1) 4 industry groups		(1) 6 industry and service sectors	(1) One industry sector (engineering and metal working)	(1) One industry sector (engineering and metal working)
Ownership		(1) Public/private†			(1) Nationality of ownership, USA/Canada	(1) Nationality of ownership (four groups)		(1) Nationality of ownership (Ireland/elsewhere)	(1) Nationality of ownership (Ireland/elsewhere)
Management type		(1) Owner-operator partnership/board of directors†							
Plant status	(1) Parent/branch	(1) Single plant/branch/main production centre†		(1) Single plant/branch	(1) Single plant/branch		(1) Single establishment local H.O./H.O. elsewhere	(1) Autonomous/dependent	(1) Autonomous/dependent
Productivity					(1) Ratio of inputs to outputs* (2) Best practice/less productive*	(exporters and growth orientated firms used only to select sample)			
Internal organisation			(1) Change/no change					(1) Presence/absence of each of 5 departments	(1) Presence/absence of each of 5 departments
Process (including scale of production)		(1) Jobbing/mixed jobbing/repetition	(1) Routine/non-routine (2) Change/no change						

* Le Heron and Schmidt (1976)
† Taylor (1974)

of product or service has been measured differently in virtually every study. Broad sectoral aggregations (secondary, tertiary, quaternary) were used in Walker's (1977) work while nine types of output in either the foundry, drop-forgings or lock and latch industries were used in the study by Taylor and Wood (1973). Two dichotomies have most frequently been used to measure ownership parameters in these empirical studies – public/private and local/overseas. Management type has been considered only in Taylor's (1974, 1977, 1978) work, while a majority of studies have recognised the distinction between single plant firms and branch plants. Occasionally main production centres have been distinguished. Amongst this sample of studies, only those by Schmidt (1975) and Le Heron and Schmidt (1976) have identified productivity as a significant aspect of organisation. Internal organisation *per se* has been treated explicitly only by Hoare (1978*a*), although Moseley and Townroe (1973) employed a crude dichotomised variable of change/no change. Finally, production process has been measured only by Taylor and Wood (1973), Moseley and Townroe (1973) and Taylor (1978) but once more only as simple categorised variables.

None of these can be considered adequate specifications of organisational structure which can be related to spatial linkage patterns, although organisational size is perhaps a surrogate for organisational structure. Ownership, plant status and corporate affiliations are not in themselves indices of structure, although they may be conceived as pressures which influence structure through their effect upon the processes of task differentiation and integration within organisations (Chapter 2). Consequently, relationships between spatial linkage patterns and organisational structure can only be inferred from the majority of linkage studies.

It can be concluded from this review that linkage studies in industrial geography have tended to treat organisational structure only by inference (Table 3.1). However, the approach has developed from a strong empirical tradition which must be contrasted with the deductive approach of organisation theory. While the study of linkages has revolved around a simplistic and fundamentally naive specification of organisational structure it enables relationships between internal structure and linkage patterns to be postulated which highlight and emphasise the interdependence of environment and organisation.

Material linkages and organisational structure

Against the background of the limited conceptualisation of organisational structure in industrial geography, the purpose of the present section is to examine the relationships between material linkage patterns and organisational attributes as these have been revealed in a range of empirical studies.

In general terms, studies that have attempted to relate patterns of material linkage with organisational characteristics can be divided into two groups; those that have used static cross-sectional data for only one point in time, and the few that have adopted a more dynamic perspective. Each has made its contribution to understanding the relationships between linkage patterns and organisational attributes, although some cross-sectional studies have given rise to dynamic inferences on the *evolution* of spatial linkage patterns and the growth of organisations which have yet to receive empirical verification.

(a) Cross-sectional studies of material linkages

Amongst the studies using single cross-sections of data, a number have concentrated upon the issue of linkage systems within industrial agglomerations. Into this category fall studies by Keeble (1969), Taylor and Wood (1973), Taylor (1971, 1973, 1974, 1975, 1977), McDermott (1974) and Le Heron (1976), for example. Keeble's (1969) study showed, from an analysis of the forward linkages of 114 establishments in North West London, that many agglomerated enterprises possess long-distance linkages. However, engineering establishments – especially small job-bing engineers – exhibited strong local linkage, with the implication that small size is a prerequisite for strong local linkage. Notwithstanding this possibility, it was the overall weakness of local linkage in North West London that led Keeble to question the validity of the external economies explanation of agglomeration which had been advanced by Hall (1962) to explain the localisation of industry in Inner London's Victorian manufacturing belt.

A more extensive analysis of linkages in industrial agglomeration was undertaken by Taylor and Wood (1973) in separate analyses for the ironfoundry, drop-forging, and lock and latch industries using ordination analysis to establish the main dimensions of the local linkage systems in the West Midlands conurbation. Although the analysis for the lock and latch industry was indeterminate, for the ironfoundry and drop-forgings industries, two dimensions of the linkage systems were identified. The first related to sales and subcontracting and the second to the purchasing of materials and equipment. Statistical and visual correlation led to the suggestion that the smallest, privately owned, single plant operations were the most strongly locally linked. Batch producers of ironcastings were also shown to be strongly locally linked, while both jobbers, as specialist producers of single castings, and repetition ironfounders, as mass producers, were far less locally linked. In contrast, producers of automobile castings were shown to be the least dependent upon other local organisations while producers of castings for the general engineering trade tended to be deeply involved in the local linkage system. From these findings, which categorised survey respondents according to organisational and technological sophistication, it was conjectured that organisational growth and development, together with increased technical complexity, was associated with expansion of firms' 'action spaces', defined by their material linkages.

A subsequent study by Taylor (1973) of the relation between simulated cost-rational linkages and surveyed patterns for ironfoundry firms in the West Midlands and East Lancashire conurbations added weight to Keeble's (1969) contention that an external economies explanation of agglomeration is wholly inadequate. Significantly, however, the study also showed the orientation of organisations' more distant linkages to be modified in a major way by ownership ties and ties of affiliation between plants in multiplant, multilocation enterprises.

These findings on local linkage systems have been confirmed and extended in a number of studies undertaken in New Zealand. McDermott (1974) used an interaction model similar to that used by Taylor (1973) to simulate the sales linkage patterns of manufacturers in five New Zealand secondary centres – Whangerei, Napier, Wanganui, Nelson and Timaru. The tendency to localise linkages was in this instance interpreted as *spatial monopoly* – the ability and desire of an organisation, based on limited spatial information, to monopolise its adjacent regional market, reinforced by its inability to meet competition on non-local markets. The study also added support to a behavioural interpretation of agglomeration and localised transactions, contending that:

It might take a particular combination of behavioural, structural and economic attributes to reduce a firm's local dependence and enable it to operate effectively on non-local markets. (p. 16)

Indeed, a more recent study of rail-transport data by Taylor and Hosking (1979) has recognised a hierarchy of functionally discrete regions within New Zealand that corresponds with the zones of spatial monopoly measured in studies by McDermott (1974), Le Heron (1976) and Taylor (1974).

The results of a survey of 259 Auckland manufacturing firms have extended these findings (Taylor, 1974). Both sales and purchasing links were found to be strongly localised, with non-local inputs referring mainly to imports and non-local sales going predominantly in Wellington, Christchurch, Hamilton and Dunedin – the largest population centres in New Zealand outside Auckland. Merchants were frequently found to be the counterparts in localised supply linkages although they played a somewhat less significant role in localised sales linkages. This pattern was ascribed to the limited spatial information possessed by many organisations and a desire on their part to minimise the risks and uncertainties of supply. Despite the differences that were observed in the spatial patterns of sales and supply linkage for organisations and establishments in different industries (Table 3.1), important regularities across sectors were also recognised. Again, organisations with the simplest structures, as measured by the surrogate variables adopted for the purpose, exhibited the strongest local linkage. It was suggested that while differences in linkage patterns between *industries* reflected the impact of economic product-related variables, differences between organisational types reflected, at least in part, the impact of firm structure and management behaviour variations. In a test of the relative significance of industry group or organisational type the latter was found to be the overwhelmingly dominant influence upon patterns of both sales and purchasing linkage, adding weight to a behavioural explanation of spatial interaction.

Furthermore, when the sales linkage patterns for Auckland firms were simulated alternately under conditions of spatial competition and economic rationality in an interaction model and under conditions of spatial monopoly in a linear transportation model, they were again shown to be related systematically to the organisational characteristics of respondents, irrespective of the products they made. While organisations with simpler management structures were shown to have sales distance-decay profiles similar to those simulated under conditions of spatial monopoly, the profiles for organisations with more complex organisational attributes were shown to be more closely related to the patterns simulated under conditions of rational spatial competition (Taylor, 1978).

Lever's (1974) study of 24 Scottish plants has added further weight to the notion of spatial monopoly, with the finding that many plants serve local markets while drawing materials from a far wider area. A generally inverse relationship was demonstrated between the value of the products of an industry and the degree to which its organisations are locally linked. At the same time, however, the extent to which findings derived at the industry level hold true for all the separate plants that make up an industry was questioned by Lever. Again small plants were shown to be the most locally dependent for purchases and, to a lesser extent, sales. Economies of scale in transport were hypothesised as influencing large plants' linkages over distances in excess of about 500 km. However, this finding could equally reflect the significant pulling power of the other main population centres in Britain in the manner suggested for New Zealand by McDermott (1974) and Taylor (1974, 1977). Indeed, this is consistent with Lever's own finding that company affiliations caused the orientation of a substantial proportion of Scottish input links towards Yorkshire, Lancashire and the Midlands.

The significance of corporate affiliation is, perhaps, the most important result from Britton's (1976) study of the separate input linkages of 73 Canadian plants. The principal conclusions were that:

(1) intracompany shipments are associated with long-distance linkage, with United States-owned branches being heavily dependent on these long-distance intracompany inputs; and that
(2) while Canadian-owned and United States-owned plants in main centres (especially Toronto) have significant local linkages, those in peripheral towns more frequently substitute corporate flows for local flows.

Hoare (1978) has similarly claimed a tendency for corporate affiliations to influence long-distance linkage in the case of manufacturing in Northern Ireland, and Stewart's (1976) study in Northern Ireland adds credence to this contention. He showed that while none of the 21 Ulster-owned firms in his sample gave preference to linkages with other plants in the company or group to which they belonged, 9 of the 24 'outside' firms had such a policy of linkage preference.

None of the studies so far reviewed, however, has considered anything other than material linkages. Britton (1974) made a significant contribution in this respect in a study of the service linkages of firms in southern Ontario. The survey sought information on the input of six office services and three plant services, with 758 linkages having been revealed for 87 plants. While 224 of the surveyed service linkages were internally supplied, 54.5 per cent of the remaining links were supplied locally by counterparts in the same urban centre. For Toronto plants, however, this proportion rose to 91.0 per cent. The data also showed, not surprisingly, that the degree of localisation varies according to the type of service linkage involved. Thus the sources of higher order services (legal, auditing and other financial services) were the least localised and most frequently supplied from Toronto, while the sources of lower order plant services (maintenance, electrical and janitorial) were almost invariably local. The similarity between spatial linkage patterns for service inputs and the patterns for material inputs was shown to extend to the impact of organisational structure since branches were found to have the longest service linkages.

This set of essentially static linkage studies dealing with the material and service linkages of firms and establishments in Britain, Canada and New Zealand, suggests a number of general relationships between organisational structure and patterns of spatial interaction. While linkage studies have considered organisational attributes in the main, rather than organisational structure, it is important that, in the studies reviewed above, size has been one of the attributes most strongly and consistently related to spatial linkage patterns, for size has been suggested previously as a reasonable surrogate for organisational structure. The studies have shown that small, single plant and privately owned firms run by owner-operators and partnerships tend to be the most locally linked types of organisation with the greatest reliance upon local customers, suppliers (especially, merchants, stockists and agents) and subcontracting services. These are the firms with the simplest management structures. Larger, more complex organisations, which are frequently publicly owned, and branches of organisations with headquarters outside the focal region, tend to be less locally linked. It can be implied that this group operates within far wider task environments and action spaces as defined by their material and service linkages. Organisations' more distant contacts have been suggested as being directionally biased towards the main population centres in a country and the locations of affiliated and associated organisations and plants – a characteristic particularly prevalent amongst branch plants. This implies that spatial linkage is influenced by information bias as much as by economic considerations. In the main spatial linkage patterns have been reckoned to reflect attempts to cope with environmental uncertainty rather than cost-rational attempts to maximise profits.

However, these static linkage studies possess a number of deficiencies and limitations of which two are particularly severe. Britton (1976), for example, concluded from an analysis of only three input linkages and four organisational attributes for a sample of 73 plants that 'company organization and management strategy appear more important variables in accounting for differences in the way linkages are assembled (p. 332)', than do plant size, nationality of ownership, input orientation and industry sector. Notwithstanding the confusion introduced by the synonymous use of the terms 'plant' and 'company', this study is a prime example of the tendency for generalisation based on limited empirical investigation which Stanfield (1976) has condemned in organisation theory. Indeed, this is a fault of all the studies listed in Table 3.1: they all draw conclusions beyond the scope of the data they employ.

There is, however, a more fundamental shortcoming involved in industrial linkage studies which concerns the comparison of linkage attributes for dissimilar operational units. All the studies reviewed above suffer in this respect, but those by Britton (1976) and Hoare (1978*a*) present the issue most clearly. In these studies, the linkage patterns for *branch plants* were compared with the linkage patterns for *single plant firms*. In the light of the definitional issue raised in Chapter 1, these studies have compared the linkage patterns for *subsystems* of larger, multilocational organisations with the linkage patterns for the *entire production systems* of other organisations. Consequently, *internal* and *external* linkages for some organisations have been compared with only the *external* linkages of others. An organisation's internal and external linkages and business contacts are obviously subject to very different pressures, constraints and opportunities. Comparisons of mixtures of these two types of contact cannot yield meaningful conclusions with respect to the management of linkages.

This issue of linkages internal and external to organisations' production systems has been touched upon by McDermott (1979), in the context of Scottish industry. Foreign firms were shown in this study to operate simply as parts of multinational production systems. Their organisation, structure and strategy could not be understood in terms of only *one* plant in *one* region, with the multinational corporation being the correct focus of attention in this particular situation. It is concluded, therefore, that the only proper foundation for the comparison of spatial linkage patterns is the 'enterprise' which possesses either complete autonomy, or at least a very major degree of autonomy, in its actions. For this reason, it is the *enterprise* which is the focus of attention in the analytical and empirical sections of the present study.

(b) Linkage change and organisational structure

A number of studies have gone beyond the analysis of static linkage patterns to examine linkage change and organisational change. The first of these studies was undertaken by Steed in connection with the development of the more general concept of the *milieu* of the firm, which equates, in part, with concepts of organisational environments. Steed (1968) identified two types of milieu:

(1) the *operational milieu* external to the firm – corresponding to the organisational environment, incorporating task, domain and societal environments and influenced strongly by technological change; and

(2) the *behavioural milieu* – referring to the internal characteristics of the firm as a decision-making unit, as this is influenced by the attitudes, views and prejudices of its management team.

For the Northern Ireland linen complex technological change in the operational milieu over a fifteen-year period was shown to have brought rapid change in sectoral input–output relationships. In separate analyses at the level of the firm, Steed showed that organisational structure (the internal behavioural milieu) was a major factor determining firms' resilience to change in the external operational milieu. Independent firms were found to be most prone to closure while larger composite organisations with wider spatial marketing arrangements were able to accommodate change through the adoption of rationalisation strategies.

Moseley and Townroe (1973) used a somewhat biased set of data (Taylor, 1978; Le Heron and Schmidt, 1976) to examine linkage change, dealing only with mobile manufacturing plants and considering only input linkages. Their study revealed a great elasticity in firms' linkages, with the relocation of branch plants being accompanied by the 'stretching' of input transactions. These findings match those on the long-distance linkage of branch plants by Lever (1974b), Britton (1974, 1976) and Hoare (1978a), for example. They do not, however, warrant the dismissal of linkage studies as of no practical significance for regional planning purposes, as was Moseley and Townroe's contention.

A more thorough appraisal of linkage change was undertaken by Lever (1974b) for a small sample of Scottish manufacturing plants, using data for the period 1966–1970. Two indices of linkage change were developed in the study, one measuring *plant linkage change* (stability in the list of customers and suppliers) and the other measuring *spatial linkage change* (stability in the regional distribution of customers and suppliers). 'New' plants were shown to exhibit greater linkage change on both indices than were 'old' plants, and branch plants were shown to make more linkage changes (especially for customers) than were indigenous Scottish plants. However, the greatest changes on both measures were associated with rapid growth, which was shown to necessitate a major search for new suppliers and expanding sales to existing customers. Because individual plants tended to score similarly on both indices of linkage change, Lever (1974b) concluded that in the search for new, but similar, customers and suppliers, organisations do not begin in the local market area and then extend their search to other regions, as has been suggested by Cyert and March (1963) and made explicit by Golledge and Brown (1967). Instead, he claimed that the spatial search and the counterpart search occur simultaneously, defined by both area and sector of operations.

A more detailed study by Schmidt (1975) of seven firms in the iron and steel industry in the Pacific Northwest of the USA examined linkage patterns between 1963 and 1970 at the plant level, using graph theory indices to measure network complexity, concentration of flows, and the spatial expansion of supply areas and markets. In part, the findings of this study run counter to those from Lever's (1974b) study, and show that, in this particular context and during periods of rapid growth, firms develop and expand new markets, more by expanding the area over which they establish linkages than by making changes in the volume of existing flows. Maintenance of existing markets and volume adjustment of existing supply and market contacts was only associated with slow growth. However, Schmidt added to Lever's findings on organisational characteristics by showing that the ability to adjust linkage patterns was related to organisational size and productivity. Within his small sample,

larger and more productive operations were able to maintain their regional competitive position and effectively compete in more distant markets. These firms possessed the technology, industry contacts, investment funds, and entrepreneurial skill to undertake the necessary production adjustments and sales efforts. (Schmidt, 1975, p. 35)

Le Heron and Schmidt (1976) extended this work on industry in the Pacific Northwest to include organisations in the plywood and veneer industry. They concluded from their analyses of fast and slow growing firms and best practice and less productive firms, that technological change induces rapid linkage change, adding weight to Steed's earlier propositions based upon the milieu within which enterprises in the Irish linen industry operate. However, Le Heron and Schmidt acknowledged that their study inadequately specified the environment confronting organisations, and suggested that more account should be taken of spatial and sectoral competition – the conditions of the domain in organisation theory. They also questioned whether the propositions they advanced on technological change, linkage change and industry growth would hold true under conditions of industry decline and industry conversion. The evidence they presented led to the conclusion that 'technical externalities' (local external economies) may be 'elusive and shortlived' as forces promoting industrial agglomeration, especially 'during periods of rapid growth and in highly competitive market areas' (p. 476).

The issue of linkage change in a declining industry has been examined by Taylor (1978) in the context of the ironfoundry industry of the West Midlands conurbation between 1968 and 1976. Firms' spatial linkage patterns were shown to evolve in a common and general direction but not in the way hypothesised in many earlier cross-sectional studies. Over the period, organisational development was accompanied by *reduced* dependence on the West Midlands for both sales and subcontracting. However, it was also accompanied by *increased* local independence for supplies of materials and equipment. It can only be conjectured that this increased dependence upon local suppliers may have been the result of increased purchasing specialisation amongst the surveyed firms or possibly, and more likely, a reaction to intensified uncertainty as a result of industry contraction and recession. Nevertheless, substantial spatial linkage change was shown to have occurred under conditions of slow technological change and economic recession, calling into question the technological determinism favoured by Steed (1968, 1971), Thomas and Le Heron (1976) and Le Heron and Schmidt (1976). For the ironfoundry firms of the West Midlands, increased organisational complexity measured in terms of employment size, ownership, management type, scale of production and type of output (the measures employed by Taylor and Wood, 1973), was shown to be related to rapid linkage change, although change had also occurred without any obvious organisational shifts. The results suggested a 'slow and steady evolution of spatial linkage, bringing increments of information to the enterprise' (p. 334). This in turn was thought to create a steadily mounting pressure for structural change within the organisation and the adoption of new management strategies to cope with environmental uncertainty. Organisational change could then promote additional rapid linkage change. In short, this study of West Midlands industry cast the organisation in an active, rather than a passive, role in its relations with the environment. It would appear that the interaction field or task environment within which an organisation operates does not necessarily influence its internal structure. Rather, through the ability engendered by the possession of an appropriate structure, the organisation may be able to define an interaction field which favours its survival and growth.

A measure of consensus exists amongst cross-sectional linkage studies on the relationship between interaction fields and organisational attributes. Strong local dependence for goods and services has characterised the linkage networks of small, simply organised enterprises, but even amongst these studies, no obvious indication has emerged as to the benefits, if any, which accrue from such arrangements. Are these benefits pecuniary external economies (localisation and urbanisation economies) or is it simply that agglomerations provide an environment of low *perceived* risk which makes business *easier* but not necessarily cheaper? Complex, multiplant and multilocation organisations have also been seen in these cross-sectional studies to possess more extensive interaction fields influenced in their spatial orientation by intragroup ties, affiliations and policies, and the pulling power of large population centres. Nevertheless, though evidence exists to suggest that an organisation's internal structure, rather than the products it makes, most strongly influences spatial linkage patterns, many studies continue to accept without question that product is the principal determinant of spatial linkage networks.

However, some conflict arises within the findings of the few studies of spatial linkage change. One body of opinion highlights the role of the technological forces of the external environment, while more recent work envisages the organisation as an active, rather than a passive, participant in the process of interaction with the environment. Indeed, no obvious pattern can be gleaned from the few studies that have examined spatial linkage change in any detail. Under some circumstances it may involve the spatial expansion of marketing linkages accompanied by retrenchment of supply linkages (Taylor, 1978), while under others it may involve the expansion of both types of linkage (Schmidt, 1975; Le Heron and Schmidt, 1976). Studies of linkage change have also left unresolved the issue of the appropriate unit upon which to focus attention (the establishment, company or corporation); an issue which has already been examined for cross-sectional linkage studies.

The few, and largely inconclusive, comparisons of linkage patterns at two points in time do, nevertheless, throw some additional light on the interrelationship between the organisation and its environment. First, they suggest those conditions under which environment is likely to determine spatial linkage patterns and thereby influence structure (a *passive adaptive response* by the firm), and second, they suggest the conditions likely to stimulate an organisation to mould its linkages to suit its objectives – when structure influences linkages (*active adaptation* to the environment). In all probability, the reasons for contradictory results between studies reflect the different environmental contexts within which organisations were operating when and where they were surveyed.

To avoid a deterministic explanation, it must also be recognised that organisations can react in different ways – either actively or passively – to the same environment. It could be contended that *active* organisations who extend, increase and multiply their linkages are the enterprises most likely to grow and succeed in static or slowly changing environments in which uncertainty is low and the opportunities are considerable for appropriately structured organisations. In more dynamic environments, *passive* firms may survive and succeed through strengthening existing linkages, at least in the short term. Indeed, fostering existing linkages may be the way in which the inappropriately structured organisation continues to survive, by reducing short term environmental uncertainty and the need for change.

Active and passive adaptation is obviously dependent upon the information which a firm extracts from the environment and acts upon in its decision-making processes. The limited specification of linkage characteristics in material linkage studies, which arose from an earlier concern for the cost of moving materials and goods, has resulted in a failure to appreciate the role of specialised information flows in defining organisations' interaction fields, although the above commentary has inferred this from the results of studies highlighting intracorporate or 'main centre' dominated flows. The potential significance of information flows has long been recognised (Wood, 1969) although all the studies cited above have dealt with only the exchange of goods, materials and services. Notwithstanding the comment by Tolosa and Reiner (1970) that information flows and economic flows are interdependent since one generates the other, very few studies have related organisations' information networks to their organisational structures or even their organisational attributes. It is equally significant that very few studies have tried to explore the perception of the environment that a firm may develop from the information it receives. The following section reviews those few studies which have considered spatial variations in the availability of information at the level of the individual organisation and enterprise, and the ways in which the environment is perceived by industrial managers.

Information flows and organisational structure

Implicit in the treatment of material linkages in the previous section is the contention that jointly these define action spaces within which organisations ordinarily operate. Differences in this action space have been associated with difference in corporate organisation. However, material linkages are not the only avenues through which information accrues to the firm. While all material linkages involve to some extent the transfer of information, the converse is by no means true. Not all organisations supplying information in a firm's environment act as its customers and suppliers. Consequently, information flows are more catholic in their coverage and may be regarded as more fundamental for decision-making.

Decision-making itself can be envisaged as an ordered process. Cyert and March have argued that it can be analysed in terms of the 'variables that affect organisational goals, the variables that affect organisational expectations, and the variables that affect organisational choice' (1963, p. 115). Ference (1970) has recognised five stages in the decision-making process:

(1) problem recognition;
(2) identification procedures;
(3) information acquisition and integration;
(4) the definition of constraints; and
(5) comparison and adaptation.

However, this framework, and others like it, are no more than elaborations of the phases in the decision process originally outlined by Simon (1960). The first phase he outlined was *intelligence* activity, and involved the recognition and anticipation of conditions that might give rise to the need for a decision. The second phase was *design*, which involved the definition of alternative solutions to a problem while the third and final phase involved the *choice* of the alternative to be implemented. Of these phases, the first is concerned with monitoring and feedback, not only of internal indicators of firm performance but also of shifts, or impending shifts, in external conditions. The second phase encompasses external search procedures in which an organisation's previous experience and level of spatial learning both play an important part in defining alternative strategies. In the third phase, the nature of the information available to the organisation and the manner in which it is used are of major significance, with internal communication becoming more important than external search. In this section of the present chapter it is the second phase of this decision process which is emphasised, especially the geographical bias of the information which accrues from external search procedures.

Few attempts have been made to monitor information flows at the individual organisation and enterprise level, or to explore their implications in terms of organisational structure, development and decision-making. Nevertheless, in the studies that have been undertaken three approaches can be detected, all of which have some bearing upon the relationship between information flows and organisational structure. These are:

(1) the analysis of spatial variations and biases in the availability of information in urban systems and urban hierarchies;
(2) organisation-centred studies of the localisation of information flows; and
(3) studies of organisational perception and the filtering of information upon which corporate decisions are based.

Propositions on the spatial biases of information within urban systems have been most fully articulated by Pred (1973). The largest metropolitan areas have been seen to possess the most pronounced advantages in access of information, with this being a self-reinforcing attribute. Spatially biased information flows have also been found to parallel interurban flows of goods, services and capital and have been thought to arise from non-local, inter- and intra-organisational multipliers. Furthermore, spatial constraints on inventiveness (Pred, 1969; Taylor, 1977), together with the process of interurban diffusion of innovation, have been cited as additional evidence of biases in information within the urban hierarchy.

Adopting this same approach, Törnqvist (1973) has drawn attention to the possibility that regional variations in information availability produce regional development differentials. Using Sweden as a case study, he emphasised the role of Stockholm as the dominant node in Sweden's regional information system, especially for the business contacts of administrators in both the public and private sectors. Given acceleration in, and growing dependence upon, the production and processing of information in post-industrial society (Schon, 1973; Bell, 1974) the localisation of information processing functions in major urban nodes has been thought to reinforce regional discrepancies in economic health (Pred, 1973; Goddard, 1975). In the British context Westaway claimed that:

Information flows may be the mechanisms through which the behaviour of firms is influenced by their local environment with this, in turn, providing the key to regional economic development. Development area firms would be . . . deprived of critical orientation contact and, to a lesser extent, planning contacts that are essential precursors to growth and change, principally because the local environment is dominated by low level functions. (Westaway, 1974*a*, p. 59)

In pursuing the implications of spatial variations in the availability of information within a general model of the growth of the urban system, Pred (1973) also discussed the impact of hierarchically directed information flows upon the orientation of material linkages. He claimed that business decisions (given the bias in content and depth of information towards major cities) act to reinforce the development of major metropolitan centres. As a result, decisions by organisations involving sales, purchasing and private investment would normally be directed towards their immediately local area or towards the upper tiers of the urban hierarchy. Thus, by following established information-circulation channels and repeatedly choosing the same locational alternatives, decision-making involving information linkages leads to a stabilisation and expansion of existing local and non-local multiplier relationships. As Pred (1974) stated:

Whatever the reason . . . in most cases non-routine operational decision-making terminates with the selection of alternatives located in places with which the organization is already familiar: this is the most readily accessible information which can be turned up by limited search, and the most readily accessible information which can be turned up is apt to be that obtainable from or near the organization's already existing local and non-local contacts of both a direct and indirect (or relayed) character. (pp 125–6)

In terms of the spatial allocation of contacts, this arrangement implies initial consideration of local opportunities and opportunities in the neighbouring areas, followed by the orientation of contacts towards major urban areas, particularly those in closest proximity. This ordering is, in fact, wholly consistent with evidence for New Zealand manufacturers (McDermott, 1974; Taylor, 1974, 1978). It suggests that an organisation's information field is fundamentally similar in form to its interaction field and that changes in the spatial distribution of material linkages will reflect a close association between the spatial learning process and the distribution of existing contacts. As part of this approach, Törnqvist (1968, 1970), Pred (1974) and Westaway (1974*b*) have also advanced the proposition that corporate location policies are influenced by spatial variations in the availability of specialised information. Yet, such a perspective cannot be accepted without reservation. As indicated earlier, studies of location decision-making and corporate organisation, for example, suggest that the organisation does not have the freedom to make location decisions on the basis of external forces alone, and that the location of facilities within the organisation as a whole is constrained by wider corporate strategies. The suggestion that spatial variations in information availability are determinants of the location of firms implies a return to Weberian determinism in which the plant is *drawn* to that location where external forces, in this case relating to information density, are in some sort of equilibrium (Bater and Walker, 1970; Smith, 1970).

A common concern of information flow studies has also been with the behaviour of the individuals making up a spatial distribution rather than with the information flows of individual firms. Such studies generally follow Hägerstrand's approach (1967) by considering the diffusion of information and innovation. The concept of the *mean information field*, by which the behaviour of the individual in the wider communication network could be ascribed to the friction effect of distance, underlies analyses of information-based spatial processes in a variety of contexts (Morrill and Pitts, 1967; Clark, 1969). The main characteristic of the mean information field is the empirically-substantiated decline in interaction which accompanies increasing distance. Nevertheless, little research has been carried out into the nature and implications of the mean information field for the behaviour of individual organisations.

Very few studies have analysed information flows at the firm level and none have attempted to relate spatial variations in information flows to organisational structure in the manner attempted for material linkages. Nevertheless, Thorngren (1970), Törnqvist (1970) and Goddard (1971) have shown organisations' information flows to be highly localised. For three large Swedish manufacturing firms located outside Stockholm, Törnqvist (1970) found that 40–50 per cent of all contact time was spent in the origin centre, with the equivalent figure for a firm in Stockholm being 71 per cent. For offices in London, Goddard (1971) showed that 79 per cent of all face-to-face contacts were highly localised and occurred within 30 minutes travelling time of the office. These studies led Taylor (1975) to conclude that organisations' information flows are more highly localised than their material linkages, and this contention was supported in Gysbert's (1974) analysis for New Zealand plastics manufacturers located in Auckland, who had 93.1 per cent of their information linkages (telephone contacts and face-to-face meetings) locally oriented but only 73.9 per cent of their material linkages similarly arranged.

Drawing on the concepts developed by Jantsch (1967), relating technological development to the structuring of information, Thorngren (1970, pp 414–16) has classified *contact systems* according to the role they play within the organisation. In *programmed* systems, previously allocated organisational resources 'interact with well-known and well-defined segments of the environment', exchanging information with 'the nearest surrounding segments of the development space'. *Planning* systems involve changes in the use of organisational resources so that interaction is less stable, less well-defined and demands 'more comprehensive connection with social groups and potential technology, as well as with the socio-economic environment and existing technology'. The evaluation of alternatives, however, is connected with *orientation* contact systems, through which otherwise disconnected elements of development space might be brought together as various alternatives are implemented.

This scheme subdivides the organisation according to its members' communication tasks and their involvement in different contact networks (Törnqvist, 1968; Rhenman, 1969). From a spatial perspective, separate surveys of London business activities (Goddard, 1973) and Swedish government agencies (Thorngren and Goddard, 1973) have demonstrated that programmed or routine contacts tend to be more highly localised than non-routine planning or orientation contacts. This point has been confirmed in Gysbert's (1974) work.

Any relationships between organisational structure and patterns of information flows are difficult to infer from existing literature and only a few partial insights can be gleaned from studies of office location, for example. The British experience, elaborated by Goddard and Morris (1976) and Goddard and Pye (1977), has shown that offices undertaking routine tasks tend to be involved in only short distance relocations in the South East owing to the importance of retention of strong contacts with central London. Daniels (1969, 1976), moreover, has shown this type of move to involve generally smaller office establishments. Long-distance relocation has been shown to occur only amongst firms with more non-local contacts than was the case with non-movers. These fragments of information suggest that spatial patterns of information flows closely resemble spatial patterns of material linkage at the firm and establishment level. Pred (1973) has reported work by Simmons (1970), Thorngren (1970), Lasuen (1969, 1971) and Gould (1970), together with unpublished Swedish work, which supports this proposition.

While Thorngren and, subsequently, Goddard (1973, 1975) have concentrated upon the alignment of contact systems with different types of activity, Taylor (1975) has proposed a model of organisational development and industrial location which was based on a spatial learning process and the incremental growth of the space within which an organisation operates. However, the interpretation of information space as relevant only to the alternatives considered for plant location obscures the importance of the spatial learning process for other aspects of organisational behaviour (Steed, 1971; Townroe, 1974; Pred, 1974). In particular it can be expected that awareness of trading opportunities will precede their realisation as contacts involving actual exchange (Lever, 1974*b*; Gilmour, 1974). While the information field may be most heavily weighted towards an organisation's local area, its outer limits must, by definition, encompass existing linkages and will usually extend beyond them.

The spatial learning process establishes a direct connection between firm development in a spatial context and work undertaken in economics, in general, and on the theory of the firm, in particular (Lamberton, 1971). Shubik, for example, called for a rethinking of models of political and economic man on the grounds that they should:

. . . fit the pattern of the uncertain decision-maker acting under severely restricted conditions of information embedded within a communication system upon which he is increasingly more dependent. (Shubik, 1967, p. 75)

Stigler (1961) examined the implications of the fact that, in all but a completely centralised or artificial market, 'no-one will know all the prices which various sellers (or buyers) quote at any given time' (p. 171). The cost of search in such circumstances reflects, in part, the geographical size of the market. Similarly, Rees (1966) pointed out that matching specialised or highly skilled crafts or professional vacancies with suitable applicants 'required search over a wide geographical area' (pp 565–6).

It has long been recognised that firms and organisations receive information but do not act upon it or use it. This is often because the information they receive does not conform with what is expected and, in consequence, it is discarded or ignored. Organisations filter the information they receive (Huff, 1960) and it can be suggested that they sometimes misread the information they do accept (Woolmington, 1975). Thus, information is not a uniform commodity with a utility perceived in the same light by all people. It means different things to different people, and it can be accepted, distorted, rejected or ignored. For this reason it is difficult to equate *action spaces* and *information spaces* with organisations' actions as they appear in the spatial dimensions of investment decisions. However, a small number of studies have addressed the question of organisational perception together with the selectivity and distortion of information in the decisions that managements make in response to pressures from the external environment.

Stafford (1973, 1974), for example, used content analysis to construct an aggregate image involving fourteen items for a small sample of businessmen in Ohio. This image was dominated by the overwhelming importance of personal contacts and the importance of labour considerations (productivity, wage rates and availability). It was presented by Stafford as a non-operational model with numerical weightings expressing each item's relative significance for locational choice. Thus,

Locational choice = f {(13.0 Personal contacts), (7.9 Labour productivity), (6.0 Labour rates), (5.5 Labour availability), (4.6 Transport facilities), (3.8 Dispersion tendencies), (3.6 Market access), (3.6 Local amenities), (2.8 Facilities and utilities), (2.7 Supplies access), (2.2 Executive convenience), (1.8 Corporate communications), (1.0 Taxes), (1.0 Induced amenities)}

The impact of labour on managerial images identified by Stafford, was also central to Picton's (1953) work on the establishment of branch factories in South Wales by West Midlands-based organisations. This study showed that branch plant location decisions were made in response to very few factors. Items referring to buildings and labour supply dominated the 'foreground' in these decisions while other items, including problems of transport and other economic considerations, occupied a secondary and far less significant place. In a study of management perception by Green (1974, 1977) it has also been suggested that larger firms and firms with large market areas have the best knowledge of Government Industry Policy in Britain. It was concluded from this study that the *subjectivity* of information on regional policy incentives was less important for decision-making than the *quantity* of that information:

it may be argued that it is the limited amount of information about the assistance available for development in the Development Areas and the spatial extent of the areas themselves which influences the amount of movement to the areas. (Green, 1974, p. 295)

Yet the conclusion that the quantity rather than quality of information is critical in decision-making does not correspond with Newby's (1971) findings. He emphasised the inappropriate image upon which managers based their relocations in the South West of England, which was an image based upon the appeal of a 'holiday area'. As it was put by Newby:

the fact that so many firms experienced so many problems reveals the extent to which this image, based on what is essentially background information, has influenced an economic decision. While these firms almost certainly took the question of accessibility into account in their location decisions many appear to have underestimated it. (Newby, 1971, p. 198)

As a consequence, Newby felt that it was necessary to pay attention to managerial attitudes to current locations in order to identify the general locational requirements of individual firms and enterprises.

A study conducted in the context of New Zealand manufacturing indicated that managerial attitudes towards various elements in the external environment were closely related to the spatial scale at which they impinged upon the organisation's operations (McDermott and Taylor, 1976). There was evidence that organisational size and complexity influenced managerial perception of some items in their environments, while attitudes to other items were based upon organisations' experiences at their different locations. A major difference in managerial perception was revealed between organisations located in

New Zealand's main population centre, Auckland, and their counterparts operating from the country's much smaller secondary centres. It was also shown that the larger organisations possessed the most polarised attitudes to items in their operational environments – basically, strong positive and strong negative attitudes in main centre and secondary centre locations, respectively. Therefore, both location and organisational structure were shown to influence managerial attitudes towards the external environment and the information upon which they operate. Information relating to localised interaction gave rise to attitudes reflecting the 'filtering' effect of location, while attitudes relating to wider levels of interaction, particularly interaction with the national market, were more obviously influenced by the nature of the organisation.

The incorporation of information flows into studies of spatial linkage has, therefore, added several important elements to the study of organisation–environment interactions. The types of information upon which an organisation operates have been recognised, and a strong distinction has been drawn between information concerned with routine monitoring of the environment and information concerned with unprogrammed decisions, planning and search behaviour. Some consideration has also been given to the question of information distortion and organisational perception, admittedly at an elementary level, but based upon an empirical appreciation which is considerably more advanced than that of organisation theory. The possible relationship between information flows and material linkages has been considered as denoting different aspects of organisation–environment interaction which may, in some cases, be translated into particular spatial investment decisions. Finally, the relationship between information flows, their content, quality and orientation in space has been alluded to, which suggests that larger, more complex organisations tend to draw information from throughout the urban hierarchy and, therefore, from wider communications fields than is the case with their smaller and less complexly organised counterparts.

The enterprise and its spatial environment

The generalisations from organisation theory, developed in Chapter 2, can be integrated with those from industrial geography, developed in the present chapter, to produce a more comprehensive, although still exploratory, model of organisation–environment interrelationships within an explicitly spatial framework. That these two sets of generalisations are essentially complementary can be illustrated with the adoption of a simple systems perspective. Figure 3.1(*a*) presents such a perspective, derived largely from organisation theory, in which the organisation or enterprise is seen as just one of a series of systems arranged in the form of a nested hierarchy.

The review of organisation theory in Chapter 2 emphasised the treatment of the organisation as a complex of subsystems internally structured through the processes of differentiation and integration in response to experiences gained from interaction with the domain and task environments. The environment itself was conceptualised in an

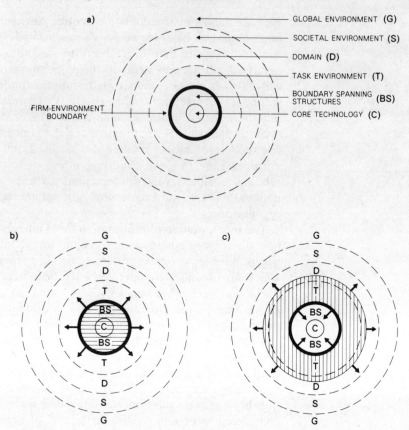

Figure 3.1 The complementarity of organisation-theory and industrial-geography approaches to organisation–environment interrelationships

essentially abstract fashion as a set of 'systems within systems', with the global, societal, domain and task environments forming a continuum through which external forces, organised at different scales, impinge upon an enterprise with increasing directness and strength. The focus of studies undertaken in organisation theory has, therefore, been the enterprise, and only with the development of contingency ideas has consideration been given to the various aspects of environment within which the enterprise must operate. In diagrammatic form, this focus and its more recent contingency theory expansion is illustrated in Figure 3.1(*b*).

Studies in industrial geography of linkages and information flows, as discussed in the present chapter, have adopted a different focus, and have refined notions of interaction, especially in the context of manufacturing firms and their task environments. In so doing, they have added an important spatial dimension to the concept of external environment, and they have gone a long way towards operationalising the concept of inter-organisational interaction. Their focus on the task environment and, to a lesser extent, the organisational domain, is illustrated diagrammatically in Figure 3.1(*c*).

The complementarity of these two sets of ideas and generalisations demonstrated in Figure 3.1 implies that the terminology and concepts of organisation theory can be reconciled with those developed within

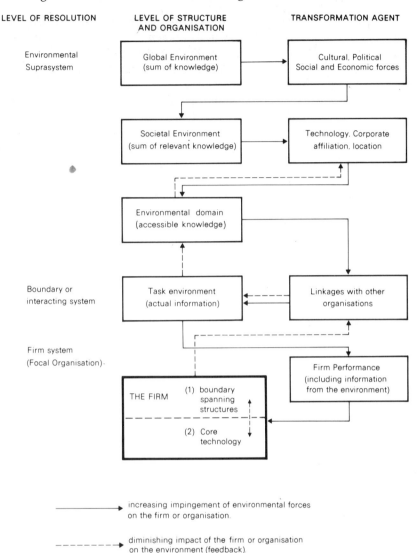

LEVEL OF RESOLUTION   LEVEL OF STRUCTURE   TRANSFORMATION AGENT
                          AND ORGANISATION

Figure 3.2 A conceptual
model of organisation–
environment interrelations
and organisation structure
within a spatial framework

→ increasing impingement of environmental forces
on the firm or organisation.

┄► diminishing impact of the firm or organisation
on the environment (feedback).

industrial geography. The result is an exploratory model of organisation–environment relationships and organisational structure in an explicitly spatial framework, which is described in this section. This model
is elaborated and tested in the empirical context of the UK electronics
industry in the remainder of the book.

The model is presented in diagrammatic form in Figure 3.2, in which
components of organisational environments, technology, linkage and
information flows, organisational structure and performance are
brought together. The organisation is conceived as being confronted at
the broadest level with a *global environment* which represents *all*
knowledge. The characteristics of this environment are modified and
transformed by the attributes and idiosyncracies of the cultural, political, social and economic systems within which the organisation operates.
The product of this transformation is the *societal environment* which

encompasses the stock of relevant knowledge upon which an enterprise can draw in its capacity as a producer. The societal environment can be regarded as the context within which technologies are embedded and evolve. It is also the context within which distinctive types of corporate form and allegiance might evolve, across a spectrum ranging from small craft producers, at one extreme, to transnational and multinational enterprises, at the other. In different societies, alternative forms and scales of organisation may prevail, holding different implications for the environments within which these enterprises operate.

An important point concerning the societal environment is that it is at this level that distinctive spatial dimensions emerge. Space is an attribute of all the environmental subsystems within the global system, and different sets of environmental information may be emphasised as a consequence of spatial 'sorting' within them. Technology, corporate and locational characteristics, can all be conceived as filters through which a societal environment is transformed into an *environmental domain* for a particular focal organisation. This domain comprises the set of organisations with which a focal organisation might potentially interact given its particular charter, the inputs it requires and the output it produces. However, the establishment of a domain requires the implicit or explicit recognition by these other organisations that it is legitimate for the focal organisation to interact with them. This so-called *domain consensus* defines for an organisation, largely on the basis of internal technology, the portion of its environment which contains the most accessible knowledge and the knowledge most relevant to its behaviour. Within the domain, an organisation or enterprise will develop a particular set of trading, business, labour and information contacts (linkages with other competing, controlling and complementary organisations) which in themselves act as further filters, creating the *task environment*. This is the most particularised level of environment within which the organisation operates and will have the most direct bearing upon its development. Thus, linkages represent the ultimate filter or transformation agent acting upon the organisational environment. Despite the concrete nature of the transformation at this level, the task environment may, nevertheless, be the most ephemeral and dynamic of all the levels of environment.

In many respects, the societal environment embodies the formative values and precedents which will ultimately impinge upon the form and behaviour of all organisations. It may also represent the level of environment to be monitored from the point of view of long-term planning. The environmental domain, however, is the area within which medium-term planning and negotiation may take place, while it is within the task environment that the day to day behaviour of the organisation occurs. Through their success, or otherwise, at coping with the external uncertainty of the task environment, organisations become differentiated one from another. Because the task environment incorporates the actual business contacts of the enterprise, it can also be considered to have a direct and immediate bearing upon *performance* in whatever way this might be measured, in terms of growth or decline, market shares and control, or resource accumulation, for example. Through the activity patterns which occur within it, the task environment embraces all the forms of information available from the global environment to a focal organisation. In this manner, the forces of environment as defined by social, economic, technological and geographical filters impinge upon the operations of the firm. The information which is finally acted upon may be distorted in the course of its transmission from the environment to the organisation and this possibility ensures that the model allows for behavioural variations in organisational response and thereby avoids deterministic overtones.

The pressure to cope with different forms and intensities of information from the environment influences organisational structure. As a consequence of this pressure, boundary spanning functions (such as marketing, sales, purchasing, finance and personnel) may become differentiated, with their internal status depending upon the nature of the segments of the environment which they confront, and following from this, their contribution to the organisation's success or failure at any one point in time. The role of boundary functions then, is to act to shield the core technology from environmental forces, maintaining the organisation in as near a closed-system state as possible (Chapter 2).

The direction, directness and form of environmental impact in the organisation is indicated by the solid arrows in Figure 3.2. These arrows suggest a reduction in the level of resolution at which different facets of the environment are viewed and acted upon by the organisation – a reduction which is accompanied by increasing relevance for those facets which do have an impact. However, owing to both the nature of the environmental information transmitted through this framework, and the differing abilities of decision-makers, alternative forms of structural differentiation (such as bureaucratisation, divisionalisation and depart-mentalisation) and different forms of internal integration (interdepart-mental co-ordination and management styles) may emerge (Chapter 2). In normative terms, the organisation copes with uncertainty in its environment by adopting a unique structure, which it creates through differentiation and integration and which subsequently influences the 'next round' of linkages it establishes. Insofar as there is a right and wrong way to structure activities for a particular set of environmental circumstances, the model in Figure 3.2 revolves around the notion of *performance*. This enables the dynamic implications of the process that is modelled to be introduced explicitly. Performance at time t establishes the antecedent conditions relevant to the model (and the organisation) at time $t + 1$. In the specification of this model, these antecedent conditions may be simulated through introduction of organisational size as an 'exogenous' variable which can be related to both linkage patterns and organisational structure.

It can be suggested that the ability of the firm to cope with the external environment, and thereby enhance its own performance, will be reflected at any point in time in the sectoral, corporate or spatial distribution of its linkages. An organisation in which external uncertainty is relatively low, or the ability to act upon environmental information is high, might be characterised by an extension of its linkages and hence its task environment. This might be achieved by extending its product mix, interacting with different types of organisation, or establishing exchange relationships in other geographic areas. For an organisation to adopt such external strategies with success implies that those of its subsystems responsible for the relevant segments of the environment have an appropriate degree of recognition and power within and without the organisation. From the linkage studies reviewed earlier in the chapter, it can be anticipated that successful organisations will be characterised by the most widespread and far reaching linkages, in spatial terms at least. Indeed, a degree of management complexity apparently enhances spatial interactions and reduces dependence upon highly localised opportunities for interaction. Geographically more widespread linkages may also result from the integration of a focal organisation into a wider corporate system, although the evidence on this point is far from conclusive. It may be that unless corporate membership precludes a degree of management autonomy in an organisation, other aspects of internal organisation will be of equal importance in determining the dimensions of interaction fields.

The relationship between material and information interaction fields may cast further light on the strength or weakness of an organisation's external linkages. A wide information field, for example, might give rise to a similarly wide linkage field, if an enterprise is able to act successfully upon the information it receives. Thus, the development of information monitoring and processing functions, such as marketing, may be more critical in effective internal differentiation than the development of those tasks more directly concerned with physical transactions, such as sales. If the departments within an organisation which deal with physical transactions gain ascendency over those dealing with information monitoring and processing, the organisation's ability to cope with a turbulent or dynamic environment may, over time, be severely impaired. It is towards these types of issue that the empirical exploration of the model in Figure 3.2 is directed in subsequent chapters of this book.

However, not only does the organisation exercise choice over the ways in which it treats the information it receives and the ways in which it structures its activities to cope with the environment, it also makes its own contribution to the texture of the environment within which it operates. The ability of an organisation to influence its own structure, and thereby influence the linkages it establishes with the environment and the information it is able to extract and act upon, establishes a feedback loop within the model. This feedback, and the fact that the organisation is itself a component of the environment of other organisations, is represented by broken arrows in Figure 3.2. Through its linkages, the focal organisation adds to the stock of information in the environmental domain and, at the same time, extends the technical, corporate and geographic characteristics of the societal environment.

While this contribution to the societal environment is not considered directly in the present study, its recognition means that the model advanced in Figure 3.2 may well provide a framework for investigating the impact of organisations upon their environments. The environmental domain, for example, may be conceived as the level at which Benson's (1975) linkage network, defined in terms of the political economics of power and control relationships rather than through simple exchange transactions and information flows, can be identified. Furthermore, while in the past it may have been unrealistic to extend the feedback loop beyond the transformations operating upon the societal environment, which would deny any organisational impact upon the global environment, it may be that major transnational and multinational corporations do operate in more than one societal environment and, in so doing, are breaking down global societal differences through extensions of their own task environments. Indeed, it may well be through the extension of individual task environments that the transnational and multinational organisations provide the mechanisms through which one society imposes its organisational norms and attendant values upon another. Within such a model the corporate strategies of multinational firms across space could be explored through, for example, analysis of the internal configurations through which they partition space and allocate responsibilities for different sets of linkages which come to define the variety of task environments within which they operate.

Against the background of the discussions of organisation theory in Chapter 2 and industrial linkages and information flows in Chapter 3, the second part of this book explores the model developed in this section. However, in order to undertake this major task, the very general and abstract tone of the first three chapters gives way to a pragmatic analysis of some of the structural and interaction concepts and interrelationships exhibited by a sample of 121 electronics firms within the United Kingdom in the early 1970s.

Part 2 Environment and enterprise structure in the United Kingdom electronics industry

4 The electronics industry in the United Kingdom

As a foundation for investigating the impact of location upon the operations and development of manufacturing organisations, the preceding chapters have developed a theoretical framework derived from organisation theory and the 'behavioural' approach to industrial geography. The framework is concerned with the structuring of organisations, their interaction with the environment, and their operations in space as defined by linkages and information flows. A number of propositions have been advanced, drawing upon a variety of theoretical and empirical studies, all of which have contributed insights into location and organisation but none of which have examined in any depth the relationships between them. The present chapter seeks to describe the character of the societal, domain and task environments confronting electronics firms in the United Kingdom as a background to the analysis of firm organisation, communication and location described in subsequent chapters. These broad environmental characteristics are discussed in light of the historical development of the industry in the United Kingdom and the technological and market conditions confronting the industry at the national and international levels (the societal environment). This is followed by a general discussion of the market and technology conditions facing the various product sectors in the industry, to provide some insight into the environmental domains and task environments within which individual organisations operate. The impact of a rapidly changing technology on the environmental domain is emphasised, and the distinctive spatial distribution of the industry which might impinge upon individual task environments within the United Kingdom is described. Having established the context within which electronics enterprises in the United Kingdom operate, the chapter describes the survey of organisations which provides the empirical material for the remainder of the book.

Origins of the British electronics industry

Within the British economy, the electronics industry falls into the group of new, science-based industries which Allen (1970, p. 20) distinguishes from those based upon traditional manufacturing techniques, and is characterised by the dynamic and unstable nature of the environment. The antecedents of the industry predate the First World War, however, when a number of companies and organisations, today among the leading United Kingdom electronic goods producers, were already

87

established. However, the electronics industry, as such, dates from the growth of the radio industry between World Wars One and Two.

Two separate origins of the industry can be distinguished: the first lay in the inventiveness of individual entrepreneurs, the second in the commercial strength of a few electrical companies established, in general, before 1920. Examples of companies founded largely upon post-1920 innovations include Mullard, Pye and Ferranti. Such companies were generally involved in the newly emergent radio industry, although Mullard Limited was established by an ex-Admiralty scientist for the purpose of manufacturing receiving valves rather than finished equipment. Pye of Cambridge had its origins in a small group of instrument manufacturers who took an early interest in radio manufacture, marketing their first set in 1922.

Guglielmo Marconi stands out as one of the leading innovator–founders of the British electronics industry, his company establishing 'the world's first radio factory' (Reynolds, 1974, p. 6) at the end of the nineteenth century. After the Second World War the Marconi Company was taken over by English Electric Limited, an enterprise which had been founded by commercial interests in 1919 to effect the merger of a variety of electrical companies. The take-over of Marconi represented the merging of a technically founded lighter electronics enterprise and a heavier electrical counterpart under a single corporate umbrella. This development was further enhanced for English Electric through its subsequent merger with Elliott Brothers under the auspices of the Industrial Reorganisation Corporation (IRC) (Young and Lowe, 1974, p. 41).

The most striking example of the attempt to effect a technical and commercial marriage within the United Kingdom electronics industry is the recent development of the General Electric Company (GEC) which, again with government encouragement provided by the IRC and Ministry of Technology, was totally transformed during the 1960s (Jones and Marriott, 1972; Channon, 1973, p. 133). Like English Electric, GEC's own origin was commercial in nature and its technology electrical. During the 1960s this 'rationalisation' of the electrical and electronics industries was pursued further by the merger of diverse interests from both industries under GEC management. The IRC was instrumental in securing the take-over of Associated Electrical Industries by GEC in 1967, further strengthening the organisation's heavier electrical engineering activities. The subsequent take-over of English Electric in 1969 with its joint legacy of Elliott Brothers and Marconi meant that major forces in English electronics manufacturing were brought together in a single, diversified enterprise based upon disparate commercially based electrical and technically based electronics backgrounds.

Although considerably smaller, the development of Thorn Electrical Industries followed a similar course. Established in 1928, this organisation entered the radio industry in 1936. After the Second World War, its interests widened to include television and other domestic appliances. Thereafter a series of acquisitions enabled Thorn to move into more general engineering, and at the same time to gain a considerable share of the television market, both through acquisition of competitors' brands and through an expanding interest in the retail and rental sectors (Hart *et al.*, 1973, pp. 43–8).

Similarly, the smaller Plessey organisation was initially established in response to commercial opportunities, undertaking large-scale component production at a time (the 1920s) when most manufacturers in the growing radio industry tended to manufacture components themselves in small quantities at high cost. In the 1960s the company set out to broaden its activities, again on the basis of take-overs (Channon, 1973, pp. 136–7). For example, two major suppliers of telecommunications equipment were acquired, giving Plessey a substantial share of the Post Office market, together with GEC and Standard Telephones and Cables (STC) (Hart *et al.*, 1973, pp. 110–11). In contrast to the other organisations, Plessey's expansion was confined largely to electronics and electronics-related activities.

The dominant British enterprises in the electronics industry have developed as a result of the merger of technically and commercially based companies and organisations since the 1940s. This has been paralleled amongst several overseas organisations which are particularly important within Britain. The Dutch Philips organisation, having established a base in the British lamp industry, subsequently developed a large and diversified British-based operation in the fields of both electrical and electronics goods. Similarly, International Telephone and Telegraph (ITT) of the United States acquired Standard Telephone and Cables in 1925. Subsequent diversification into the electronics field has been achieved through the establishment of directly controlled subsidiaries manufacturing components, private communications equipment and consumer goods.

American-controlled organisations are particularly important in the manufacture of computers and active components in the United Kingdom (Table 4.1). Conceivably American domination of employment and sales in computers would have been even greater had it not been for two forms of government intervention. Firstly, there has been resistance within the government, the largest single UK customer, to sales by the American IBM company (Malik, 1975, pp 323–4). Secondly, the government, through the IRC (Young and Lowe, 1974) restructured the indigenous computer industry by creating International Computers Limited. ICL was developed through ten years of mergers of computer activities, partly from within a number of more diversified electronics companies (Tugendhat, 1973, pp 85–7), a rationalisation based upon common and complementary technology which ran counter to concurrent movements towards greater product and organisational diversity in other major electronics enterprises (Channon, 1973, pp 124–5).

While Table 4.1 indicates that overseas-controlled companies produced almost half of Britain's components, between 1958 and 1968 the share of United States subsidiaries rose from nil to an estimated 58 per cent of the active component market, with a further 22 per cent in the hands of European-controlled companies. This trend, together with the

Table 4.1 *Overseas ownership in the British electronics industry*

	Instru-ments	Com-ponents	Consumer goods	Computers	Capital goods	Total	Overall %
American							
Number	24	33	2	10	6	75	25.2
Sales (£m)	89.5	80.0	2.2	236.6	15.6	423.9	25.0
Average sales (£m)	3.7	2.4	1.1	23.6	2.6	5.6	
Other foreign subsidiaries							
Number	11	9	1	—	3	24	8.1
Sales (£m)	33.1	93.6	3.3		24.0	154.0	9.1
Average sales (£m)	3.0	10.6	3.3		8.0	6.4	
All firms							
Number	135	89	25	18	30	297	100.0
Sales (£m)	535.3	356.7	166.0	407.1	233.0	1698.1	100.0
Average sales (£m)	4.0	4.0	6.6	22.6	7.8	5.7	

Note: Based upon companies with turnover exceeding £½m
Source: NEDO, 1974, Table 41.

fact that active components comprise the core of electronics technology, was probably instrumental in the decision by the British government to support the establishment of microelectronics development in Britain, most notably through the £50m backing provided to the newly formed Inmos company in 1977.

At a general level, then, a number of features can be identified which contribute to the level of turbulence implicit in the electronics environment in the United Kingdom during the 1970s. These include the impact of major corporate reorganisations within the United Kingdom, which were acting through the 1960s and 1970s to create entirely new technical and commercial coalitions and alignments within and amongst indigenous electronics enterprises and markets. Under the threat of external competition and eroding markets, commercial structures associated with the longer established, rather more stable electrical engineering industry were imposed upon organisations in which technical uncertainty and the speed of technological change had tended to dominate organisational structures and organisation–environment relations to the extent that technical excellence was not in many cases supported by appropriate marketing accomplishments.

At the same time the industry had been experiencing a high level of direct and indirect government involvement: as a customer; as a supplier of technology; as a regulator, especially through the imposition of quality standards; as an integrating agency; and as an investor. Finally, during the 1950s and 1960s an increase in technological and marketing uncertainty was accompanied by high levels of overseas investment in the industry. The 1970s have been marked, then, by the growth within the United Kingdom of organisations which depend upon strategy and technology developed elsewhere.

Table 4.2 *Private and public companies in the British electronics industry*

	Instruments	Components	Consumer goods	Computers	Capital goods	Total	Overall %
Overseas-owned							
Number	35	42	3	10	9	99	33.3
Sales (£m)	122.6	173.6	5.5	236.6	39.6	577.9	34.0
Average sales (£m)	3.5	4.1	1.8	23.6	4.4	5.8	
Public UK companies							
Number	11	7	3	3	2	26	8.7
Sales (£m)	74.4	72.7	9.2	157.4	10.9	324.6	19.1
Average sales (£m)	6.8	10.4	3.1	52.5	5.4	12.5	
Private UK companies							
Number	19	9	8	2	3	41	13.8
Sales (£m)	32.1	7.5	10.3	2.3	8.5	60.7	3.6
Average sales (£m)	1.7	0.8	1.3	1.1	2.8	1.5	
Subsidiaries of UK electronics companies							
Number	23	5	2	1	9	40	13.5
Sales (£m)	59.3	35.9	66.7	0.8	64.6	227.3	13.4
Average sales (£m)	2.6	7.2	33.3	0.8	7.2	5.7	
Subsidiaries of other UK companies							
Number	47	26	9	2	7	91	30.6
Sales (£m)	246.9	67.0	74.3	10.0	109.4	507.6	29.9
Average sales (£m)	5.2	2.6	8.2	5.0	15.6	5.6	

Note: Based upon companies with turnover exceeding £½m.
Source: NEDO, 1974, Table 41.

The result of these features is the domination of the environment by a relatively small number of very large corporations, despite the presence of a larger number of medium sized organisations and a host of smaller enterprises and firms. Table 4.2 indicates that the gap between the medium scale companies and the dominant companies in each sector of the industry is very large, with the implication that the environmental conditions facing the many small and medium sized organisations will depend, very largely, on the fortunes and favours of the few large ones. For example, nineteen private companies in the instrument sector accounted for less than half the market share achieved by eleven public companies. This gap between the public and overseas organisations, on the one hand, and the medium or small private organisations on the other, is most pronounced in the component sector. Just as small manufacturers produce only passive components of relatively low unit value, so in the computer sector smaller firms and enterprises do not compete with mainframe computer manufacturers. Rather, they concentrate upon the development of specialised peripheral devices and custom systems.

Thus, the medium-sized enterprise survives and grows by concentration upon more limited, specialised, and often less technologically demanding markets than its larger counterparts. While this may reduce external uncertainty in the short term, the pace of technological change within the industry, and the increasing concentration of control over invention and innovation, associated with the huge resource demands of research and development programmes, means that long-term uncertainty remains high for the majority. It also means that, while the societal environmental described in this section may be relevant to an understanding of broad industry trends, an understanding of the development and organisation of individual enterprises requires an appreciation of the particular environmental domains within which they operate.

Products and markets: the electronics environment   The *functional* definition of the industry adopted for the purposes of this study (Chapter 1) accepts that if the transmission, storage or manipulation of information is the primary role of a product, then its production comprises electronics manufacturing. If, on the other hand, electronics technology is incorporated as a control function in equipment designed to perform a mechanical task, then the production of that equipment does not constitute electronics manufacture.

Using this broad definition it is possible to identify a number of 'electronics' sectors at Minimum List Heading level within the Standard Industrial Classification. Before the 1968 revision of the SIC, electronics activities were allocated to either MLH 363, 'Telegraph and telephone apparatus', or MLH 364, 'Radio and other electronic apparatus'. The growth of the electronics industry and its internal diversity were recognised in the 1968 classification, so that today the following Minimum List Headings are distinguished:

MLH 363 'Telegraph and telephone apparatus' (telecommunications);
MLH 364 'Radio and electronic components', including active and passive, professional and consumer components, subassemblies, circuits, and printed circuit boards;
MLH 365 'Broadcast receiving and sound reproducing equipment' (consumer goods);
MLH 366 'Electronic computers' and computer peripheral equipment;
MLH 367 'Radio, radar and electronic capital goods' (HMSO, 1968).

Parts of MLH 354, 'Scientific and industrial instruments and systems' and MLH 338, 'Office machinery', also encompass electronics technology and should be allocated to the industry. Because they are only elements of wider MLH categories, meaningful published statistics are not readily available for them. Therefore, the following discussion of environmental domains is oriented primarily towards sectors MLH 363 to 367.

Table 4.3 presents various measures of industry growth over the 1960s, disaggregated according to the five major sectors. All sectors experi-

Table 4.3 *Growth of the United Kingdom electronics industry, 1963–1971*

	Establish-ments	Enter-prises	Employ-ment	Gross turnover £m	Turnover per enterprise £ thousands
Telecommunications					
1963	96	48	87100	152.8	3183.3
1971	151	97	98100	349.2	3559.5
% change	57.3	102.0	12.6	128.6	11.9
Capital goods					
1963	316	223	75300	175.9	788.8
1971	457	372	85400	398.3	1070.7
% change	44.6	66.8	13.4	126.4	35.7
Computers					
1963	48	32	10400	40.3	1258.0
1971	95	86	23500	186.1	2163.8
% change	98.0	168.8	126.0	362.8	72.0
Consumer goods					
1963	157	115	36000	173.6	1509.5
1971	198	174	47400	412.0	2367.9
% change	26.1	51.3	31.7	137.3	56.9
Components					
1963	444	345	84700	149.1	432.2
1971	949	827	125700	501.5	606.4
% change	113.7	139.7	48.4	236.3	40.3
All sectors					
1963	1061	763	293500	691.7	906.5
1971	1850	1556	380100	1798.3	1155.7
% change	74.3	104.0	29.6	160.0	27.5

Sources: Census of Production, 1968, Reports 73–7 (HMSO, 1971)
          Census of Production, 1971, Reports PA363-PA367 (HMSO, 1974)

enced considerable growth in all indices, gross output, employment and number of establishments. Relative growth was most pronounced in the computer sector, albeit from a limited initial base, and was also marked in the components sector. In the three remaining equipment sectors, telecommunications, capital, and consumer equipment, similar rates of growth were recorded which, although lower, were still substantial.

Between 1963 and 1971 the increase in establishments did not match the increase in enterprises, suggesting considerable entry of new firms. The reduced average size of enterprise is consistent with a number of smaller organisations becoming active in the industry at the same time as the dominant organisations were increasing in scale and diminishing in number as a result of rationalisation and merger. In all but the consumer goods sector the value of output per employee rose substantially, suggesting that in this sector expansion was less capital intensive than in the remainder. The marked shift in the component sector reflects the establishment in the United Kingdom of a number of capital intensive American-owned manufacturers of active devices during the period.

Table 4.3 also indicates that, by 1971, the initial lead in terms of the value of total production held by capital goods and consumer equipment manufacture in 1963 was usurped by component manufacture. While this reflects in part differential market growth, it also results from the technical advancement of active components during the 1960s and the fabrication of many more electronic functions at this level rather than at the finished equipment level. In 1971 there were also twice as many enterprises and establishments in the components sector than in any of the others, emphasising the centrality and significance of component manufacture to the electronics industry as a whole.

Figure 4.1 presents enterprise size distributions for each sector in 1971. Unfortunately the employment size classes used vary between sectors, confounding comparison. In addition, gross output figures are aggregated for the three size categories containing firms with less than 100 employees. The concentration of enterprises at the lower end of the size distribution and the concentration of output at the upper end is clearly a feature common to each sector. The conclusion that a very high share of output is accounted for by a very small share of enterprises in each case is reinforced by the fact that some enterprises controlling establishments in the largest class intervals presumably control smaller establishments as well.

Figure 4.2 indicates the changes in the cost structure of each sector which took place between 1963 and 1968 and between 1968 and 1971. The omission of organisations employing fewer than 25 people in the compilation of these data introduces relatively little distortion to the cost structure per unit output. However, Figure 4.2 presents very generalised profiles, which may have only limited relevance for the numerically dominant very small enterprises. Some comparisons between sectors are useful, however. In each sector the cost of materials and fuel rose to 50 per cent of total costs, at least, and as high as 80 per cent in consumer goods. Subcontracting was relatively unimportant in all but the computer sector, although even in that sector its importance declined between 1963 and 1971. Both transport costs, which make a very minor contribution to total costs, and the level of capital investment were stable over the final three years. The increase in the cost of materials was offset primarily by the relative decline in wages and salaries, a trend which is consistent with the higher value per unit and the greater range of functions associated with recent generations of electronic components.

Table 4.4 reveals that the electronics production in industrial sectors outside the Minimum List Headings considered in this study, is very limited (7.3 per cent of domestic production, 4.9 per cent of domestic

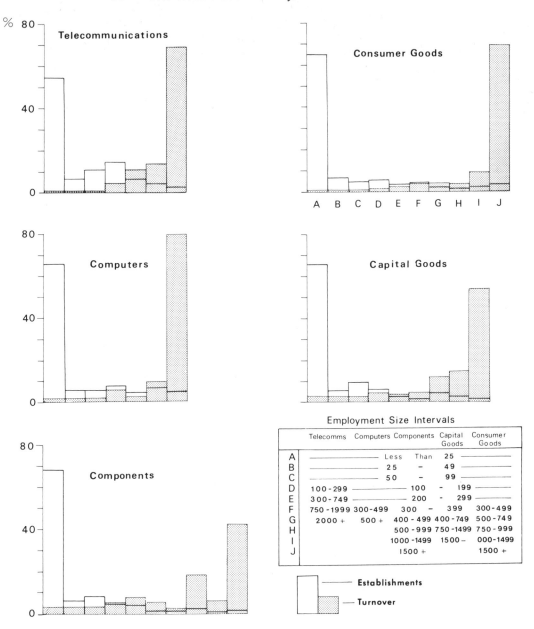

Figure 4.1 Size distribution of enterprise in the British electronics industry, 1971

demand). This is particularly the case for consumer goods, demonstrating the importance of specialised mass-production technology in this sector. The low level of imports of telecommunication products and, to a lesser extent, capital equipment, are consistent with the small part played by imports in public authority expenditure. According to the 1970 input–output tables less than 1 per cent of electronics purchases by public authorities were met by imports (HMSO, 1974*f*). The proportion

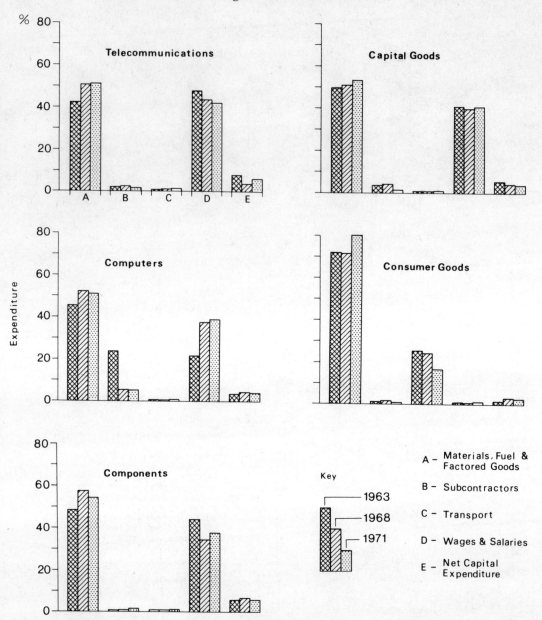

Figure 4.2 Cost structure of the British electronics industry, 1963, 1968, 1971

of electronic capital goods derived from other sectors, however, suggests that relatively high levels of purchasing in the public sector from non-electronic industries (10 per cent in 1970) is especially important with respect to capital products.

Perhaps the most significant factor to emerge from Table 4.4, however, is the very high level of imports in 1973. Imports are high in both the component and consumer goods sector. However, they are even more important in the computer sector. Input–output statistics

Table 4.4 *The demand for electronics products, United Kingdom, 1973*

Product classification	Firms in appropriate MLH £m	%	Other manufacturers £m	%	Imports £m	%	Total domestic demand £m
Telecommunications	343.955	90.96	13.061	3.46	21.111	5.58	378.127
Capital goods	248.515	69.35	34.372	21.05	75.452	0.90	358.339
Computers	248.765	46.46	27.276	5.10	259.337	48.44	535.378
Consumer goods	394.494	61.38	6.112	0.95	242.093	37.67	642.699
Components	383.002	53.54	47.010	6.57	285.352	39.89	715.364
Total	1618.731	61.55	127.831	4.86	883.345	33.59	2629.907

Source: Business Monitor Series PQ363–PQ367 (HMSO, 1975)

indicate that imports accounted for only 15 per cent of total demand in 1968, and 16.6 per cent in 1971 (HMSO, 1973, 1974*f*). Despite the limited nature of this evidence, it can be concluded that electronic imports expanded into the United Kingdom at a faster rate than local production in the early 1970s.

In order to evaluate the impact of the international network of electronics markets and producers in the United Kingdom it is necessary to consider not only the impact of imports on local demand, but also the role of exports in the sales of UK producers. Table 4.5 indicates that in those sectors which can be described as production – rather than development-oriented, namely telecommunications, consumer products and components (see NEDO, 1974, Table 30), the levels of services sold and non-MLH production are low. However, factored goods play an important part in the computer and component sectors. The highest levels of export were achieved by those sectors faced, in 1973, with the greatest levels of import competition on the local market: computers and components. However, in contrast with the level of competition from imports in the consumer goods sector, the level of exports recorded was low.

This section has established in very broad terms the environmental domains facing organisations when they are classified to major product sectors. Clearly the component sector is dominant in terms of total supply and demand, while change has been most pronounced in the computer sector. The division of organisations into the very large and the very small, alluded to in the preceding section, was most pronounced in the consumer goods sector. With respect to market uncertainty, in so far as the general level could be described according to competition from imports or competition from other sectors such as computers, components and consumer goods, all manufacturers appeared to be faced with difficult market conditions. However, in attempting to establish the likely relationships established between organisations and their task environments it is important, in the context of the electronics industry, to appreciate the role of a dynamic

Table 4.5 *Sales by the United Kingdom electronics industry*

Production sector	Sales of								Total sales £m
	Non-electronic products £m	%	Factored products £m	%	Services £m	%	Exports £m	%	
Telecommunications	24.1	5.5	15.7	3.6	12.4	2.8	13.5	9.9	439.6
Capital goods	86.8	17.3	27.5	5.5	31.4	6.3	107.3	21.4	501.4
Computers	28.2	6.6	63.4	14.7	14.3	3.3	161.6	37.5	431.3
Consumer goods	11.3	2.5	25.8	5.7	0.6	0.1	23.4	5.1	455.5
Components	29.8	4.6	68.8	11.0	4.2	0.7	141.7	22.6	630.8
Total	180.1	7.3	201.2	8.2	62.9	2.6	447.4	19.4	2458.6

Source: Business Monitor Series PQ363–PA367 (HMSO, 1975)

technology, the responsibility for which lies, in the initial stages, with remarkably few organisations.

Technology, markets and task environment relationships

Major innovations within the electronics industry occur predominantly in the development of active components. Each resulting 'generation' of components transmits external technological 'shocks' into the various equipment sectors bringing about the need within individual organisations for a redefinition of products in terms of specifications, tolerances, costs and applications. Subsequent generations of equipment effectively create new markets so that, over and above the natural growth of existing markets, a high degree of 'technology-induced' market expansion has characterised the industry.

At the same time, market force plays a major role in *initiating* technological development sequences. The dominant customers for the industry, the military and aerospace sectors, make considerable demands in terms of product performance and reliability. The resources which they bring to bear directly influence the rate of innovation. The very high capital costs of research and development, the institutionalised nature of innovation, and the economic benefits of scale production, together with the purchasing power of the defence and aerospace agencies in America, in particular, have favoured United States manufacturers. Not only do major institutional customers emerge as the initiators and sponsors of component innovation but, given their willingness to pay for product performance, they also dominate sales in the post-innovation development and early marketing stage of the product cycle. In this manner they reduce the risks for the component supplier and obviate the need for early price-cutting to increase or secure demand. The resulting opportunities for developing scale production economies can lead to the eventual reduction of costs for a particular generation of components, to a level at which significant growth in commercial demand can occur (Golding, 1971). The international advantage this distinctive high technology product cycle has bestowed upon United States producers since the 1950s is compounded by the fact that the United States intermediate and consumer home markets are large enough to support the indigenous manufacture of a variety of active components in quantities sufficient for the reinforcement of initial large-scale production advantages (Mulligan, 1974). This sequence of technology development and diffusion clearly places government agencies in a central position within the industry, triggering growth by fostering innovation and supporting subsequent development (Rosenberg, 1969).

Should large-scale production reduce costs sufficiently, a new generation of electronic technology can be incorporated into consumer products. In the consumer market the reduction of marginal costs associated with production is likely to be more critical than the technical tolerances associated with professional or non-consumer markets. The diffusion of a generation of component technology away from the highly specialised, easily defined, low-risk, 'government' market sector, through the intermediate sector (comprising industrial and commercial users) towards the consumer sector, therefore, implies the reduction of product-based technological uncertainty for the organisations involved but possibly an increase in production and market-based uncertainty.

It is possible to distinguish at least three major generations within the technological history of the electronics industry which fit into this pattern of government-induced innovation. Initially *valves* comprised the main electronic input to equipment such as high frequency radio transmitters (in the professional sphere) and radio receivers and, eventually, television receivers (in the consumer market). The second generation of components comprised *semiconductors* in the form of transistors which, like valves, were 'stand alone' components wired into circuits. Their discrete nature distinguishes them from third generation *microelectronics*, in which a series of 'active' functions are fabricated upon a single silicon 'chip'. *Large-scale integrated circuits* bring together the functions of a complex series of active and passive components upon individual microcircuits and may be construed as a fourth generation.

Against this technological background it is useful to summarise the types of relationship which occur between organisations in different sectors of the industry and their customers. Government agencies which act as major customers for electronic equipment in Britain are health and education authorities, on the one hand, and the Post Office, the aerospace sector and the Ministry of Defence, on the other. The first two have demands similar to those of the intermediate market sector, which is considered below. On the other hand, the defence, aerospace and Post Office sectors support the development of advanced and specialised equipment. The contacts between producers and these government agencies tend to take place at a variety of levels within the organisations involved. Although, for administrative purposes, purchasing may be centralised within particular government departments, the contacts which influence purchasing decisions occur, as often as not, in the field, often between engineers. This reflects a need for continuous customer feedback and technical direction as well as the large size of the organisations and transactions involved. Given the specialised requirements of government agencies, much of the technical input derives from customer capabilities in particular fields of applied electronics. In this context the existence of specialised boundary tasks for the establishment, negotiation and maintenance of customer linkages may be neither necessary nor appropriate. Commercial control in the electronics organisations involved tends to be centralised and hierarchical, while the onus for satisfactory boundary regulation falls upon technical, rather than marketing, personnel. Customers are relatively few, even internationally, and have easily defined (although technically demanding) needs. Competition is also readily identified, and, in any case, limited.

Given this heavy dependence upon government purchases, the telecommunications sector operates in a relatively stable market environment, especially in light of the limited number of producers and customers involved. For example, the Post Office accounted for 63.4 per cent of 1973 United Kingdom sales (HMSO, 1975a). Although exporting is limited, the level of imports is also low. Other electronic capital goods manufacturers, however, tend to operate in a relatively more complex market environment. In 1973, 20 per cent of sales were derived from activities other than the manufacture of capital equipment, indicating a considerable level of diversity within the sector. At the same time, local organisations were faced with considerable competition from imports and from activities classified to other MLH categories. On the other hand, the range of customers was still limited. It is estimated that as much as 34 per cent of sales of all electronic capital goods were dependent upon government expenditure in 1973, or 48 per cent of all production of capital goods within MLH 363.

Other manufacturers, commerce and some government agencies, such as the health and education departments and local authorities, comprise the intermediate market. Their demands are twofold: electronic equipment and circuits may be purchased as input for their own products in the case of other equipment manufacturers (OEM), while instruments and data processing equipment may also comprise a substantial proportion of their capital outlay. Requirements of the intermediate customer are not as technically demanding as those of the government sector. Nor are customers as likely to possess a similar pool of electronics expertise. Nevertheless, their individual needs will often involve the electronics manufacturer in considerable modification of existing products. The necessity to meet individual customer requirements suggests that the technical ability of the manufacturer will be at least as important as commercial prowess in the establishment and maintenance of market linkages.

The greater number of potential customers and competitors in the intermediate market increases market uncertainty. Thus, there is a need for the development of activities within an organisation, oriented towards regulation of the customer environment. There is also scope for product standardisation, particularly in the areas of instrument, computer and computer peripherals manufacture. The more standardised the product and its applications, the less critical the engineering capability of the sales force becomes, and the greater the importance assumed by commercial and marketing functions. Within the intermediate sector, then, the nature of the customer boundary structure and policies should reflect the level of standardisation of both demand and technology for particular products and, especially, the degree to which technology is internalised, although by no means insulated, within the organisation.

Thus, as noted in the preceding section, the market environment in the UK electronics industry appears the most 'open' in terms of penetration by imports for the computer sector. The role of overseas ownership is also particularly important in the computer sector, so that the high levels of imports and exports may reflect the international movement of goods within wider corporate networks. It is of note that in 1973 production of computer mainframes, rather than peripherals, accounted for 33 per cent of the total, of which 44 per cent was exported (HMSO, 1975a). Mainframe computer production within the United Kingdom was at the time in the hands of only four or five significant manufacturers, of which only one, ICL, was owned within the United Kingdom.

In the manufacture of consumer electronic equipment the result has been the creation of a large, structured organisation, in which large size and considerable internal differentiation has been the response to high levels of market uncertainty. How appropriate this may have been is yet to be seen, although the subsequent spectacular market and technical success of a number of far smaller and less obviously differentiated manufacturers in this sector raises doubts about such a strategy (Chandler, 1966; Channon, 1973). Production tasks may become even further divorced from marketing functions than in manufacturing for international markets. Product technology is at its most stable and most clearly buffered from the environment by other levels of organisation. The limited elasticity of consumer demand means that engineering objectives are directed towards maintenance of the lowest production costs commensurate with 'acceptable' levels of product design, performance and durability. Indeed, the boundary between manufacturing enterprises and customers may itself be mediated by a formal network of wholesale and retail outlets. Selling is based upon costs, performance, appearance and commercial arrangements between producer and vendor. The establishment of sales linkages is not completely dependent upon the nature of the product, and, because of its standardised nature, selling can be undertaken almost wholly by technically unqualified personnel drawing upon only occasional support from servicing departments. Given the nature of the customer boundary, marketing can be expected to emerge as a dominant activity within organisations manufacturing consumer equipment. Co-ordination is likely to be based upon forward planning and policy control through which the marketing function may straddle the internal technical functions, which it may direct, and the external market environment.

The electronic consumer goods sector, in which the importance of marketing as a boundary spanning and integrating task is paramount, appears the least successful in terms of international market performance in the United Kingdom (Table 4.4). While the components sector was faced with competition from similarly high levels of imports, it still managed to achieve a reasonable level of exports. However, the pattern varied considerably within the sector, perhaps revealing greater variability in the relationships between technology and marketing. In active components 29 per cent of production was exported in 1973, compared with imports which met almost 50 per cent of local demand. In terms of integrated circuits, the most technologically advanced area of component production, the value of imports almost equalled the total value of indigenous production and, in fact, accounted for 54 per cent of UK demand (HMSO, 1975b).

Location of the industry in the United Kingdom

The preceding discussion has outlined the societal and technological contexts within which United Kingdom electronics organisations operate. It has also covered some of the major market features which will impinge upon the external and internal relations of these enterprises. The present section reduces the focus of discussion yet further, in order to consider the distribution of the industry *within* the United Kingdom, and to introduce a geographic perspective to the environmental domain within which individual organisations define their particular task environments.

Smith (1971) demonstrated that despite 'a very considerable spatial variation in operating costs' the aggregate cost surface for electronic equipment manufacturing in the United States bore little relation to the distribution of employment in the industry. This does not mean that the industry is 'footloose' in the sense that variability in the availability and price of factor inputs or access to markets is unimportant to location decisions. Indeed, within the United States the industry is highly concentrated in California and in an area extending from Massachusetts and New Jersey through to Maryland. Smith suggested that these geographic concentrations reflect such 'difficult-to-cost' factors as accessibility to appropriate government agencies (cf. Nourse, 1967), close contact with research establishments, and access to existing concentrations of the industry (Smith, 1971, pp 383–7). It appears, then, that information availability and exchange is a major factor underlying the distribution of the United States electronics industry.

Keeble's (1976) analysis of shifts in the distribution of employment in the United Kingdom electronics industry between 1959 and 1971 was not limited by the partial approach adopted by Smith, who emphasised only spatial cost variations and location decisions. Keeble's conclusions were similar, however, and again regional information advantages apparently underlie the spatial pattern of the industry described. Thus, Keeble attributed the traditional dominance of the South East to the region's 'unique environmental advantages for innovative, information-hungry activities . . . exceptional market accessibility . . . the quality and skill of its residential labour force'. Of considerable importance was the role played by government demand, especially through the early development of broadcasting in the South East and defence expenditure and, as a result, the development of an industrial 'seed-bed' environment for electronics enterprise in North West London (Keeble, 1976;

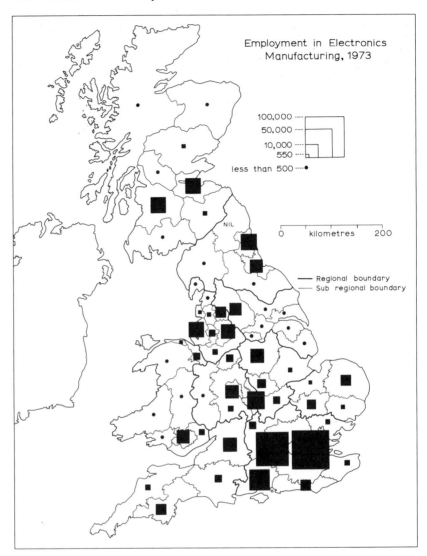

Figure 4.3 Geographic
distribution of British
electronics employment,
1973

Martin, 1966). Some dispersal of employment in electronics manufacturing has been taking place during the past two decades, however,
primarily at an intra-regional level *within* the South East, augmented by
the induced growth of the industry evident in Scotland. Other than the
latter trend, which is based primarily upon externally controlled investment, and partly in response to regional development policies (McDermott, 1979), Keeble suggested that the shifts observed reflected the
growing importance of semi-skilled female labour for more production-
intensive activities and the importance of residentially attractive locations within other parts of the South East as a means by which firms in
more technologically intensive production might attract qualified personnel.

Figure 4.3 shows the distribution of electronics employees across
planning subregions of the United Kingdom in 1973. The dominance of

Table 4.6 *Regional distribution of electronics employment within Britain, 1973*

Standard regions	All manufacturing	All electronics	Telecoms	Capital goods	Computers	Consumer goods	Components
Northern	5.22	**6.34**	**16.15**	0.92	2.35	3.84	**5.77**
Yorkshire and Humberside	10.09	2.33	0.23	1.28	0.52	8.73	1.69
East Midlands	7.77	4.76	**9.30**	3.65	0.43	0.98	5.68
East Anglia	2.62	**3.20**	0.00	**3.36**	0.08	**5.35**	**5.20**
South East	27.18	**48.61**	**27.27**	**72.92**	**53.07**	**53.35**	**44.24**
South West	5.38	**5.50**	1.09	2.74	1.15	**13.47**	**7.44**
West Midlands	14.12	8.39	**20.89**	1.54	8.39	8.74	4.10
North West	14.67	9.38	**14.83**	3.72	**15.07**	1.23	11.61
Wales	4.34	4.03	**4.89**	2.26	0.23	3.97	**5.84**
Scotland	8.64	7.43	5.35	7.57	18.70	0.77	8.25

Note: Regional shares exceeding share of all manufacturing industry in bold type.
Source: Department of Employment

the South East, in particular, the continuing importance of Greater London and the emergence of the Outer Metropolitan Area (OMA) and Solent subregions, all trends noted in Keeble's study, are confirmed. The North West forms a secondary concentration based upon the Manchester and Merseyside areas, while inclusion of telecommunications employment means that the Coventry subregion also emerges as a significant area of electronics employment. Scotland accounted for over 7 per cent of British electronics employees in 1973. The minor concentrations in South Wales, the Bristol area, Nottinghamshire, East Anglia and the Outer South East are consistent with Keeble's suggestion that any dispersion which has taken place away from the hearth areas of the South East has favoured adjoining areas rather than peripheral regions.

Disaggregation of the employment data shows how the extent to which the South East dominates the industry's distribution varies between sectors (Table 4.6). Thus, the most technically diversified and demanding sector, producing capital goods, was also the most strongly localised with 73 per cent of all employees located in the South East. Of these, 40 per cent were located in the Greater London, 47 per cent on the OMA, and 9 per cent in the Solent subregions. This concentration can be interpreted, in part, as the geographical outcome of the need for close technical liaison between government and company engineers as the basis for boundary regulation in the capital equipment industry.

The rapidly growing computer sector was also marked by distinctive concentrations of employment, primarily in the South East, with 25.6 per cent of employees found in the OMA in 1973, 18 per cent in London and 8 per cent in Solent. A further 19 per cent of computer employees were found in Scotland, with 15 per cent in the North West. While less dynamic and technologically intensive than the preceding two sectors, the electronic consumer goods sector was also concentrated in the South East. Employment in the Greater London subregion was three times that of the Outer Metropolitan Area, reflecting, perhaps, a high degree of locational inertia for this long-established sector. In addition, the distribution of consumer goods manufacture may represent a conflict between the need for a high degree of market accessibility and access to reserves of semi-skilled, lower-cost labour for the purposes of product assembly. The latter requirement gives rise to the secondary concentrations of consumer product employment in West Yorkshire, the West Midlands and East Anglia. East Anglia and the South West are locations in which the relatively low-cost labour force associated with less industrialised regional environments is available in areas with reasonable proximity to the major markets in the South East.

Component manufacture was the most *wide-spread* of all sectors and may be construed as potentially the most footloose. However, the telecommunications industry might be considered the *least centralised*, given its association with the traditional industrial areas of the Midlands, particularly in the Nottinghamshire/Derbyshire subregion, and Coventry, the North West, centred on Merseyside, and in the Northern region. Presumably this distribution is associated with various metal-working and engineering sectors out of which the telecommunications sector has evolved and with which it still maintains strong ownership and material input linkages.

Despite the facts that transport costs are a relatively low component of costs in the electronics industry (Figure 4.2) and that spatial variations in input costs and market access do not obviously influence the distribution of the electronics sector, distinctive concentrations both in the United States and the United Kingdom demonstrate the importance of an information-rich environment to the spatial evolution of the industry.

The survey of electronics firms   The preceding discussion established the broad environmental contexts within which United Kingdom electronics organisations operate. The brief description of the distribution of the industry suggests that location within the United Kingdom will also influence the operation of these individual organisations and their constituent firms, particularly insofar as location affects the information to which they might be exposed. The relationship between organisational location and information monitoring and development within the wider industrial environment is the concern of the empirical part of the study, which is based upon a direct survey of electronics enterprises.

Data were gathered during 1974 and 1975 from 121 electronics manufacturers with their operations based in Greater London, the Outer Metropolitan Area of South East England (the OMA), or Scotland. London was selected as the traditional hearth of the UK electronics industry (Keeble, 1976, p. 194). The OMA comprises a rather more arbitrary economic planning subregion, yet forms a distinctive transitional area between the intensive urbanisation of Greater

London and the more extensive rural and agricultural areas of the Outer South East and East Anglia (Keeble, 1972*b*, p. 139). Constraints imposed by time and resources meant that it was only feasible to gather data from organisations operating in the east, north and west of the OMA, however, from Reading through to Southend-on-Sea. Scotland, although hardly a single region in general terms, offers the advantage of clear delineation in a UK context. In addition, its economic record and the designation of all parts of Scotland as Development or Special Development Areas after 1966 means that it is valid to treat it as a single unit in the present study. As indicated earlier, Scotland is also the one regional development area which has experienced considerable post-war growth in electronics manufacturing.

Data were gathered from organisations selected randomly from all known electronics manufacturing enterprises in each area. For this purpose a comprehensive list was compiled from a number of sources, including government-published directories (HMSO, 1971; NEDO, 1973; Scottish Council, 1973), research registers (Firn, 1975; Wray *et al.*, 1974), and trade association membership and product directory lists (RECMF, 1974; Peregrinus, 1974; Eurolec, 1974; Technical Indexes Limited, 1974). As a result, the derived list was considerably more comprehensive than any of the individual sources upon which it drew.

In order to survey only manufacturing units which could be considered as 'independent' enterprises, several conventions were observed. The existence of a manufacturing function together with significant additional manufacturing support and management tasks including, for example, purchasing, design, production and development engineering, personnel, and sales, was the major criterion for the inclusion of an organisation. As the study is concerned with 'self-contained' manufacturing organisations the definition of enterprise adopted does not coincide with the Census definition, which rests solely upon ownership. The final list therefore included single-plant firms, multiplant firms, subsidiaries, and some semi-autonomous divisions of large organisations. Because the sample was not restricted to organisations operating at a single location, the additional inclusion criterion was observed that 'head office' and some manufacturing functions took place within the region. While a number of divisions of larger corporations met these criteria, and were included in the sample, the terms *enterprise* and *organisation* are used interchangeably to refer to respondents in the description of the study.

Emphasis upon the enterprise defined in this way raises the issue of the level of autonomy necessary to distinguish 'self-contained', fully functional units from branch plant operations. There is no simple means of deciding whether or not an establishment is autonomous. No organisation can be conceived as acting with complete freedom, its behaviour being conditioned by the linkage network within which it operates and its status in that network. In a branch plant the overwhelming relationship is often, but not always, with the parent company. In a subsidiary or division certain links in the network may be more formalised or constrained by virtue of corporate allegiance, yet these may not unduly influence the operation of the organisation other than in the field of, say, finance. While autonomy may be considered, therefore, a continuous rather than a discrete property, no major difficulty was encountered in the course of the survey in applying the above criteria once contact had been made with a respondent. If corporate influence was subject to negotiation and if responsibility for a wide range of external links rested with the organisation under consideration it was accepted as an enterprise for the purpose of the survey.

The survey was conducted amongst Scottish organisations in August and September, 1974, and in the South East of England between May and September, 1975. From each respondent information was sought in the course of an interview on:

(1) the history and structure of the organisation;
(2) the organisation's activities, encompassing factors such as market orientation, sales and purchasing linkages, financing and growth;
(3) the external communications of the executive with main responsibility for customer and market contact (the Chief Marketing Executive).

The first items were derived from an open, structured discussion with an executive, usually the Managing Director, but occasionally the Chief Marketing Executive. Information on the operations of the organisation was sought through the use of a standardised questionnaire which was completed, where possible, during the interview. Otherwise the questionnaire was left for subsequent attention, a procedure which, unfortunately, reduced the information received, despite the use of follow-up letters. The attempt to measure information flows involved a request for the Chief Marketing Executive – often the Managing Director himself – to maintain a prepared diary in which all external communications were recorded for a period of five working days.

This threefold approach enabled very detailed data to be gathered from a majority of respondents. Inevitably, however, there were gaps – most notably with respect to the contact diary information which was obtained from only 52 organisations. While this places limits on subsequent analysis and interpretation the following section is concerned only with the representativeness of the total sample of 121 respondents.

The data   Emphasis upon enterprises rather than establishments, and upon enterprises defined in functional rather than legal terms, limits the degree to which official or published statistics could be used to evaluate the sample. Such information is generally available at a national level only, and most usually for establishments employing more than 25 people. In any case, as information was gathered to test hypotheses rather than to describe the industry, it is more important that the sampling framework be adequate for the experimental purpose, than that the sample should be representative of the total industry. Further, the rationale underlying the study suggests that there will be regional differences in the nature of

organisations, so that comparison of the characteristics of a geographically biased sample with the characteristics of the entire industry is
contradictory. Nevertheless, an attempt was made to assess the nature
of the sample in relation to the industry as a whole.

The list of organisations compiled as a basis for sampling indicated
that as many as 80 might be eligible in Scotland, 300 in the OMA, and
250 in Greater London. It turned out that a considerable proportion of
these comprised branch plants or sales offices only. Others were
untraceable as a result of movement or closure, discrepancies which
indicate the difficulty of identifying functional manufacturing enterprises from registers compiled for other purposes. However, on the
basis of these early estimates sample targets of 40 organisations in each
region were set.

Discussions with trade, government, and research sources in Scotland
indicated that there were considerably fewer than 80 electronics enterprises there. The final total, 58, almost certainly encompassed all
operations which met the inclusion criteria outlined above. All these
enterprises were approached: the 39 interviews conducted therefore
represented a 76 per cent success rate.

Given the larger populations of electronics organisations in London
and the OMA, random sampling was undertaken in these regions, with
adequate allowance made for replacement of inappropriate contacts or
refusals. In the case of London the 39 interviews conducted represent
approximately 20 per cent of all potential participants. It is further
estimated that the 43 interviews recorded in the OMA cover at least 15
per cent of eligible OMA organisations, and as many as 30 per cent of
electronics organisations in the part of the region to which the survey
was restricted. Over the three regions the 121 interviews derived from
173 appropriate contacts represent a 70 per cent success rate, with the
highest regional rate having been achieved in Scotland. Comparison
of respondent into non-respondent, as far as the nature of the latter
could be determined, revealed no evidence of a statistically significant
difference between the two groups.

The distribution of respondents by sector within the industry can be
compared with that of non-respondents, as far as the latter could be
determined from directory and industrial sources and from telephone or
letter communications. Table 4.7 indicates considerable similarity between the distribution of respondents and non-respondents, both at a
regional level and across the entire sample. Although capital goods
manufacturers formed a substantial proportion of non-respondents in
the OMA and instrument/computer manufacturers in Scotland, there is
no evidence of any statistically significant difference between respondents and non-respondents.

The most obvious way to utilise official data to assess the representativeness of the survey at the regional level is through consideration of
employment coverage. Using figures supplied by the Department of
Employment at the subregional level for 1973, two comparisons were
undertaken. Assuming no significant change between the 1973 distribution and that of 1974–75 Table 4.8 compares absolute employment

Table 4.7 *Distribution of respondents and non-respondents by sector*

	London		OMA		Scotland		Total[1]		Refusals as % of approaches
	No.	%	No.	%	No.	%	No.	%	
Capital goods									
Surveyed	3	7.7	6	14.0	6	15.4	15	12.4	25.0
Refused	—	—	5	23.8	—	—	5	9.6	
Instruments									
Surveyed	9	23.1	11	25.6	6	15.4	26	21.5	33.3
Refused	5	26.3	3	14.3	5	41.7	13	25.0	
Consumer goods									
Surveyed	7	17.9	1	2.3	—	—	8	6.6	27.3
Refused	3	15.8	—	—	—	—	3	5.8	
Components									
Surveyed	20	51.3	25	58.1	27	69.2	72	59.5	30.1
Refused	11	57.9	13	61.9	7	58.3	31	59.6	
Total									
Surveyed	39		43		39		121		30.1
Refused	19		21		12		52		

Note: [1] $\chi^2 = 1.42$, 3 d.f., not significant.

Table 4.8 *Employment coverage of survey by region and sector*

	London	OMA	Scotland	Total
Total Electronics Employees, 1973	93357	97695	38531	229583
Survey Coverage (1974–1975)	47891	13196	11174	72261
Coverage as % 1973 Total	51.30	13.51	29.00	31.47
%Distribution electronics employees				
Capital goods				
Total 1973	34.49	33.55	27.99	
Surveyed	34.33	28.24	27.99	12.4
Instruments				
Total 1973	25.86	38.91	41.75	
Surveyed	5.47	31.52	33.34	21.5
Consumer goods				
Total 1973	19.58	8.40	1.37	
Surveyed	50.83	1.90	0.00	6.6
Components				
Total 1973	20.07	19.14	28.79	
Surveyed	9.37	38.34	38.66	59.5

Source: Department of Employment

coverage with total employment. On the further assumption that the relative distribution of employees between sectors has not changed, the sectoral distribution obtained through the survey is compared with that recorded by the Department of Employment. These comparisons are prejudiced by the fact that the official data are based upon *all* establishments, while the sample data are drawn from functional enterprises only. It appears, nevertheless, that the sample covered approximately 13 per cent of all UK electronics employment, and about 31 per cent of employment in the three regions considered. Within these regions the shares vary between a low 13 per cent in the OMA and a high 51 per cent in London, this last figure being a function of the sampling of several particularly large organisations in the London area.

With respect to sectoral distribution, employment coverage in London is biased towards consumer manufacture and away from instrument and component employment (Table 4.8), reflecting the occurrence of several large consumer goods producers in the sample. While organisations in the other sectors dominate the sample in terms of numbers of enterprises, they are generally much smaller than consumer goods manufacturers. In both Scotland and the OMA the higher coverage of component and instrument/computer manufacturers is a function of the frequent occurrence of branch establishments in the other sectors, and does not indicate any bias in the sampling procedure.

According to the Census of Production there were 1556 electronics 'enterprises' active in the United Kingdom in 1971. Assuming this to be a reasonable estimate of functional units in existence in 1974 the sample represents approximately 8 per cent of the total. The distribution of the sample across sectors and size classes can also be compared with equivalent distributions derived from the 1971 data (Table 4.9). Because of the small number of respondents in the telecommunications sector and the similarities between the manufacture of telecommunication equipment and capital goods, respondents from these two sectors were amalgamated for the purposes of subsequent analysis. In addition, a considerable number of instrument manufacturers were encountered in the course of the survey. No mainframe computer manufacturers co-operated in the study so that instrument and computer peripheral manufacturers were also allocated to a common category. In an attempt to reduce any distortion which this procedure might introduce in the comparison of the sectoral distribution of firms, the value of chi-square was calculated on the basis of a further amalgamation between the computer/instrument sector and the capital goods/telecommunications sector. Accepting that these adjustments give rise to a degree of imprecision in the test results, it is concluded, nevertheless, that the sectoral break-down of organisations obtained in the sample is not significantly different from the national distribution (Table 4.9). The sample is dominated by component producers, although to only a marginally greater extent than the national distribution, with consumer product manufacturers in the minority. However, there is evidence to suggest that the sample is also slightly biased towards larger organisations, as the very smallest size category is under-represented and every other category over-represented (Table 4.9).

Despite the difficulty of evaluation, a number of factors, including sample size, the high response rate and comprehensive source listing, the similar distribution of participant and non-participant organisations, and the reasonably full employment coverage obtained, give sufficient

Table 4.9 *Size and sector distributions of surveyed organisations*

	1971 Census		1974–75 Survey		%
	No.	%	No.	%	Difference
Employment size					
1– 24	974	62.60	23	19.01	−43.59
25– 49	111	7.13	18	14.88	7.75
50– 99	145	9.32	23	19.01	9.69
100–199	98	6.30	14	11.57	5.27
200–299	70	4.50	12	9.92	5.42
300–749	86	5.53	18	14.88	9.35
Over 749	72	4.63	13	10.74	6.11

$\chi^2 = 90.90$, 6 d.f.
  Significant at 0.001 level

Sector					
Telecommunication	97	6.23			
Capital Goods	372	23.91	41	33.88	−1.79
Computers	86	5.53			
Consumer Goods	174	11.18	8	6.61	4.57
Components	827	53.13	72	59.50	− 6.37

$\chi^2 = 4.50$, 2 d.f.
  Not significant

Source: *Census of Production*, 1971, Reports PA363–PA367 (HMSO, 1974)

grounds for accepting the survey data as suitable for subsequent analysis. The only obvious discrepancy between the sample and official statistics with respect to the nature of the industry was the under-representation within the survey of the very smallest employment size interval.

Corporate attributes of the sample

Given the general representativeness of the survey, the sampled organisations can be classified according to a number of corporate characteristics: the location of ownership (determined with reference to 'ultimate' ownership in the case of corporate hierarchies with more than two tiers); the status of the organisation within a corporate context; the origin of ownership; whether or not a respondent belonged to a public group; and spatial organisation (Table 4.10). On the basis of these indices a general image emerged of predominantly locally controlled organisations, many still under the control of their entrepreneur-founders, although only 35 per cent were single-plant, independent firms. One-fifth were overseas-owned, predominantly American. While half the respondent organisations were themselves subsidiaries, only 15 per cent owned subsidiaries. Despite a relatively complex pattern of origin and ownership, only 27 per cent of enterprises surveyed operated at more than one location.

Table 4.10 *Corporate characteristics of surveyed organisations*

Variable	Categories	Respondents No.	%
Location of ownership	Head Office	59	48.8
	Elsewhere within region	24	19.8
	Elsewhere within UK	14	11.6
	Europe	9	7.4
	United States	15	12.4
Corporate status	Independent (single-plant firm)	43	35.5
	Independent with subsidiaries	6	5.0
	Subsidiary	61	50.4
	Subsidiary with subsidiaries	11	9.1
Holding	Public	29	24.0
	Private	92	76.0
Origin of ownership	Private – entrepreneur	52	43.0
	Corporate	35	28.9
	Take-over by UK principal/s	13	10.7
	Take-over, overseas principal/s	21	17.3
Spatial organisation	Single location	88	72.7
	Single manufacturing location, sales office, etc. elsewhere	8	6.6
	Multiple manufacturing locations	25	20.7

A number of interesting differences in the regional distribution of organisations emerge on these indices. For example, considerably more London organisations were multilocational than was the case in the other regions, an outcome consistent with London's history as an electronics hearth area and with government effort devoted to encouraging organisations to remove manufacturing facilities from London (Figure 4.4). A larger proportion of Scottish organisations operated at single locations compared with the situation in the other two regions. Yet, the level of local control and within-region ownership was considerably lower in Scotland (Figure 4.5). Overseas ownership was

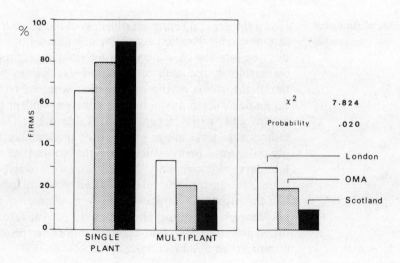

Figure 4.4 Spatial organisation of surveyed enterprises by region

Table 4.11 *Regional distribution of respondents by sector*

	London		Outer Metropolitan Area		Scotland		Total
	No.	%	No.	%	No.	%	
Capital Goods	3	7.7	6	14.0	6	15.4	15
Instruments	9	23.1	11	25.6	6	15.4	26
Consumer Goods	7	17.9	1	2.3	0	0.0	8
Components	20	51.3	25	58.1	27	69.2	72

$\chi^2 = 14.55$, 6 d.f., significant at 0.05 level

relatively common, an observation consistent with the policy-induced nature of the industry in Scotland (McDermott, 1976). Head office control was most common in the OMA, although the level of within-region control was highest in London. In keeping with its record as an electronics enterprise hearth area, London was also an administrative centre within the industry; hence, the relatively high proportion of OMA organisations falling into the 'Elsewhere UK' category were all controlled by London-based groups. Consistent with the pattern revealed in Figure 4.4 is the fact that 16 London respondents (41 per cent) were members of publically-listed groups, compared with eight in the OMA and five in Scotland ($\chi^2 = 9.56$, significance = 0.008). While the absence of statistically significant variations between the corporate status and origins of organisations in the three regions means that no sweeping conclusions can be reached, several broad differences are of note. Amongst Scottish organisations there was a low level of local control, limited entrepreneurial activity and considerable external ownership. In London overseas ownership was unimportant, the high proportion of subsidiaries there reflecting membership of troups of predominantly London-based *British* corporations. In the OMA there was evidence of a high level of entrepreneurial activity (McDermott, 1978).

There was also significant variation in the sectoral distribution of organisations by region (Table 4.11). Component producers dominated each region, although they made up almost 20 per cent more of the Scottish than the London sample. The distribution of consumer goods

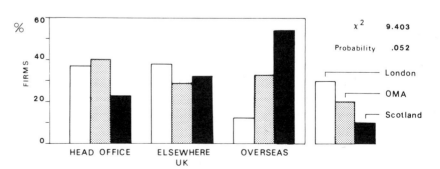

Figure 4.5 Location of ownership by region

producers was reasonably consistent with their overall distribution, but this does mean that there was a difference in their contribution to the sample between regions. Only one consumer goods producer was recorded in the OMA and none in Scotland. The instrument/computer sector was less important in the Scottish sample than in the other regions, the capital goods/telecommunications sector less so in London.

It can be concluded, then, that spatial variations in both the corporate ownership characteristics of respondent organisations and their sector affiliations within the industry might underlie any differences which may otherwise be attributed to location in subsequent analyses. Indeed, these broad organisational attributes, together with location, appear to define respondents' particular environmental domains and, as a result, are included in the attempt to specify the structural contingency model in Chapter 7. The next two chapters, however, narrow the focus of the study to consider the internal structure of sampled organisations and the definition of their task environments through linkage and information fields.

5 Measuring organisational structure, performance and development

Having established in Chapter 4 the broad dimensions of the domain within which electronics enterprises and the electronics industry operate in Britain, this chapter explores the internal characteristics of individual electronics organisations. Drawing on the postulates of the structural contingency model from organisation theory (Chapter 2), these characteristics have already been suggested as important determinants of the form, functioning and performance of individual organisations and enterprises. Therefore, through the analyses of this chapter it is hoped both to clarify and to specify these internal attributes of electronics enterprises so that they can be incorporated into an empirical test of the *a priori* model of organisation–environment interaction proposed in Chapter 3.

The first consideration is organisational structure. This is the most basic element of the contingency model and yet it is the aspect of organisation which has received the least attention in industrial geography. Rather than using a handful of randomly chosen variables to depict only hopefully salient aspects of organisational structure, the present study adopts a multivariate approach and a base of 40 variables to undertake these analyses.

The second consideration is organisational performance. This is an internal index of an enterprise's success, unlike the externally judged index usually referred to as 'effectiveness' (Pfeffer and Salancik, 1978), and is again a basic element of the structural contingency framework. Finally, an attempt is made to draw together these structural dimensions of electronics enterprises into a development sequence, again adopting a multivariate approach.

Organisational structure

To explore organisational structure in the context of the electronics industry, information was gathered on the general form or configuration of each respondent enterprise; the nature of the transformation process undertaken within it; the existence, role, organisation and control of development functions; the existence, organisation, control and differentiation of selling and marketing tasks; and the integration of development, sales and marketing functions. Forty more specific attributes of these general dimensions of organisational structure were defined, the presence or absence of which were recorded as a series of binary variables for each respondent. The complete list of these attributes is outlined in Table 5.1. This is a considerable advance over the specification of organisational structure in those few studies in

115

Table 5.1 *Organisational structure; orthogonally rotated components*

| | Component Loadings[1] | | | | | | |
	I Differentiation	II Delegation	III Integration	IV Production flexibility	V Production complexity	VI Marketing	h^2
Attributes[2]							
(1) Departments	−0.580	0.381		−0.255			0.590
(2) Divisions	0.399	0.209	0.244	0.452	0.416		0.651
(3) Vertical integration	0.496	0.260	0.302	0.361		0.217	0.583
(4) Custom products							0.063
(5) Fabrication	0.561	−0.221	0.246	0.461			0.661
(6) Small batches	−0.711		−0.208				0.586
(7) Large batches					0.736		0.585
(8) Mass production	0.506	0.262	0.432	0.240			0.570
(9) More than one technology	0.212		0.240		0.598		0.536
(10) New products	0.220			0.783			0.675
(11) Original product	−0.650						0.478
(12) More than one product line				0.786			0.707
(13) Product development	−0.471	0.554			0.258		0.635
(14) Process development	0.710				0.261		0.616
(15) Advanced development	0.769		0.221				0.726
(16) Outside technology	0.695	−0.217					0.604
(17) Manager controls technology		−0.357	−0.485	0.209	−0.461		0.627
(18) Marketing controls development				0.215		0.722	0.571
(19) Customer based development							0.073
(20) Corporate technology			0.787				0.690
(21) Sales office		0.773				0.222	0.672
(22) More than one sector				0.244			0.124
(23) Sales by area	0.350	0.569					0.466
(24) Sales by product			0.641	0.211		0.208	0.554
(25) Use UK agents	0.551	−0.267					0.396
(26) Overseas agents		0.212		0.204			0.110
(27) Sales office elsewhere	0.700	0.230	0.283				0.665
(28) Sales office overseas	0.833		0.209				0.775
(29) Manager controls sales		−0.691			−0.248		0.603
(30) Marketing controls sales	0.506		0.274		0.222	0.440	0.593
(31) Sales office manager		0.718	0.254				0.603
(32) Corporate sales support			0.873				0.799
(33) Marketing information function		0.311				−0.212	0.160
(34) Marketing uses customer information	−0.249	0.428				0.336	0.396
(35) Marketing uses secondary information	0.340	0.238				0.594	0.575
(36) Marketing discrete function	0.653		0.400	0.225		0.275	0.779
(37) Sales controls marketing		−0.498					0.318

Table 5.1 *Organisational structure; orthogonally rotated components—(contd)*

	Component Loadings[1]						
	I	II	III	IV	V	VI	
	Differentia-	Delega-	Integra-	Production	Production	Market-	
Attributes[2]	tion	tion	tion	flexibility	complexity	ing	h²
(38) Marketing executive director	0.481					0.623	0.690
(39) Marketing function by sales	0.461	0.531			0.324		0.591
(40) Corporate marketing support	0.331		0.758				0.723
Eigenvalue	10.881	4.758	2.310	1.994	1.681	1.468	
% of variance	27.2	12.0	5.8	5.0	4.2	3.7	

Notes:

[1] Loadings below 0.2 omitted.

[2] Full description of attributes in Table 5.3

industrial geography which have considered this issue explicitly (McDermott, 1977; Hoare, 1978; Marshall, 1979).

As there are alternative structural forms which an organisation might adopt, it is likely that the particular combination of such characteristics within an individual organisation will be both a consequence of previous development and an influence upon future development. Therefore, it is the purpose of this section to investigate interrelationships amongst the 40 variables describing structure to identify different dimensions about which the internal structuring of activities take place amongst the electronics manufacturing organisations.

Principal components analysis has been used to identify distinct clusters of structural attributes. However, there was a problem in selecting the appropriate transformation for the original incidence matrix, given that the Pearson product moment correlation coefficient was inappropriate for the point dichotomous data upon which the analysis was based. A number of alternatives have been suggested in the literature, usually derivatives of the appropriate product moment coefficient, phi (Carroll, 1961). In the present study both attributes and organisations can be considered members of well-defined, meaningful sets, so that attention can be restricted to coefficients which accommodate mutual absence. Three such coefficients have been described by Sneath and Sokal (1973), two of which are based upon the cross-product of the two-by-two table, the Yule and phi coefficients, and a proportional coefficient introduced by Hamann (1961).

Both the frequently used phi coefficient, and the long-standing Yule coefficient are sensitive to the distribution of marginal frequencies. As the distribution of cases on one or both of the dichotomous items becomes more uneven these coefficients become less reliable indicators of the internal relationship. Furthermore, the Yule coefficient becomes completely meaningless if zero occupies one of the cells. While a procedure has been suggested for adjusting phi to overcome marginal inequalities (Cureton, 1959), there is neither statistical nor mathematical justification for this (Guilford, 1965).

Amongst the surveyed electronics firms, however, many attributes of internal structure appeared infrequently, although it is still likely that they played a central role in organisational development. In addition, it is only to be expected that in considering relationships between all 40 attributes of structure in the present study some cells in the 780 two-by-two contingency tables will record zero occurrences. For this reason the Hamann coefficient has been used (Tinkler, 1971). While this coefficient is directly analogous to phi when the marginal frequencies are evenly distributed, it remains a reliable indicator of relationships *within* the table when the distribution of these marginal frequencies is uneven.

The coefficient, H, is defined as follows:

$$H = \frac{(a + d - b - c)}{(a + d + b + c)},$$

Where a, b, c, d are the (clockwise) cell frequencies in the two-by-two contingency table. It possesses the advantage of ready interpretation, comprising the differences between matched and mismatched firms on each pair of attributes expressed as a ratio of total firms. Complete coincidence of attributes, whether based upon mutual presence or absence, or both, gives rise to a perfect positive relationship, $H = 1$. Complete disassociation, regardless of the direction in which it might occur, gives rise to a perfect negative relationship, $H = -1$.

Nine principal components with eigenvalues exceeding unity were extracted from the matrix of Hamann coefficients. Loadings exceeding 0.2 for the 40 attributes on six of the rotated factors are presented in Table 5.1. In terms of overall importance the first three components made the greatest contribution to explanation and are worthy of considerable emphasis (accounting for 27.2, 12.0 and 5.8 per cent of variance respectively). The second three components formed a secondary set of meaningful dimensions and justify an attempt at interpretation. The final three were based either on one, or at most, two variables from the set of 40, and were not conducive to generalisation. The communalities presented in Table 5.1 have been adjusted accordingly, to reflect the involvement of variables on only six components. These components represent the main dimensions of organisational structure that can be distinguished from the survey of electronics enterprises.

The first component is the major structural dimension and parallels the first component derived by the Aston study (Pugh *et al.*, 1968) labelled the 'structuring of activities'. It loads positively on attributes which indicate increasingly specialised technical and boundary functions and the allocation of tasks to identifiable subsystems within, and even outside, the firm. In other words, it relates to the differentiation of departments to deal with homogeneous segments of the external environment. Indeed, it is tempting to interpret the component as a dimension of specialisation and differentiation within the organisation, and it is useful to label it accordingly. However, although variance was not distorted by the split of the data on the various attributes as a result of the use of the Hamann coefficient the first component does resemble an 'artifactual' factor (Horst, 1965, pp 513–6; Rummel, 1970, pp 303–5), as it is positively associated with less common attributes and negatively associated with the more common ones. It is difficult, therefore, to attribute this component wholly to the nature of the surveyed organisations and not, in part at least, to the nature of the attributes that were recorded and to likely underlying correlations with scale. As a result it must be regarded as yielding little insight into particular forms of internal structuring within this particular set of organisations.

The second component (Table 5.1) is more meaningful. Variables denoting managerial control over technology, sales and marketing load negatively upon it, while the establishment of a sales office, the appointment of an internal sales office manager and the organisation of sales by territory all load positively. The undertaking of product development and association with an information-oriented marketing function under sales office jurisdiction suggest that Component II reflects the emergence of structure as a function of the decentralisation of authority within the business enterprise. It is analogous to the second dimension of the Aston study although, given the nature of the attributes used in the present study, is more appropriately considered as a measure of *delegation* than the more physical notion of decentralisation.

The third component reflects the *integration* of tasks within the organisation on the basis of whether or not it has access to a wider corporate system. The component is associated with group assistance, support, or control of technology, marketing and selling. It extends the idea of lateral movement of information between subsystems within the organisation to incorporate flows taking place within a wide corporate framework. However, Component III also accommodates some elements of the organisation of production, particularly mass production and vertical integration, and therefore implies that corporate dependence and technology come together, not as determinants of structure, but as integral components of organisational structure (Pugh *et al.*, 1969).

The fourth component is related to those aspects of technology which indicate *production flexibility*, i.e. the establishment of additional product lines since 1969 and the production of more than one such line. Component V is also associated with production processes, although more as an indicator of *complexity*, given positive loadings with attributes denoting large batch production, more than one technology, and organisation in product divisions. This is also consistent with a negative loading with direct manager control of technology. These two dimensions of organisational structure are, in fact, closely related but it is significant that they should emerge separately in this analysis. Component IV closely parallels the continuum proposed by Harvey (1968) to measure technological complexity in organisations while

Component V is a direct parallel of that devised by Woodward (1965) with which Harvey so strongly disagreed. Finally, Component VI emerges as an indicator of *marketing development* with high loadings associated with a managerial role played by a distinct marketing function. It confirms the significance attached to marketing functions in firms and organisations by Hower and Lorsch (1967) and Thompson (1973) for example.

Organisational performance

Performance can be regarded as a key element of the structural contingency model from organisation theory since structure has been held to influence performance on the one hand and the effectiveness of the organisation in the environment within which it operates on the other. As such, performance assumes a pivotal role in the *a priori* model advanced in Chapter 3 as a possible foundation for a more broadly based geography of business organisations. However, the difficulty of specifying performance is an additional legacy from the structural contingency model.

Because of the difficulty of conceptualising and measuring organisational performance, the size and growth of enterprises are treated in the present study as surrogate indicators. In a regional context, the size and growth (or decline) of organisations are of interest owing to their association with the provision of employment and maintenance of regional economic welfare. From the perspective of organisation theory, organisational size and growth measure performance insofar as survival is contingent upon the ability of the enterprise to accumulate and retain resources within its boundaries (Katz and Kahn, 1966, p. 150).

While a variety of accounting measures could be used as indices of performance, variations in book-keeping procedures from one firm to another, the piecemeal introduction of current cost accounting, the less accessible nature of these data, and the noise which they might introduce are such that there may be considerable loss of information in attempting to utilise more sophisticated scales to measure performance (see Grinyer and Norburn, 1975, pp 74–5). In the present study all respondents supplied employment totals for 1974, 67 provided two years' figures, and 61 furnished accurate data for 1969, enabling employment change over five years to be measured for over half the surveyed electronics enterprises. For turnover, 77 respondents provided 1974 figures, 60 provided 1973 figures, but only 51 provided information for 1969. To make use of all these indices it is necessary, therefore, to assume that response bias within the sample for the incomplete items was either regular or random across the three regions. The consistency of the results which were derived from these data suggests that one of these conditions is satisfied. Inspection of the data indicated that a log to the base ten transformation was necessary to derive approximately normal sample distributions for the various size and growth variables.

Using these data, an attempt was made to derive more general indices of organisational size and growth, and hence performance. A variety of variables was developed for this purpose, measuring aspects of growth

Table 5.2 *Size and growth; orthogonally rotated components*

Variable[1]	Component Loadings[2]		
	I Size	II Growth	h^2
Age in years	0.238	−0.834	0.735
Employment 1974	0.904		0.839
Turnover 1974	0.982		0.971
Turnover per employee 1974	0.549		0.303
% Employment shift 1973–1974		0.882	0.798
% Turnover shift 1973–1974	0.253	0.782	0.676
Eigenvalue	2.476	1.846	
% of variance	41.3	30.8	

Note: [1] All variables transformed to log base 10
       [2] Loadings below 0.2 omitted

and change and, together with the age of firms, reduced to two more general indices using principal components analysis (Table 5.2). Prior analysis indicated that the measures of one and five year change were highly correlated and, therefore, the former was retained for subsequent analysis to ensure as wide a coverage and as large a sample as possible.

The principal components procedure extracted two major clusters of variables from the data which together accounted for over 70 per cent of the total variance. The axes defining these clusters were then rotated by the varimax procedure to an orthogonal position for the purposes of interpretation and further analysis (Table 5.2). This procedure rendered the components mathematically independent so that scores on the growth component could be treated as independent of the organisational size component. With respect to the loadings of variables on these two components, the ratio of turnover per employee is positively associated with organisational size, which suggests that in the electronics industry the largest enterprises are also the most capital intensive. Age, however, is negatively associated with the growth component, holding the implication that, while the size of an enterprise is not necessarily associated with the length of time it has been in existence, recent growth tends to have been the prerogative of younger firms.

Scores on these two components could be calculated for a total of 67 firms. In addition, in an attempt to assess the generality of the component of short-term growth, respondents' scores on this component were correlated with the variables measuring growth over a five-year period. The results, $r = 0.81$ (51 cases), between the scores on the growth component and growth of turnover over five years, and $r = 0.88$ (54 cases) between the scores on the growth component and the five-year increase or decrease in employment, confirm that the composite variable is a meaningful measure of differences in firm performance during the early 1970s. Consequently, these two measures of organisational size and organisational growth would appear to be adequate surrogates to calibrate performance in the subsequent exploration of the *a priori* model of organisation–environment interaction based upon the surveyed electronics firms.

Organisational development

The forty variables used in the present study to describe organisational structure allow alternative structural forms to be recognised from the tendency of these variables to cluster into interpretable subsets. The identification of these clusters has already been attempted using principal components analysis. The general level of firm development may relate not simply to the interrelationships among subsets of these variables, however, but also to the way in which they are structured with respect to an ongoing *development* continuum. In part this could be measured just by the density of attributes by summing their occurrence (or non-occurrence) with regard to *a priori* interpretation of each item's contribution to organisational development. However, while the number or density of attributes for individual electronics enterprises should indicate their *general* levels of development, the scores derived from simply summing down respondents' profiles would accord each attribute equal weight. This procedure makes the implicit assumption that the incorporation of any particular function or task into an organisation or enterprise, as denoted by the presence of any one of the attributes, would be treated as no more difficult, or likely, than incorporation of all others into its operations. As this is clearly unrealistic, an attempt is made in the present section to scale organisational development, and subsequently to order electronics enterprises themselves, on the basis of the relationship between attributes and a single central development component. The topological analysis which is described below quantifies the complex notion of development which is implicit in all the more common indicators of organisational performance. Indeed, the derivation of a central development component in the present analysis can be incorporated as a third dimension of performance, building on the two developed in the previous sections.

R. H. Atkin has developed concepts from set theory and algebraic topology into a general, although elaborate, technique for the identification and analysis of mathematical relations based upon the type of binary transformation of qualitative information undertaken in the collection of data on respondent organisations (Atkin, 1974*a*, 1974*b*, 1974*c*, 1976). In the present context, a development continuum can be postulated, whereby some general order emerges with respect to the likelihood of any organisation possessing a particular subset of the 40 original attributes and its relative position on that continuum, defined in this case by the full set of respondents. Both organisations and attributes have a role to play in defining development which, in Atkin's language, is manifest in the attributes (as *simplices*) sharing common business organisations (as *vertices*). Following Atkin's terminology, a pair of attributes is defined as *q-near* if they share $q + 1$ organisations in common. For example, two attributes are *10-near* if they jointly characterise 11 enterprises. The set of two or more attributes so related comprises a *simplicial complex* and forms *q-connected components*. Unlike factor analytic methods which seek to partition variation, Atkin's method, then moves towards *q-connected components* whereby all simplices in the complex (in this case, attributes of firms) are connected to a greater or lesser extent, and where the level of connection is quantified by the value of *q*. The convergence of simplices and the emergence of a single comprehensive component through the process of *q*-connection makes the method appropriate for the analysis and measurement of development.

Without describing the philosophical and theoretical basis of Atkin's *q*-analysis, an attempt is made in the following discussion to incorporate the conventions and terminology associated with it (Atkin, 1974*a*). For a technical description of this form of analysis the reader is referred to Atkin (1974*a*). The extent of the discussion is limited, however, to that necessary to enable elaboration on the results achieved.

Table 5.3 outlines the attributes recorded for electronics enterprises, most of which are self-explanatory. Within the table they have been grouped according to more general, higher order dimensions of organisation derived on an *a priori* basis. Departmental differentiation was the most common attribute, although in some cases specialisation followed both departmental and divisional, or product-based, lines. Over 80 per cent of respondents undertook small batch production with assembly line or mass production being the least common transformation processes. There is little evidence of recent shifts in production activity, with original product lines still the main focus of 80 per cent of respondents and only 30 per cent having made any major product change or addition since 1969. Control and direction of many of those respondent organisations fell to a single Managing Director, while in less than 40 per cent of the sample enterprises did marketing exercise any significant control over development. Indeed, a high proportion of respondents based their technical development efforts only on known customer needs.

With respect to boundary spanning activities, sales offices were generally small; the existence of a full sales office with separate back-up functions such as telephone order-receiving, order-processing and sales co-ordination, was by no means universal. Many electronics enterprises did not possess the sales personnel which might have enabled them to decide whether to sell by area or product. The result was usually, but not always, geographical limits on the market area in which they operated.

In a number of organisations the Managing Director retained responsibility for customer relations as one of a range of executive responsibilities. The most common arrangement for marketing as such was its integration with selling, either subordinate to it (31 per cent of firms) or spanning it (20 per cent). However, most organisations paid lip service to the marketing function, but only 59 per cent acknowledged it as a distinctly information-oriented task. The generally low status of marketing is reflected in its considerable dependence upon customer feedback in the few instances in which it existed as a function in its own right, and

Table 5.3 *Selected attributes of organisation and q-analysis*

	I		II	III
	Incidence			
Attributes	No. ($\hat{q}$ + 1)	%	$\check{q}$	Eccentricity
Configuration				
(1) Organised by department; functional specialisation	103	85.12	85	0.1977
(2) Organised by division; product specialisation	32	26.45	28	0.1034
(3) Vertical integration of manufacturing	29	23.97	27	0.0357
Technology				
(4) Produce custom products, prototypes, etc.	72	59.50	63	0.1250
(5) Undertake fabrication of materials, engineering tasks, etc.	18	14.88	16	0.0582
(6) Undertake production of small lots/batches	99	81.82	82	0.1928
(7) Undertake production of large batches	57	47.11	48	0.1633
(8) Undertake assembly line, continuous or mass production	30	24.79	29	0.0000
(9) Involved in more than one process; e.g. chemical, mechanical, assembly, etc.	46	38.02	40	0.1219
(10) A new product line established since 1969	37	30.58	33	0.0882
(11) Still manufacture original product line	101	83.47	85	0.1744
(12) Produce more than one product line	37	30.85	33	0.0882
Research and development				
(13) Undertake development of existing products	93	76.86	80	0.0882
(14) Undertake research and development of process or processes	20	16.53	18	0.0526
(15) Undertake advanced R and D, without immediate market applications	18	14.88	17	0.0000
(16) Buy-in external expertise, use technical consultancy, etc.	15	12.40	14	0.0000
Control of technology and development				
(17) Technology responsibility of, or controlled by, the Managing Director	51	44.63	49	0.0800

Table 5.3 *Selected attributes of organisation and q-analysis—(contd)*

	I		II	III
	Incidence			
Attributes	No. $(\check{q} + 1)$	%	$\check{q}$	Eccentricity
(18) Development undertaken primarily in response to marketing initiative	46	38.02	40	0.1219
(19) Development only in response to known customer needs or customer initiatives	17	58.68	64	0.0923
(20) Technical direction and/or support and assistance from corporate sources	49	40.50	46	0.0426
Sales function				
(21) Full and separate sales office	73	60.33	67	0.0735
(22) Selling into more than one market sector; e.g. government, intermediate, consumer	47	38.84	43	0.0682
(23) Sales force and selling effort organised by area	59	40.40	44	0.0889
(24) Sales force and selling effort organised by product or by individual customers	41	33.88	36	0.1081
(25) Use of selling agents within the UK	22	18.18	19	0.1000
(26) Use of selling agents overseas	53	43.80	49	0.0600
(27) A spatially separate or additional sales office within the UK	26	21.49	25	0.0000
(28) An overseas sales office	15	12.40	14	0.0000
Control of the sales function				
(29) Under Managing Director	63	52.07	58	0.0678
(30) Part of a wider, overriding marketing function	25	20.66	22	0.0370
(31) Separate Sales Office Manager	68	56.20	63	0.0625
(32) Selling direction and/or support from corporate sources	42	34.71	38	0.0769
The marketing function				
(33) Defined as an information-based and oriented function	71	58.68	65	0.0758
(34) Customers the main source of market information	77	63.65	69	0.1600
(35) Extensive use of secondary information sources for market projection, planning, etc.	37	30.58	34	0.0571
(36) Marketing a separate and discrete department	16	16.22	15	0.0000

Table 5.3 *Selected attributes of organisation and q-analysis—(contd)*

	I		II	III
	Incidence			
Attributes	No. ($\hat{q} + 1$)	%	$\check{q}$	Eccentricity
Control of the marketing function				
(37) Under Managing Director	43	35.54	39	0.0750
(38) Chief Marketing Executive of director status on basis of his marketing function	27	22.31	25	0.0385
(39) Marketing a function performed within, or under a wider overriding selling function	39	32.23	35	0.0833
(40) Marketing direction and/or support and assistance from corporate sources	32	26.45	30	0.0322

in the few enterprises in which the Chief Marketing Executive enjoyed director status on the basis of the marketing task.

The real value of a topological approach to organisational development only emerges with consideration of the *chains of q-connection*, the connection of attributes by common vertices, or enterprises. At this stage of analysis attention is shifted from $\hat{q}$(q-top) to $\check{q}$(q-bottom) (Table 5.3, column II). Two attributes, departmentalisation and the manufacture of the original product line, with $\hat{q}$ values of 102 and 100 respectively, combine to form a single component based upon 86 respondents within which there were common features. As a result they share $\check{q}$-values of 85. Small batch production, $\hat{q} = 99$, joins the q-connected component, $\check{q} = 82$. Of the 86 organisations holding the first two attributes in common, 83 undertook small batch production. At $\check{q} = 82$ there are also a number of disconnected components, that is simplices with $\hat{q} \geqslant 82$ but which are 82-connected neither to the main component nor to each other.

By $\check{q} = 50$, the attributes defining the central component and their order of connection clearly indicate the initial direction of organisational development (Table 5.3, column II). Thus, there is evidence of the emergence of internal technical development capacity, although this is still related to the original product line and confined mainly to small batch production, and there is evidence of some formalisation and differentiation of the selling function, although this is still under the control of the Managing Director. At this stage, a marketing task may have emerged, but not as a fully differentiated function within the enterprise. Attributes joining the component thereafter are increasingly representative of advanced levels of internal differentiation and specialisation within the organisation. Mass production or assembly is 29-connected, divisional specialisation 28-connected and vertical integration 27-connected. Process improvement and advanced development joined at $\check{q} = 18$ and $\check{q} = 17$ respectively. The establishment of an overseas sales office and a fully differentiated marketing department, together with the subcontracting-out of development needs, are the attributes defining the lower limits of the complex. Thus, a component has been defined along which attributes are ordered, not so much in terms of their diminishing occurrence within the sample, as in terms of their integration in the sequence of development implicit in the cross-section of enterprises surveyed.

The q-connection of each attribute does not fully define its relationship with the simplicial complex. For example, it would appear that the establishment of a sales office elsewhere in the United Kingdom, for which $\hat{q}$ and $\check{q} = 25$, is more intimately associated with the development sequence than the establishment of a full sales office in the first place, for which $\hat{q} = 73$ and $\check{q} = 67$, although the former is obviously a less frequent attribute. Unlike the latter attribute, however, the occurrence (or non-occurrence) of a physically removed sales office can be completely attributed to the position of an organisation on the development component. To measure the extent to which simplices may or may not 'stand-off' the component, Atkin defines a simple measure of *eccentricity*:

$$\text{ecc} = \frac{\hat{q} - \check{q}}{\check{q} + 1}$$

Eccentricity tends towards zero the more closely an attribute is associated with the development sequence (Table 5.3, column III). Indeed, there is a relatively low degree of eccentricity amongst the 40 attributes recorded, indicating considerable consistency in the direction of development amongst the surveyed organisations. The most common attributes, departmentalisation, manufacture of original products, and small batch production, tend to stand-off more than most, suggesting a higher level of variation in *early* development. Other items with relatively high levels of eccentricity include production of customised items, involvement in more than one production technique, development of existing products, development in response to marketing initiatives, the use of agents for UK selling, and the use of customer-derived market information. The last two items can be considered as short-term forms of adjustment which enterprises might make in order to avoid the complete set of organisational changes necessary to cope fully with market uncertainty, thus explaining their more peripheral role in the development sequence.

While the coefficient for eccentricity is 'scale-free', examination of Table 5.3 suggests that, in this case, it diminishes with reduction in the order of simplices. Simple regression analysis yields the following relationship:

$$\text{ecc} = 0.009 + 0.0018q, \text{ for which } r^2 = 0.5177.$$

There is a strong tendency for eccentricity to increase at higher values of q. That is, the less common the attribute, the more closely it is likely to be connected with the development component. It follows that more developed business organisations have less 'freedom' in the organisational adaptions which they may make than their less advanced counterparts, a result consistent with the convergence of organisational form (Katz and Kahn, 1966, Chapter 2), and the principle of equifinality in open-systems theory (Haas and Drabeck, 1973).

Attributes for which eccentricity was markedly overestimated by the regression equation include the establishment of marketing as an information-oriented function (63 per cent error), the establishment of a full sales office (73 per cent), the presence of a Sales Office Manager (92 per cent) and sales by agents overseas (59 per cent). Thus, tasks associated with the existing customer–organisation interface – the sales as opposed to the marketing function – appear to be particularly important in the development sequence as their eccentricity values show them to be more closely associated with the development component than their $\check{q}$ values might otherwise imply. The one attribute with eccentricity considerably higher than estimated by the regression equation was the use of agents within the United Kingdom. Agents have been found to mitigate against good consumer–producer relations (Taylor, 1969) confusing rather than facilitating steady development. This practice was neither common, nor closely associated with the component, confining its marginal contribution to enterprise development.

For many values of q, $101 > q > 13$, there were a number of minor components, each comprising single simplices or attributes. The total number of components at each successive level of q defines the *structure vector*:

$$Q = \{Q_p Q_{p-1} Q_{p-2} Q_{p-3} \ldots Q_1, Q_0\}$$

The *obstruction vector*:

$$Q = \{Q_p - 1, Q_{p-1} - 1, Q_1 - 1, Q_0 - 1\}$$

denotes the number of q-connected components for each complex, without regard to their internal structure. It measures 'obstruction' insofar as it indicates for each value of q the number of simplices requiring to be connected in order to return to a single, integrated component (Table 5.4).

In the present analysis stability was first achieved at $\check{q} = 80$, at which state some technical competence in terms of the ability to modify the existing product line was introduced. After $\check{q} = 73$ this stability diminished, with separate components associated primarily with boundary spanning activities. Thus, the occurrence of the peak of obstruction at $\check{q} = 70$ suggests that while early forms of technical specialisation, such as small batch production, departmentalisation, and improvement of the original product line, are relatively easily integrated into the main component, the means by which control might be established over external relationships are less easily adopted. The first such attribute is introduced into the general component at $\check{q} = 69$, the use of customer feedback as a source of market information (for which $\check{q} = 77$), followed by the establishment of a sales office at $q = 67$ ($\check{q} = 73$). Obstruction to

Table 5.4 *Obstruction vector for the development component*

```
                                              103
                                    Q =      {0      0      0
100
   1     1     2     2     2     2     2      2      3      3
 90
   3     3     3     3     3     2     2      2      1      1
 80
   0     0     0     0     1     1     1      1      2      3
 70
   5     4     4     4     4     3     2      0      1      1
 60
   1     1     0     0     1     1     1      2      3      3
 50
   3     1     2     2     2     4     3      2      3      4
 40
   3     2     2     2     4     3     2      0      0      2
 30
   1     1     1     0     1     0     1      1      0      1
 20
   1     1     0     1     0     0     1      0      0      0
 10                                                                0
   0     0     0     0     0     0     0      0      0      0      0}
```

development again diminished at $q = 58$, suggesting that at this stage there exist within organisations distinctively defined technical and boundary tasks. The departure from stability at $54 > q > 34$, reflected, in part, the persistence of separate simplices for management control of technology and marketing. At this level management failure to delegate responsibility may obstruct enterprise development.

It is tempting to interpret increases in obstruction at different levels of development with threshold models of organisational growth. The possibility of a threshold associated initially with the need to cope with external relationships is consistent with the notion of enterprises rearranging their internal structure, and particularly the arrangement and status of boundary spanning functions, to break out of a spatially constrained action space (cf. Taylor, 1975). A subsequent threshold, which occurs at a later stage of development, may be more closely related to internal relations insofar as it appears to hinge upon integrative functions within enterprises in which the shift to an outward-looking structure has already been effected.

With the progressive connection of attributes associated with integration and control, especially those implying membership and co-operation within a wider corporate group, obstruction diminished. The evidence of general stability below $q = 34$ confirms that as development takes place within the organisation, so the alternative forms of organisational adjustment become more limited.

The q-analysis provides considerable insight into the development sequence implicit in the distribution of attributes within the cross-section of surveyed organisations, indicating:

(1) the relatively unsophisticated form of many firms and enterprises;
(2) the disparate nature of early forms of internal differentiation and their convergence with more advanced development;
(3) the tendency for organisations to become organised firstly with reference to technical tasks and, secondly, with reference to boundary spanning tasks, the latter level of organisation possibly imposing a developmental threshold;
(4) the highest levels of development of both these task areas – the establishment of overseas sales facilities and advanced product and process research – are only recorded after attributes which imply a considerable degree of internal integration are connected to the component;
(5) the possibility that failure by management to delegate responsibility to specialised subsystems impedes their continuing progress at particular points on the development continuum;
(6) the fact that membership of a wider, multilocational, corporate system can enhance internal integration.

This development sequence can be built into the testing of the *a priori* model of organisation–environment interaction proposed in Chapter 3 as an index of performance calibrated according to the density of topologically ordered attributes, with higher scores denoting increasingly complex forms of organisation.

Conclusion　The analyses undertaken in this chapter have enabled a very full specification of the internal characteristics of a sample of electronics enterprises to be made using a multivariate approach. From 40 variables, six dimensions of internal structure have been revealed which, despite problems of technique, are broadly similar to structural dimensions that have been recognised in studies adopting the structural contingency approach in organisation theory. These dimensions referred to:

(1) the structuring of activities;
(2) delegation of responsibility within the organisation;
(3) the integration of tasks;
(4) production flexibility;
(5) production complexity; and
(6) development of the marketing function.

Related to these dimensions of internal structure, three measures of organisational performance were developed. Using principal components analysis of data for UK electronics firms, two surrogates for performance were recognised, the first as organisational size, the second as organisational growth. However, topological analysis of the 40 variables describing structure also allowed an organisational development sequence to be distinguished which can be used as a third index of performance.

These nine composite variables describing structure and performance represent the compression of a large quantity of detailed information into a usable form. They also represent an improvement on the specification of organisational structure in industrial geography. Indeed, the composite variables distinguished in this study depict aspects of organisational form and functioning that have been barely recognised in industrial geography. More importantly, however, they allow the internal structural characteristics of the *a priori* model of organisation–environment interaction which was developed in Chapter 3 to be specified and calibrated so that the fusion of structural contingency notions from organisation theory and industrial linkage notions from industrial geography can be tested to determine their adequacy as a basis for a more broadly based geography of business organisations.

The present chapter has focused upon the performance, development and internal structural dimensions of electronics organisations. It is necessary to turn now to the measurement and calibration of their interactions with their task environments. These questions are addressed in the following chapter through consideration of the spatial and contextural dimensions of linkage and communication fields.

6 Defining task environments through linkages and information contacts

In the attempt to amalgamate concepts derived from studies of industrial linkage with the structural contingency model of organisations, it was pointed out in Chapters 2 and 3 that industrial geography's potential contribution to a more broadly based geography of organisations derives from its refinement of the definition and measurement of organisations' interactions with their immediate task environments. Studies of the spatial arrangement of material linkages have defined business organisations' *interaction fields* and have, to some extent, equated their form with organisational structure. Studies of information flows via letters, telephones, telex, face-to-face meetings and so on, have defined *information fields* to much the same end, and tentative attempts have been made to equate these spaces with organisations' *decision fields*. In these two types of study somewhat different approaches to measurement have been adopted and only rarely have interaction fields and information fields been measured in the same study (e.g. Gysberts, 1974), notwithstanding the fact that both material linkages and information flows are but two aspects of the same phenomenon – inter- and intra-organisational communication interaction.

The present chapter attempts, therefore, to develop a uniform methodology for the measurement and description both of interaction fields and of information fields in the context of the UK electronics industry. In so doing, it facilitates the specification and calibration of two of the vital components of the *a priori* model of organisation–environment interactions which was proposed in Chapter 3.

The distribution of purchasing and sales linkages

The present study does not equate linkages with the *movement* of goods, services, or finance between organisations or locations, but with the *distribution* and broad nature of major external 'transactional' contacts, insofar as these provide insight into the nature of the organisation itself (Wood, 1969; Taylor, 1971, 1973). In these terms several straightforward methodological precedents exist for measuring linkage. Keeble (1969) simply asked respondent firms in North West London whether they maintained links with other organisations in the same area. He was thus able to classify respondents according to the extent of their local dependence. The study indicated quite clearly the importance of these local contacts to smaller, engineering 'service' companies. Taylor (1971, 1973, 1974, 1978) and McDermott (1974) recorded sales purchasing and subcontract linkages in terms of the locations of counterparts, and

132

developed intervening opportunity models to identify differences between actual spatial linkage patterns and predicted patterns generated from data on transport costs and the spatial pattern of market opportunities. In a somewhat different study, Taylor and Wood (1973) examined the impact of local linkage in West Midlands-based establishments engaged in metal-working activities by collecting data on a standardised list of linkages embracing inputs, sales and subcontract work, with unity being ascribed to local links and zero to non-local links.

In the present study no such standardised list has been employed and respondents in the electronics industry were required to name the locations of their major suppliers and customers (input, backward, or purchasing linkages and output, forward, or sales linkages), defined as those who, individually, accounted for more than 5 per cent of the respondent's total purchases or sales in the year preceding the survey. The origin or destination sector for each linkage was also recorded, as well as whether or not the transaction involved was subject to a medium or long-term agreement (for example, in excess of six months forward ordering or call-off arrangements).

Unfortunately, not all respondents supplied complete sets of linkage data, and therefore, to test for bias, respondents were compared with non-respondents. It was found that London-based organisations, capital goods manufacturers and UK subsidiaries of foreign firms were less forthcoming than the other types of respondent. However, there was no significant difference between respondents and non-respondents on the basis of firm size. It was also concluded that output data from 90 enterprises and input data from 86 enterprises would be sufficient for the following analyses if they were suitably structured.

The interaction fields for all respondents in each of the survey regions are described in Table 6.1. Particularly prominent is the fact that Scottish respondents had more sales and purchasing contacts with foreign organisations than their English counterparts. More of their purchasing and sales linkages were orientated towards Europe and they displayed dependence on overseas sources of inputs – especially North America. This difference can be explained by the motivation of US producers with manufacturing subsidiaries in Scotland. In most of these cases the Scottish operation has been established to lead, or support, American penetration of British and European markets, often on the basis of components or subassemblies supplied from within wider, multinational, corporate groups (cf. Blackbourn, 1974).

Table 6.1 also demonstrates the continued dominance of London as the major single market centre and source of supply for UK electronics manufacturers. Over one-third of purchasing linkages established by London firms were with suppliers in the local area. In addition, 25 per cent of the purchasing linkages established by OMA firms, and 16 per cent of these same links for Scottish firms were also oriented towards London. For sales linkages, London customers accounted for a greater proportion of OMA contacts than customers in the OMA itself, and of all the non-local sales linkages established by Scottish respondents, 20 per cent were directed towards London. However, Scottish manufac-

Table 6.1 *Distribution of linkages at the regional level*

	London		OMA		Scotland	
Origin/Destination	No.	%	No.	%	No.	%
Purchasing linkages						
London	46	35.9	55	26.4	18	16.5
OMA	20	15.6	63	30.3	4	3.7
Scotland	4	3.1	10	4.8	31	28.4
Remainder UK	42	32.8	53	25.5	34	31.2
EEC	8	6.2	12	5.8	9	8.3
Elsewhere overseas	8	6.2	15	7.2	13	11.9
Total	128	100.0	208	100.0	109	100.0
Sales linkages						
London	43	29.2	81	27.8	17	11.7
OMA	33	22.4	75	25.8	13	9.0
Scotland	5	3.4	16	5.5	59	40.7
Remainder UK	60	40.5	98	33.7	31	21.4
EEC	5	3.4	11	3.8	23	15.9
Elsewhere overseas	1	0.7	10	3.4	2	1.4
Total	147	100.0	291	100.0	145	100.0

turers were also highly dependent upon their local area for the disposal of goods. Over 40 per cent of their surveyed linkages were oriented towards Scotland itself, although Scotland could never account for such a high proportion of the market opportunities in this industry in the UK as a whole. However, supply linkages were less concentrated in the region, which is more in keeping with the suggestion that the Scottish industrial infrastructure cannot provide the range of opportunities available elsewhere for scientific manufacturing activity (James, 1965).

The data for UK electronics manufacturers demonstrate the three characteristics of spatial linkage patterns that have been well established in other empirical studies. The first is local dependence, the orientation of linkages towards local customers and suppliers. The second is the impact of distance in interaction fields, which appears to be a particularly heavy constraint, while the third is an urban hierarchy or map effect reflecting, in this particular case study, the importance of London in all organisations' interaction patterns.

In part, these general characteristics of spatial linkage patterns can be summarised in linear regression analyses. To use the linear model, however, the distance-linkage data has had to be transformed. For the data sets for London and the OMA, logarithmic transformation was found, by inspection, to capture these relationships most efficiently. Since, in these cases, the rate at which contacts diminished was reasonably uniform it might be inferred that distance decay was not strongly influenced or distorted by any map effect. For Scottish respondents, however, untransformed distances were found to be most

Table 6.2 *Linear regression estimates of localisation and distance decay of aggregate interaction fields*

	Constant (localisation)	Regression coefficient (distance decay)	Standard error	r^2
Purchasing linkages				
London	−13.038	41.178	3.736	0.976
OMA	−9.434	39.124	5.271	0.952
Scotland	−43.023	41.533	6.727	0.907
Sales linkages				
London	−17.285	44.270	2.862	0.987
OMA	−30.171	49.142	6.230	0.946
Scotland	−37.584	40.722	5.962	0.931

appropriate for both purchases and sales. This would imply a weaker friction effect of distance, in this instance possibly as a result of a stronger map effect owing to the 'pull' of London.

Table 6.2 presents the appropriate linear regression equations for these three regions enabling the isolation and comparison of the effects of local dependence (through the constant intercept values) and distance decay (through the slope coefficients). From these analyses it is clear that local dependence for supply linkages is at its lowest in Scotland, although local input dependence emerges as slightly more pronounced for OMA manufacturers than it does for their London counterparts. However, particularly interesting results emerge from the analyses of output linkages. Notwithstanding a considerably higher level of within-region orientation, Scottish manufacturers record the lowest *overall* levels of local dependence. Local dependence amongst OMA manufacturers is not much higher than that of their Scottish counterparts, but it is considerably more marked amongst London respondents.

The differences between slope coefficients are far less pronounced. In fact, *t*-tests established that none of the differences between these six coefficients (Table 6.2) were statistically significant. It might therefore be concluded that the impact of distance alone, notwithstanding the impact of the map effect, is essentially similar from place to place.

Figure 6.1 presents the distance-decay curves for the input or purchasing linkages of respondents in Scotland, London and the OMA which make explicit some of the contrasts implied by the coefficients reported in Table 6.2. A low level of local dependence is immediately obvious for Scotland, with very few input contacts recorded within about 15 km of the respondent. Small increases in the density of contacts between about 80 and 150 km represent linkages with the industrial areas of the north of England and the Midlands, while the very steep rise in the curve at around 400 km represents the impact of London and the South East. The impact of London and the South East also explains the low level of distance decay recorded for London-based

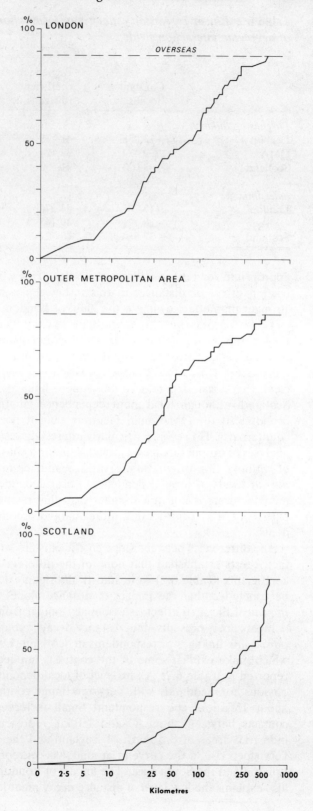

Figure 6.1 Frequency of
purchasing linkage and
distance from the firm

respondents and the tendency towards a sigmoidal curve for OMA manufacturers. The Scottish curve is also terminated at a lower level than the others, reflecting the greater significance of overseas purchasing contacts.

Figure 6.2, which plots sales linkage frequencies against the transformed distance axes, also represents distance decay from the London region essentially as a straight line. While very few contacts are recorded within the 5 km closest to any respondents, 20 per cent of these contacts occur within 10 km. Thereafter, decay in contacts takes place rapidly and constantly. However, the rate of decline is more rapid for respondents in the OMA. The impact of sales opportunities in the South East in general, and in London in particular, is also reflected in the very steep facet of the curve for this region between 15 and 80 km. The lower density of contacts established by OMA-based firms with customers elsewhere in the UK is then reflected in the flattening out of the curve beyond about 150 km. Again, the urban hierarchy effect is most pronounced for Scottish respondents, with the virtual absence of local links and the overwhelming significance of customers in the South East of England at distances over about 500 km.

But distance, parochialism and the map effect are not the only factors influencing the spatial distribution of organisations' sales and purchasing linkages. Three other factors must also be taken into account: the industry within which an organisation operates; the internal structure of the organisation itself; and the technology it employs. Traditionally location has been treated as the most important determinant of linkage length, especially in the neoclassical literature which has emphasised the impact of transport costs (e.g. Smith, 1971). However, a variety of contextural factors could also generate aggregate spatial distributions of linkages which might otherwise be attributed to location. For example, technology can be considered to influence linkage patterns in that it defines the network within which a firm or organisation is involved and, therefore, the macro-relationships with which it is faced (Benson, 1975). Indeed, a macro-economic approach to the movement of goods also suggests that differences in the nature of items being transferred will influence the distances over which the transfer can take place (Hoover, 1971, pp 41–7). Thus, the increase in value in manufactured electronics goods as opposed to input components and materials suggests that forward linkages will be generally longer than backward linkages (cf. Black, 1971).

The most obvious technology variable is the sector or sectors in which an organisation is involved. Product and production characteristics influence the linkage network and their spatial form by limiting the range of customers and suppliers involved in organisations' environmental domains. Specialised and high value-added manufacture generally requires specialised inputs and may serve potentially fewer outlets than other forms of production. The resulting absolute constraint on the availability of opportunities to establish contacts may manifest itself in more wide-spread linkages in space. In less specialised, more ubiquitous forms of manufacture both customers and suppliers may be plentiful and

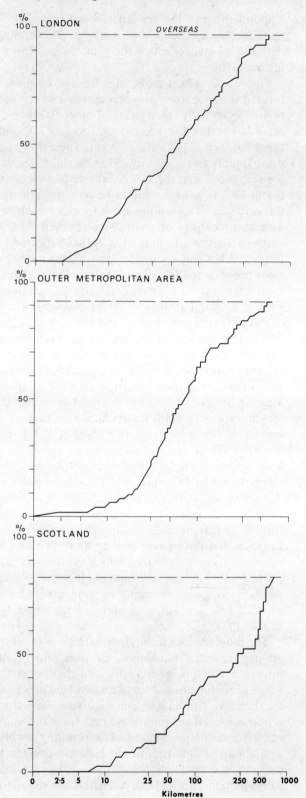

Figure 6.2 Frequency of sales linkage and distance from the firm

the capacity and needs of the firm may be met from within a relatively small geographic area.

The corporate framework within which an organisation operates also influences the form of its linkage network. Knowledge of opportunities for interaction and familiarity with a wider range of locations may result from the support provided by membership of a multilocational corporate organisation. As a result it is to be expected that linkages established with other members of a corporate organisation will operate over longer distance. Indeed, the results of previous linkage studies would lend support to this contention (Taylor, 1973, 1978; Gilmour, 1974).

Within the present study, the relative importance of these contextural factors of location, sector, negotiability of linkages and linkages with enterprises belonging to the same corporate group can be explored and estimated through comparison of the Euclidean distances over which they have been established by respondent organisations. With the length of individual linkages transformed to the logarithm (base ten) to achieve an approximately normal distribution, analyses of variance have been used to make these comparisons, and situations in which statistically significant differences have been revealed in the distances over which linkages have been established are displayed in Figure 6.3.

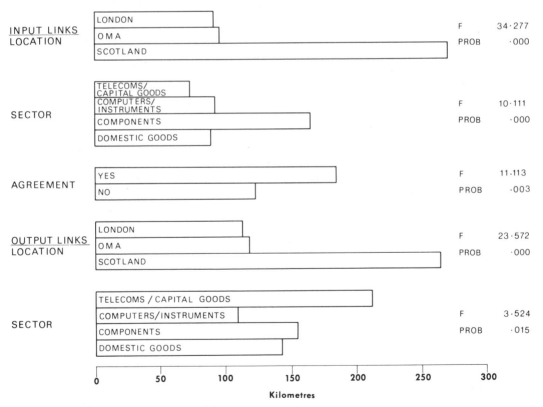

Figure 6.3 Variations in the length of sales and purchasing linkages

Regional location is obviously the major contextural influence upon mean purchasing linkage length, with a mean for Scotland of 270 km. In terms of sectoral affiliation the longest input linkages have been established by component manufacturers, a finding consistent with the proposition that opportunities to establish purchasing linkages are more constrained and therefore established over longer distances at less advanced stages in the production chain. However, some support for the importance of the items involved in the exchange emerges from the main contrast with capital goods manufacturers, which involve the purchase of generally heavier, lower-value inputs (Figure 6.3). The only other factor to influence significantly the mean length of input linkages is the negotiation of supply agreements. Although agreements were involved in only 20 per cent of recorded linkages, they were found to apply to transactions taking place over longer distances, suggesting that interaction with more distant organisations is associated with a negotiated reduction of uncertainty in environmental relationships.

Compared with purchasing linkages, a higher proportion of sales linkages (25 per cent) are subject to some form of medium or long-term agreement, yet these links have not been established over significantly greater distances than the remainder. Variations in the spatial distribution of sales linkages according to the location of respondents are clearly significant, with Scotland again recording by far the longest mean linkage length (Figure 6.3). Sectoral variations in linkage length are also statistically significant, although in this case the longest links characterise the firms manufacturing the 'heaviest' products, the capital goods sector. Presumably this situation arises from the fact that capital goods production is the most specialised of the sectors in the electronics industry, manufacturing custom-built equipment for a relatively small number of potential customers. The shortest sales linkages are recorded by consumer goods manufacturers, a result consistent with their spatial concentration, both at the industry-wide level and within the sample, near the centre of the consumer market in the South East.

In this section it has been shown that the spatial linkage patterns of UK electronics manufacturers broadly correspond to the patterns that have been revealed in other linkage studies (Chapter 3). A range of influences was identified including distance, location, parochialism and an urban hierarchy (map) effect, together with a range of contextural factors embracing technology, internal structure, sectoral and corporate affiliation, together with the negotiated characteristics of linkages. From these results it can be concluded that any analysis of the relationship between organisational structure and spatial linkage patterns should also take account of the characteristics of organisations' domains as these might be defined by location, technology and, in the case of inputs, supply agreements.

Given these general characteristics of material linkages it is necessary to develop a consistent methodology for their measurement and calibration so that they can be incorporated into the testing of the model of organisation–environment interaction at the level of the individual organisation, as proposed in Chapter 3. This is the task of the following section.

The interaction fields of organisations

The preceding discussion has concentrated upon electronics manufacturers' material linkages aggregated by region, and the main contextural sources of variation in the distribution of distances over which they were established. The present section uses the same data to develop descriptive measures of the spatial interaction fields of individual firms as defined by the configurations of their input and output linkages.

In the past, two approaches to the measurement of the linkage patterns of individual organisations have been adopted. The first has emphasised the value or proportion of sales or purchases made within a given area (e.g. Lever, 1974*a*; Stewart, 1976; McDermott, 1976). The second has attempted to develop composite measures to describe the spatial dimension of organisations' operations. This latter approach has usually been based upon multivariate ordination techniques (e.g. Taylor, 1971, 1978; Taylor and Wood, 1973; Britton, 1976), although Schmidt (1973) has employed indices from graph theory. The application of this approach can be criticised for the demands it makes upon the data that have been used. These demands have tended to introduce noise into the analyses largely as a result of collecting data on a common number of linkages for all respondents. Thus, respondents with more than, say, five contacts may have only five considered; those with less than five have the difference made up with notional local contacts (Taylor and Wood, 1973). The present approach adopts a similar technique but attempts to reduce such distortion by using all the linkage information provided by electronics manufacturers through the higher analysis of summary statistics based upon the linkage data and not through direct analysis of the linkages themselves.

Before deriving these summary statistics it has been necessary to adjust the surveyed linkages for the known impact of location, sectoral affiliation and purchasing agreements. For this purpose these nominal variables were transformed into binary form. They were then used to generate, through simple least squares regression, an 'expected' linkage length. The difference between the expected and actual linkage length in each case was standardised and treated as input into the subsequent description and analysis of interaction fields at the organisation level. This transformation procedure can be summarised as follows:

(1) Regression estimate of linkage length (y'),
   $y' = f$ (location, sector, agreement) for input linkages;
   $y' = f$ (location, sector) for output linkages.
(2) 'Compare estimate with actual length (y) Residual $y = y - y'$.
(3) Standardise results:
   $$\text{Transformed } y = \frac{\text{Residual } y \times 100}{y'}$$

The last step ensures that the weighted linkage scores are not affected by the different mean values associated with the various regions and sectors.

Table 6.3 *Reduction of influence of context upon linkage length; regression weighting*

Dichotomous variable	Constant (mean without increments)	Regression coefficient (increment)	Standard error
Purchasing linkages	1.15275		
Scotland		0.56453	0.07177
Instruments		0.25612	0.11764
Components		0.30614	0.06641
Contract		0.21105	0.07650
Multiple r = 0.469			
Multiple r^2 = 0.220			
Sales linkages	1.53079		
Scotland		0.41398	0.05879
Capital Goods		0.36189	0.10272
Multiple r = 0.313			
Multiple r^2 = 0.098			

Table 6.3 presents the results of this procedure applied to both input and output linkages, together with the dummy variables used to measure variations in sector, location or contracts (agreements). For input linkages the regression equations were built up in three stages; for output linkages they were built in two stages. The variables entered into the equation at each stage were ordered in terms of their relative explanatory importance derived from prior multiple analyses of variance. Thus, for input linkages location was entered at the first step and sector at the second step. In both cases the effect of location was measured simply as a dummy variable denoting whether or not a respondent was based in Scotland. In the case of inputs, two dummy variables were used to incorporate the impact of sector, namely instrument and component manufacture. The contract variable was already in binary form denoting the presence or absence of a supply agreement. In the case of output linkages a single dummy variable was used to measure the influence of sector, whether or not an organisation belonged to the capital goods sectors of the electronics industry.

The results indicated that the amount of variance in linkages associated with the contextural variables is rather limited. Furthermore, a series of one-way analyses of variance demonstrates the statistical effectiveness of the transformation (Table 6.4). The new indices of linkage length remain closely related to the original Euclidean measure of distance and yet are totally unassociated with variations in location, sector and, in the case of inputs, agreements. It is of interest that even these transformed variables are not influenced by corporate associations. That is, even with sectoral and locational variation held constant corporate contacts do not differ in length from the remainder. One further benefit of the transformation process described is the fact that the new variables are approximately normally distributed about a mean of zero (Table 6.4).

Table 6.4 *Statistical efficiency of linkage length transformations*

Summary statistics	New purchasing linkage variable	New sales linkage variable
Mean	−0.045	0.002
Standard deviation	40.077	34.390
Range	218.25	166.992
Skewness	−0.179	−0.042
Kurtosis	−0.062	−0.035
Probability of no association with[1]:		
(1) Location	0.917	0.435
(2) Sector	0.870	0.821
(3) Contract	1.000	0.042
(4) Corporate affiliation	0.194	0.471

Note: [1] Based upon one-way analyses of variance.

A total of seven statistics can be calculated which summarise the set of transformed linkage scores obtained for each respondent. The first is the *mean score* which indicates the general spatial orientation of linkage patterns, a higher mean denoting the importance of more distant contacts. Obviously, however, similar scores can be from geographically quite different linkage distributions. For example, a relatively high mean can be achieved in cases involving a large number of local contacts and either only one linkage over a considerable distance, or with several linkages over only moderate distances. In the former case the mean is influenced by, but does not accurately reflect, the furthermost boundary of the interaction field. A direct measure of this latter characteristic is the length of the *longest linkage* recorded by a firm and this constitutes the second summary statistic. Further, the existence of a number of linkages established some distance from a firm can be detected through measuring the proportion with scores exceeding zero, that is, exceeding the mean for the particular subgroup of organisations (e.g. Scottish component manufacturers) to which the respondent belongs. This is treated as a third measure of the general *spatial orientation* of enterprises. An index which measures the level of 'spatial monopoly' in an organisation's linkage pattern (i.e. interaction with organisations in closer proximity than might have been expected on the basis of the contextural variables) is the *shortest transformed linkage* and this is used as the fourth summary statistic. Furthermore, as the analyses and transformations in the previous and present sections have involved only linkages within the UK, the proportion established with *overseas* counterparts can be introduced as a fifth measure of geographical orientation.

A firm maintaining a number of linkages over a wide range of distances, and therefore locations, is likely to maintain more stable external transactions than a firm with contacts in only one or two locations. To measure this type of variation, the *standard deviation* and *range* derived from the linkages for each firm are used as the sixth and seventh summary statistics. These depend not only on the variability implicit in a set of linkage scores, but reflect also the number of linkages, with the standard deviation and range both reaching zero in those cases when only one linkage was established by a firm.

Although these measures summarise the interaction fields of firms and enterprises, they also remain 'one-dimensional' measures of interaction since the linkage data from which they are derived have been collapsed onto a single distance continuum. Terms such as 'orientation' and 'variability' thus refer only to the distribution of points on a vector with the focal organisation at the origin. However, this is a meaningful basis for the comparison of interaction fields between firms and organisations in that a cluster of points – or a single point – around the origin of the vector suggests a high level of local dependence and, by implication, considerable uncertainty in external transactions. In contrast, the distribution of a number of linkages along the vector suggests considerably more flexibility and spatial knowledge underlying external interaction.

The seven summary statistics described above have been calculated for each respondent across the number of linkages recorded, separately for purchasing and sales transactions. This produces two sets of data, both of which have been subjected to principal components analyses. Not surprisingly, the two analyses give rise to similar results in terms of numbers of components, eigenvalues, loadings and communalities (Table 6.5). For input interaction fields, the first component, which accounts for 43 per cent of total variance, reflects the variability of distances over which linkages were established, the highest loading being with 'range', followed by 'standard deviation' (Table 6.5a). It is of interest that a variable interaction field within the UK is negatively associated with the proportion of linkages established with overseas suppliers, suggesting that those firms with few or clustered linkages within the country tend to be ones which establish contacts overseas. An overseas orientation would appear to replace, rather than supplement, wide-ranging UK supply contacts. It can be inferred that the import orientation is not so much a function of a widening of the interaction field beyond national boundaries by United Kingdom organisations, but, rather, reflects the presence of foreign-controlled enterprise operating within international linkage networks.

Component II measures input linkage orientation. The highest loading is recorded by the mean distance variable, with moderate loadings also recorded by the percentage of linkages of above 'average' length and the length of the longest link. The component represents a measure of the level of spatial monopoly in supply transactions, with positive scores suggesting a limited dependence upon local suppliers and negative scores indicating considerable local dependence and a strong distance constraint upon interaction.

The loadings reported in Table 6.5b suggest that exactly the same interpretation can be placed upon the two components derived for sales interaction, with the first denoting variability in the interaction field,

Table 6.5 *Deriving interaction fields; orthogonally rotated components*

| | Component Loadings[1] | | |
(*a*) Purchasing linkages	I Variability	II Orientation	h^2
Mean length		0.971	0.944
Standard deviation	0.940		0.899
Maximum length	0.732	0.625	0.927
Minimum length	−0.723	0.653	0.950
% Non-local		0.876	0.768
Range	0.990		
% Overseas	−0.216		0.048
Eigenvalue	3.008	2.511	
% of variance	43.0	35.9	
(*b*) Sales linkages			
Mean length	−0.268	0.936	0.948
Standard deviation	0.958		0.922
Maximum length	0.463	0.852	0.940
Minimum length	−0.854	0.444	0.926
% Non-local		0.919	0.885
Range	0.973		0.974
% Overseas	−0.392		0.183
Eigenvalue	3.208	2.570	
% of variance	45.8	36.7	

Note: [1] Loadings below 0.2 omitted

and the second orientation. The overall level of explanation achieved in the analysis of sales linkages is higher, however, at 82.6 per cent. A contrast with the input linkage analysis is the negative association of mean distance with the first component which, while small, nevertheless suggests that the more widely distributed sales linkages are founded upon a degree of local dependence. That is, the ability to extend the task environment to incorporate more distant points of sale is enhanced by a reasonable base of local sales transactions.

In this section, therefore, four composite variables have been derived to describe the spatial patterning of electronics manufacturers' material linkages. *Purchasing variability* and *purchasing orientation* are indicative of distance decay and levels of localisation, respectively, for input linkages while *sales variability* and *sales orientation* are equivalent measures for output transactions. The method adopted for the definition of these summary measures has avoided the worst limitations and shortcomings of the methods used to calibrate spatial linkages in previous studies, and the measures themselves can be readily incorporated into the model of organisation–environment interaction proposed in Chapter 3.

Patterns of market communication

Rather more than is the case for material linkages, the measurement of information exchanges at the firm level presents methodological and conceptual difficulties for which there are only limited, although diverse, precedents (Connell and Pye, 1973; Pye, 1973). Techniques available include, for example, questionnaire analysis, direct observation, laboratory experiment, attitude testing and perception measurement. For this study it was decided to use a standardised contact diary to monitor a sample of the external communications maintained by electronics manufacturers. To reduce demands upon individual respondents and to obtain information directly comparable between them, this exercise was confined to the Chief Marketing Executive from each respondent enterprise.

The design of the diary reflected two prerequisites for analysis:

(1) the amount of information collected for each contact should be sufficient to enable meaningful classification;
(2) the amount of information requested should prejudice neither response reliability nor the number of diaries that were kept.

Therefore, an approach which gathers a considerable amount of data regarding individual communications was combined with one which attempts to gather rather less data for a larger number of contacts. Examples of the detailed approach include studies by Törnqvist (1970) and the Communications Studies Group (Pye, 1972; Collins, 1972). In these analyses only face-to-face contacts were considered. Detailed studies were feasible given the limited number of contacts on which respondents were required to give information and because of restriction to face-to-face communication.

The second approach uses participant records of all interactions over a period of time (Hesseling, 1970, p. 50). Each contact may be recorded in terms of duration, content, type of exchange, and even in terms of effectiveness (e.g. Stewart, 1965; Marples, 1967). Participant-kept diaries emphasise quantitative, rather than qualitative, information (Graves, 1972) and may incorporate all modes of contact, including letters, telephone calls, meetings and memoranda (Burns, 1954). Weinshall (1966) described the use of a contact diary in which each telephone call and face-to-face communication was recorded on a separate page. Thorngren (1970) adopted this approach in the analysis of meetings with external parties among Swedish business organisations while Goddard (1973) extended it to include telephone contacts in his survey of London office functions. The diary for the present study drew upon these precedents, particularly the last two in light of their concern with 'external' contacts. The format was streamlined so that a number of contacts could be recorded on a single page with each separate communication, other than a meeting, occupying a single line only. Because previous studies have demonstrated that indices of meeting duration and intensity of contacts are highly sensitive to response bias, no attempt was made to measure these characteristics. In addition, the placement of diaries with Chief Marketing Executives only automatically directed coverage more or less to planning and orientation contacts, so that it was considered important to include all external

Table 6.6 *Distribution of information contacts at regional level*

| | Location of respondents | | | | | |
| | London | | OMA | | Scotland | |
Origin/Destination	No.	%	No.	%	No.	%
London	407	38.3	403	23.7	128	13.2
OMA	207	18.5	483	28.4	88	9.1
Scotland	22	2.1	38	2.2	439	45.3
Remainder UK	271	25.3	521	30.7	200	20.6
EEC	86	8.2	158	9.3	71	7.3
USA	11	1.0	23	1.4	25	2.6
Elsewhere overseas	60	5.6	73	4.3	19	1.9
Total	1064	100.0	1699	100.0	970	100.0

communications irrespective of the means by which they were conducted, whether by letter, meeting or telephone.

Despite an initial willingness on the part of management to take part
in the contact exercise – with over 80 diaries placed in the course of 121
interviews – only 52 usable diaries were returned. However, simple
one-way analysis of variance of the employment size of respondent
organisations revealed no statistically significant difference between
participants in the contact diary exercise and the remainder of the
sample, although the respective means of the two groups suggested that
the former tended to be somewhat smaller than the latter.

The 52 organisations participating in the contact diary exercise
provided information on 3733 separate communications – 1064 for
London respondents, 1699 for the OMA, and 970 for Scotland.
Although the majority of diaries were kept for the full five days
requested, a few were maintained for only three or four, an outcome
consistent with Goddard's observation that, after three days, recording
tends to become less reliable (1973, p. 155). The mean number of
contacts recorded was 72, with a standard deviation of 43, a minimum of
12 and maximum of 213. As it had been decided to disregard contact
intensity all 52 diaries contributed to the following analyses.

Each contact was allocated to the region from which it originated or
towards which it was directed, and the more general distributional
characteristics of these aggregate information fields (Table 6.6) are
broadly comparable with those observed for sales linkages discussed in
the previous section (Table 6.1). However, the material linkage data
refer only to the most important sales contacts established or maintained over a full year whereas the communication data are based upon
external communications involving the Chief Marketing Executive over
no more than a week. In addition, the communication data are drawn
from considerably fewer organisations. Nevertheless, it is useful to
undertake such a comparison.

It is of interest that for London and Scottish respondents, at least, the
extent of localisation is more marked for communication fields than for

sales linkages, although for OMA respondents this holds true only if London and the OMA are considered to comprise a single 'local area'. Despite a presumably smaller local information base, localisation of information contacts is most evident in Scotland. However, together London and the OMA account for over 50 per cent of contacts established by firms in each of those two regions.

Table 6.6 also indicates that for respondents in each region, organisations in the remainder of the UK provide far more input into market information systems than do overseas organisations. Indeed, the remainder of the UK is a more important source of information for OMA firms than either the local area or London alone. London and OMA firms also appear to maintain wider contacts than their Scottish counterparts, as well as a considerably higher level of foreign information exchange. This pattern contrasts with that for sales linkages (Table 6.1), for which the highest proportion of overseas contacts was recorded by Scottish respondents.

Examination of the detailed subregional distribution of information contacts suggests that much of the pattern of aggregate communication fields could be attributed to the same three interrelated factors that influence material interaction fields:

(1) dependence upon local information;
(2) relatively rapid decline in the proportion of contacts established over increasing distances; and
(3) emphasis upon the important centres of electronics manufacturing and marketing opportunities, particularly in the South East (the map or urban hierarchy effect).

As in the analyses of material linkages, the significance of these factors can be estimated using graphic and regression analyses.

To construct Figure 6.4, all information contacts have been converted to the straight-line distances between their origins and destinations, and their cumulative frequency has been plotted against a logarithmic transformation of these distances. The distance decay of London's information field again approximates a straight line as was previously found to be the case with sales linkages. Indeed, this linear tendency is emphasised by correlation between contact frequency and distance of $r = 0.996$. Similarly paralleling the analysis of sales linkages, the graph of OMA-based respondents' information contacts assumes a strongly sigmoidal form, while the J-shaped curve which described the sales interaction field of Scottish manufacturers is particularly pronounced for their information contacts.

Although broad similarity is evident between patterns of sales and information contacts based on visual comparison, it is also useful to examine these distributions in terms of the regression equations which describe them, and this is attempted in Table 6.7. From the figures in this table it is evident that in each of the three study regions the rate of decay for the communication field is less than that for the equivalent sales interaction field, suggesting, not surprisingly, that the breadth of the information fields of firms exceeds that of their interaction fields.

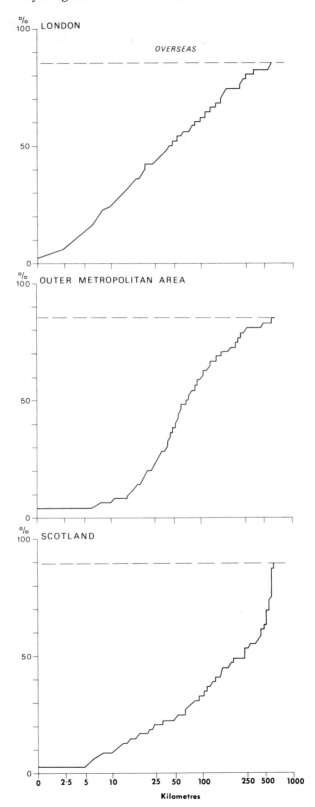

Figure 6.4 Frequency of communications contacts and distance from the firm

Table 6.7 *Localisation and distance decay; comparison of aggregate market information and sales interaction fields*

	Regression intercept (localisation)	Regression coefficient (distance decay)	Standard error	r
London				
Sales linkages	−17.285	44.270	2.862	0.993
Information flows	0.093	34.656	1.400	0.996
OMA				
Sales linkages	−30.171	49.142	6.230	0.972
Information flows	−22.412	44.400	4.976	0.972
Scotland				
Sales linkages	−37.584	40.722	5.962	0.965
Information flows	−29.033	38.657	8.343	0.926

Furthermore, the slope coefficients indicate that the effect of location relative to the geographic centre of market information (London) has tended to increase the overall rates of distance decay recorded for Scotland and the OMA, compared with London.

Comparison of the intercepts derived for aggregate information fields and interaction fields also confirms that communication contacts are relatively more locally orientated than material sales linkages in both Scotland and London, but not in the OMA. In terms of the factors underlying the aggregate fields, therefore, it is concluded that local dependence is a marginally more important element in the sales linkage based field. This result suggests that quantitatively, at least, marketing information tends to be dominated by contacts available in relatively close proximity to the firm, although the absolute limits on spatial learning are not likely to be set by the pattern of more tangible sales linkages.

While the present study is concerned only with the communication patterns of marketing executives and is thereby confined largely to a high proportion of planning, search and non-routine contacts, the possibility remains that the distribution of contacts is influenced by the nature of exchanges recorded. Therefore, the remainder of the present section investigates variations in the average distance over which communications were conducted, according to the context within which they were established and the role they played.

Table 6.8 presents the distribution of contacts according to various measures of communications mode, context and content recorded in the diaries. Contacts are also disaggregated according to the precise role of the Chief Marketing Executive in the firm, a role which may range from owner–manager (with a wide variety of responsibilities but answerable only to himself) and professional manager (also with wide-ranging responsibility but answerable to a corporate principal) to a specialised

Table 6.8 *The nature of information contacts*

	Contacts recorded	
Variables	No.	%
Position of diary respondent (Chief Marketing Executive)		
Owner–manager	958	25.7
Professional Manager, General Manager, etc.	1092	29.3
Sales Manager, Sales Office Manager, etc.	1088	29.1
Sales or Marketing Director	595	15.1
Mode of contact		
Telephone	1756	47.1
Telex or cable	301	8.1
Letter	1157	31.0
Other, including memos, brochures, etc.	210	5.6
Face-to-face	309	8.3
The correspondent		
Initiated by respondent	1984	55.0
With member of same firm	160	4.3
With member of associated firm	277	7.4
Content of the exchange		
With customer or potential customer	2191	58.7
With salesman or sales support services	377	10.1
With a supplier	632	16.9
To do with recruitment, labour, etc.	38	2.1
With non-customer institutions (local authorities, government bodies, trade associations, etc.)	77	2.1
With competitors	21	0.6
With technical service supplier of technical services	62	1.7
With supplier of professional services	199	5.3
With management or concerning management issues other than covered above	136	3.6
Purpose of exchange		
Giving information (by respondent)	1615	43.3
Receiving information	1241	33.3
Giving instruction	522	14.0
Receiving instruction	538	14.4
Involved in discussion	657	17.6
Involved in negotiation	210	5.6
Arranging a meeting	191	5.1
Total	3722	100.0

Sales Manager, and Senior Sales or Marketing Executive. Nearly 90 per cent of contacts were with personnel entirely outside the organisation from which the respondents came. Indeed, only 4 per cent of the surveyed contacts were with counterparts belonging to the same enterprise and most frequently these counterparts were salesmen in the field.

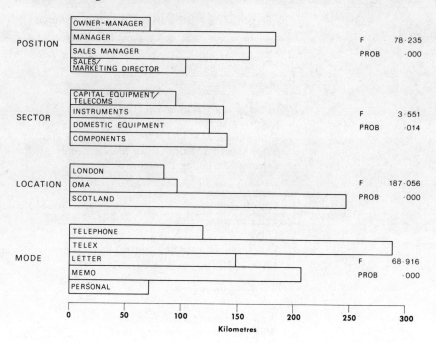

POSITION
OWNER-MANAGER
MANAGER
SALES MANAGER
SALES/MARKETING DIRECTOR
F   78·235
PROB   ·000

SECTOR
CAPITAL EQUIPMENT/TELECOMS
INSTRUMENTS
DOMESTIC EQUIPMENT
COMPONENTS
F   3·551
PROB   ·014

LOCATION
LONDON
OMA
SCOTLAND
F   187·056
PROB   ·000

MODE
TELEPHONE
TELEX
LETTER
MEMO
PERSONAL
F   68·916
PROB   ·000

0   50   100   150   200   250   300
Kilometres

Figure 6.5 Variations in communication contact length by context

The dominant mode of communication was by telephone, followed by letter, and face-to-face contacts were infrequent.

The content of the communications recorded suggests that the diary exercise successfully captured specialised market-boundary exchanges. Thus, over 58 per cent of contacts were established directly with customers, while a further 10 per cent were with correspondents who were offering some form of customer support. However, the often unspecialised or diversified role of the Chief Marketing Executive in the respondent organisation is betrayed by the importance of contact with suppliers and, to a lesser extent, professional services and managerial personnel in a non-customer role. Furthermore, the majority of contacts involved information exchange or discussion, while the giving or receiving of instructions – more routine functions – were considerably less important. Also, insofar as they may be indicated by negotiation or the arrangement of meetings, orientation activities were infrequent.

Analysis of variance has been used to examine the relationships that exist between contact distance (transformed to the log base ten) and the characteristics of these information contacts as outlined in Table 6.8. The significant differences which emerged from this analysis are depicted in Figures 6.5 and 6.6.

The location of the participating (respondent) organisation together with its sectoral affiliation are also included as broad indices of organisations' domains and task environments (Figure 6.5). On average, the information contacts of Scottish respondents were established over distances almost twice as long as those located in the OMA, while the latter exceeded those based in London firms by a small margin, again demonstrating the importance of London in all three fields. Professional managers tended to maintain communications over the

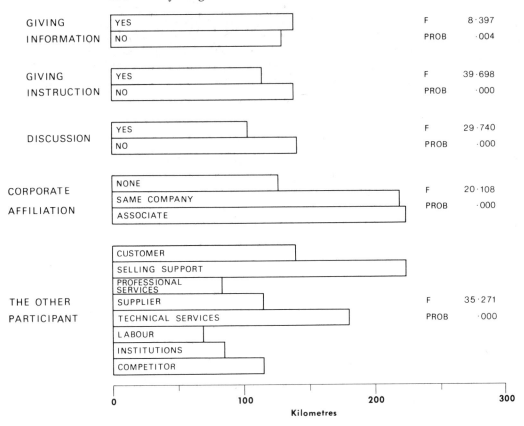

GIVING INFORMATION — YES / NO — F 8·397 / PROB ·004

GIVING INSTRUCTION — YES / NO — F 39·698 / PROB ·000

DISCUSSION — YES / NO — F 29·740 / PROB ·000

CORPORATE AFFILIATION — NONE / SAME COMPANY / ASSOCIATE — F 20·108 / PROB ·000

THE OTHER PARTICIPANT — CUSTOMER / SELLING SUPPORT / PROFESSIONAL SERVICES / SUPPLIER / TECHNICAL SERVICES / LABOUR / INSTITUTIONS / COMPETITOR — F 35·271 / PROB ·000

0   100   200   300
Kilometres

Figure 6.6 Variations in communications contact length by content

longest distances, with owner–managers operating within the most restricted information fields. The most specialised sales personnel fell between these two extremes, with Sales Managers operating within a wider information space, on average, than generally higher-level Marketing Executives with Director status. This finding is consistent with the possibility that the higher the level of control held by the marketing function, the more the person charged with that authority will come to depend upon information passed upward through the organisation and the less he will be directly involved in external communications. Thus, as the Chief Marketing Executive becomes less directly responsible for external search and more directly concerned with orientation functions, so his personal sphere of direct communications might contract.

This last observation is at variance with the findings of Goddard (1973) and Thorngren (1970) which previously have indicated that programmed or routine contacts are generally the most localised. Yet the observation is also supported by variations in the distance over which information linkages have been established according to the mode of communication involved (Figure 6.5). Thus, written communication, telex, 'other' information contacts (comprising mainly memoranda and brochures) and letters, recorded longer mean distances than verbal communications, either by telephone or via face-to-face contacts (Table 6.8). Indeed, meetings involved participants who were, on average, based less than 80 km from the respondent's place of work. Insofar as written communications are generally less efficient than verbal communication (although this varies according to their precise role: Short, Williams and Christie, 1976, Chapters 6 and 7) it can be suggested that the furthermost contacts within the UK will also tend to be the least effective. Not only might local information flows dominate the information fields of the Marketing Executives in quantitative terms, but they may also be qualitatively more important. This contention holds the implication that information drawn from a business organisation's local area may dominate its decision-making, although this does not deny the importance of distant information contacts at an earlier stage of the decision-making process.

With respect to the role of the other participant in any contact, communications with sales-support organisations or salesmen tended to take place over greater distances, on average, than did communications with correspondents from the other categories distinguished (Figure 6.6). In keeping with the advanced technological status of the electronics industry and the need for specialised information, contacts with agencies providing technical services were also established over long distances. Next in importance were direct contacts with customers or potential customers, and competitors. Thus, the types of communications central to the marketing function generally took place over the longest distances. In contrast, contacts involving labour, professional services, institutions such as local or central government, and contacts with managerial or administrative agencies or organisations, tended to take place much closer to the respondent's place of work. Contacts with participants from the same or an associated company took place over considerably longer distances, on average, than those with participants with whom there was no corporate affiliation. To assess the relationship between length of information contact and the content of the communication, a series of separate analyses of variance was undertaken for each of the items denoting the content of communication, as the categories of these items (Table 6.8) are not mutually exclusive. The results of these analyses are reported in Figure 6.6. Only three aspects of communication content were significantly different in average length from the remainder – giving information, giving instruction and discussion – and these three again suggest that less routine communications take place over shorter distances. While contacts in which the respondents themselves gave information were marginally longer than the remainder, those involving the issue of instruction and, particularly, those involving discussion took place over a considerably shorter distance (Figure 6.6).

Before commenting on these results it is necessary to consider the possibility that the effect of location impinges upon them all, as there may be some variation in the 'mix' of contacts recorded between respondents at different locations. For this purpose the descriptive categories in Figures 6.5 and 6.6 were included as independent variables in a series of two-way analyses of variance, together with location. The results indicated that in each case the effect of the respective indices denoting the role or content of communication acted independently of location, although in each case the explanation attributable to location was the greater.

It can be concluded that while the three components of distance decay, local dependence, distance friction and map effect (location within the urban hierarchy), dominate aggregate communication fields, a number of contextural and content variables also play an important part. In particular, it appears that less routine communications, involving verbal contact, discussion, or non-customer participants, tend to take place in closer proximity to respondents' locations than other types of communication. This finding suggests that in its day-to-day external communications the marketing subsystem of an organisation maintains relatively wide spatial horizons with respect to those functions for which it holds primary responsibility – the maintenance and monitoring of customer relations. However, in less routine functions, functions which may well be more critical in terms of the firm management and alignment of the enterprise as a whole, respondents are more constrained in their spatial interaction and apparently more dependent upon local communication.

The communication fields of Marketing Executives

Against the background of these general characteristics of the information fields of electronics manufacturers it is necessary to develop summary measures consistent with those for material interaction fields so that this significant aspect of inter-organisational interaction can be incorporated in the testing of the model of organisation–environment interaction. To achieve this end a methodology has been employed similar to that previously elaborated for the analysis of material linkages.

The first step involves the use of a regression weighting procedure to reduce the effect of a respondent being located in any of the three study regions on the length of its information contacts. However, amongst these information contacts the overriding importance of location upon the distances over which contacts were established and the considerable range of other influences identified, were such that it was decided to eliminate the map hierarchy effect only. Thus, the weighting procedure was equivalent to expressing each contact as a deviation from the mean length of contacts recorded by all respondents in a particular region. That is, the intercept or constant in the regression equation represents the mean achieved by the reference variable, or the dummy variable not included in the equation which in this case was set as location in the OMA. The expected lengths of contacts for London or Scottish respondents are derived by making the adjustment indicated by the appropriate regression coefficients. Each contact was measured as a deviation from the expected length and then converted to a proportion of expected length, in order to reduce the impact of absolute variations between the means across the three regions.

Because of the simple nature of the transformation process and the fact that virtually every respondent recorded at least some contacts within close proximity, the shortest contact and the range between the shortest and longest were not included as indices of spatial communications activity in subsequent analyses. However, a set of summary statistics was derived for each respondent describing aspects of the distance distribution of information contacts first adjusted by the regression weighting procedure:

(1) the mean (weighted) distance over which contacts took place;
(2) the most distant contact;
(3) the standard deviation derived from all contact lengths recorded within a diary (indicating the degree of concentration of contacts within the vector of distances over which they were recorded);
(4) the percentage of contacts with a weighted distance value exceeding zero, i.e. above the mean established by all contacts recorded for respondents in the region;
(5) the percentage of all contacts established for the exchange of information directly overseas.

The relative localisation and the strength of distance decay in the communication fields of individual respondents were measured using the regression procedure earlier employed at the regional level. For each respondent, an ordinary least squares regression line was fitted to the distribution of points denoting the cumulative percentage of contacts at various distances, the latter measured on a logarithmic scale. Although an arbitrary procedure, this yielded estimates of distance decay in the form of the slope coefficients and of local dependence in the form of the intercepts, both of which were statistically significant at the 0.001 level in every case. Indeed, the lowest correlation coefficient achieved using this procedure was $r = 0.773$, corroborating at the individual firm level the relationship observed between distance and information flows at the regional level. Moreover, it yielded for every firm two variables which are not only aligned with the foregoing discussion of the components of spatial interaction, but which also directly incorporate the importance of overseas contacts. The maximum value which the dependent variable in the regression equation, the percentage of contacts, might assume will be influenced by the proportion of contacts established with overseas counterparts. Thus, a high proportion of foreign contacts would act to depress the intercept and thereby reduce the measure of local dependence.

The nature of these two derived variables can be demonstrated diagrammatically (Figure 6.7). Firm (1) in Figure 6.7 is a Scottish organisation dependent almost entirely upon information obtained from a customer less than 8 kms away, the high score recorded for the intercept providing evidence of the importance of local information exchanges. Over and above the role of the customer in the immediate area, remaining information contacts have been established with the parent company, some 96 kms distant. Beyond this distance no contacts were recorded. The result is a relatively high rate of distance decay, as

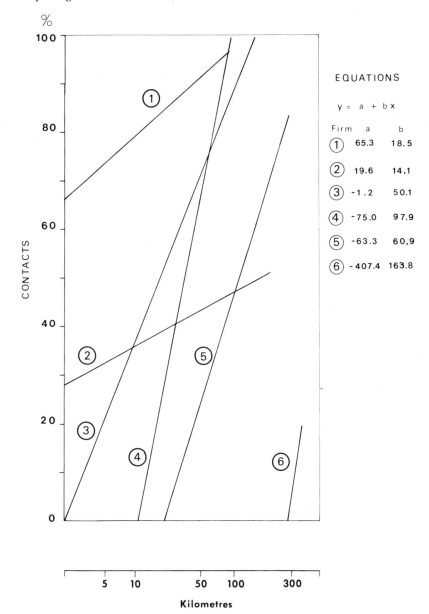

Figure 6.7 The
communications fields of
individual firms: regression
analyses

indicated by the slope of the regression line. Firm (2) was a highly
specialised capital equipment manufacturer located in South London.
The majority of market information contacts were with a major
government corporation, also located in London. Over and above those
London contacts there is no evidence of a pronounced distance friction
constraint upon other information contacts, which occurred throughout
the UK. In addition, a number of contacts are maintained with an
American subsidiary. The impact of this pattern on the regression line
shown in Figure 6.7 is to suggest that a high level of local dependence is
accompanied by a relatively low level of distance decay.

Firm (3) manufactures passive components. Also located in South London, the firm is dependent upon localised communications with a relatively constant decline in contacts away from the local area. Operating in a non-specialised product area the firm acts in a servicing role for producers within a radius of approximately 50 kms, upon whom it is dependent for most of its marketing information. At the time of interview expansion problems had encouraged Firm (3) to consider relocation, although the alternatives considered all fell well within the radius described by customer information contacts.

Firm (4) is located in a new town in the OMA and also acts as a service or subcontract manufacturing enterprise with customers confined to surrounding towns. Because Firm (4) has developed from the merger of two separate enterprises originally located in neighbouring towns, it has no important contacts at its current location. As a result there is evidence of a relatively low level of local dependence, but a very rapid friction of distance effect in communications thereafter.

The lowest levels of local dependence in the entire sample are recorded by Firm (5), a relatively long-established subsidiary of an American instrument and component manufacturing group in the east of Scotland. The contact diary maintained by the Marketing Director reflects two distinctive elements in the firm's operation: a very high level of overseas communication, and frequent contact with sales organisations and customers in London. The result is a completely non-localised information field which, given the predominance of London linkages within the UK, is, nevertheless, subject to a rapid rate of distance decay.

The procedures described in the preceding paragraphs provide seven indices summarising the form of the communication fields of firms. The two principal components with eigenvalues exceeding unity extracted from the product moment correlation matrix generated from these indices are presented in Table 6.9. The first component, accounting for 43 per cent of total variance, is clearly a measure of the orientation of the information field, bringing together the mean distance of information contacts, the percentage of contacts exceeding the regional mean, the percentage established overseas, the distance over which the longest contact was recorded within the UK, and the value of the intercept for the distance decay curve. Bearing in mind that a lower intercept value is associated with a low level of local dependence, the loadings are all consistent with discrimination upon Component I between firms with highly localised market information fields – high negative scores – and those with completely non-localised fields – high positive scores. As such, the first component parallels the second component in the equivalent analyses of sales and purchasing linkages (Table 6.5).

The second component is associated with the notion of distance decay, the loading of the slope coefficient suggesting that a positive score is consistent with a field in which the friction effect is not marked. This is supported by the loading of the standard deviation, indicating that firms recording high scores upon Component II will possess the least spatially concentrated information contacts. The loading for the

Table 6.9 *Market communication fields; orthogonally rotated components*

Information contact variables	Component Loadings[1]		
	I Orientation	II Variability	h^2
Mean length	0.942		0.895
Standard deviation		0.910	0.859
Maximum length	0.536	0.669	0.734
% Non-local	0.879		0.789
% Overseas	0.798		0.642
Localisation (regression intercept)	−0.518	0.793	0.900
Distance decay (regression coefficient)		−0.818	0.700
Eigenvalue	3.008	2.511	
Variance	43.0	35.9	

Note: [1] Loadings below 0.2 omitted

longest linkage suggests that this variable indicates the range over which contacts are established. The positive loading of the intercept upon Component II infers that a high degree of spatial variability in information contacts is associated with some initial local dependence. This component is accepted, therefore, as a measure of spatial variability in communication fields and corresponds with the first component in the analyses of sales and purchasing linkages. A negative score indicates that the Chief Marketing Executive's information was drawn from a restricted range of distances and, it might be inferred, from a limited range of locations.

This section has, therefore, reduced a variety of measures describing the spatial form of communications fields to two composite variables which are directly comparable with those developed for material linkages.

The texture of communications

Since the urban hierarchy or map effect was controlled for in the analyses of the previous section, the exact form of the communications fields described by the indices that were developed is likely to depend upon:

(1) the quality and quantity of information available locally; and
(2) the nature of the respondent organisations, their information needs, and the communication systems in which they are involved.

These two elements are obviously interdependent. The greater the proportion of relatively underdeveloped or unstructured organisations or enterprises in an area, the greater the role which local information is likely to play in their communication fields. However, in order to investigate the relationships between organisational structure and information fields, which are considered in the following chapter, it is necessary to examine an element of communications activity which might come between the two – the nature or 'texture' of communications activities. The role of the Marketing Executive in his external communications, the information network in which he is involved, and the nature of the exchanges which he makes, might be expected to reflect the type of organisation with which he is associated, on the one hand, and the spatial form of his communication field, on the other. The present section is therefore concerned with the communications activities of the Chief Marketing Executives who returned contact diaries.

Two possible approaches could be employed to summarise the 'texture' as opposed to the spatial form of communications activities. The first would involve the multivariate analysis of the individual contacts, classifying and scoring them according to indices derived directly from 'profiles' of each of the 3733 contacts recorded for the sample, and averaging these scores across the diaries of each respondent. In its emphasis upon individual contacts this approach is similar to that adopted by Goddard (1973), Thorngren (1970) and the London Communication Studies Group (Short, Williams and Christie, 1976), for example. However, averaging the scores of each respondent is a tenuous procedure, which may involve the loss of considerable information. The approach also presents analytical problems, firstly in selection of an appropriate analytical technique (latent structure analysis (Lazarsfeld and Henry, 1967; Goddard, 1973), multidimensional scaling (Kruskal, 1964a, 1964b) and factor analysis being the main alternatives (Gibson, 1961; Pye, 1973)) and secondly in selection of appropriate similarity coefficients for initial transformation of the contact data.

For these reasons a second approach has been preferred. This involves expressing the frequency of each item as a percentage of all contacts recorded within each diary. This procedure has the effect of standardising diaries so that contact frequency is unimportant. It yields profiles of communications activity based upon the relative occurrence of different characteristics of information contacts. For the present analysis eighteen items have been distinguished describing the content and the purpose of information exchange, and the role of the counterpart in any contact (Table 6.10). The 52 profiles created from these data can then be subjected to principal components analysis: the standard procedure employed elsewhere in the study. Table 6.10 presents the loadings of the eighteen indices of communications activity upon the varimax rotated components derived from principal components analysis. In all, six components with eigenvalues greater than unity emerged from the analysis, and together these account for 72 per cent of total variance.

The first component is associated primarily with the frequency of contacts with suppliers and labour, and with the issuing of instructions. The receipt of information and the frequency of interaction with organisations providing both professional and technical services also load positively, although less strongly on Component I. In addition, the component is associated with higher proportions of externally initiated, or incoming, contacts. It appears, therefore, that Component I identi-

Table 6.10 *Dimensions of communications activity; orthogonally rotated components*

Variables	I Diversity	II Obliquity	III Orienta-tion	IV Institu-tional	V Adminis-tration	VI Subord-ination	h^2
				Component Loadings[1]			
Respondent initiated	−0.305	−0.217	−0.468	0.260		0.427	0.609
Give information						−0.832	0.747
Receive information	0.561					−0.227	0.429
Give instruction	0.732	0.205	0.206				0.634
Receive instruction		−0.283		−0.316	−0.223	0.605	0.615
Discussion		0.261	0.484	0.382			0.689
Negotiation			0.863				0.793
Arranging meeting			0.808				0.703
With customer	−0.688	−0.567		−0.322	−0.234		0.954
With sales support		0.895					0.832
With supplier	0.764	−0.230		−0.207			0.761
With labour	0.523				0.581		0.660
With institutions				0.869	0.202		0.821
With competitors			0.328		0.806		0.772
With technical services	0.482	−0.316		0.215		0.218	0.454
With prof. services	0.204			0.803		−0.268	0.784
With management		0.449			0.788		0.836
Eigenvalue	3.701	2.542	2.023	1.903	1.650	1.110	
% Variance	20.6	14.1	11.2	10.6	9.2	6.2	

Note: [1] Loadings below 0.2 omitted.

fies communication patterns associated with non-customer, routine exchanges, with a high score implying that the Marketing Executive is involved in a relatively high proportion of non-marketing tasks, an interpretation enhanced by the negative loading on the component of contacts with customers. It is therefore labelled as a component measuring the *diversity* of communications with the implication that diversity acts against strong market or customer orientation and that Chief Marketing Executives who are strongly involved in this pattern of contacts deal with many segments of the external environment.

The proportion of customer contacts also loads negatively on the second component (Table 6.10). However, the proportion of contacts with market support agencies or personnel has a high positive loading, as does contact with associates. There is evidence that this second component also relates to discussion and the issuing of instructions although respondents involved with this pattern of communication appear unlikely to initiate external contacts. Component II can be said to describe communications which incorporate a high degree of market information without a high level of direct customer contact. Firms with high component scores are characterised by a developed marketing function based upon information moving upward through the organisation, drawn from associate companies and from sales and marketing servicing agencies. The Chief Marketing Executive, whose communication patterns are thus described, presumably undertakes planning using information supplied or filtered by organisations and personnel interposed between him and the market place. The converse comprises a pattern of relatively simple-structured communications taking place directly between the Chief Marketing Executive and customer or potential customer. For convenience of reference the component can be described as a measure of the *obliquity*, or indirectness, of market communications, a high positive score implying a relatively low level of direct contact with customers although communications are primarily concerned with market information.

The third component is more closely related to the content and especially the complexity of communications than either Component I or Component II. The main loading occurs for contacts involving negotiation, followed closely by those involving the arrangement of meetings. Also important are contacts involving discussion and, to a lesser extent, communication with competitors and the issuing of instructions. Component III therefore describes *orientation* activity within organisations' communications network.

The fourth component also involves contacts through which discussion was conducted. More important, though, is the strong emphasis upon contacts with *institutions* of various kinds involving, for example, local and national government departments, trade associations, and professional services. Component IV implies involvement with institutions which tend to be more peripheral to the day-to-day operations of an enterprise than its customers, although they are of importance for long-term development owing to their ability to control or regulate the organisation's external environment.

Component V complements the second and third components as it involves variables indicative of orientation towards the wider corporate context and competition, management and labour. The component appears to identify communications activities associated with routine administrative communications, an interpretation confirmed by inspection of the scores for individual respondents' contacts through which instructions are sought. It is negatively associated with the exchange of information and involves communication with technical but not professional services. Although relatively unimportant in terms of its share of total variance, interpretation of this component is of interest. It is indicative of low-level, routine flows whereby external communications largely take the form of initiatives upon which the focal organisation might act. It suggests dependence upon established lines of communication through which the organisation seeks to respond to externally defined requirements or routine technical information. Strong involvement in this component may well reflect a high level of dependence upon external technology, in which case the marketing function may become dominated by the need to seek technical guidance, rather than acting to exploit internal technical competence. The component is labelled, therefore, as a measure of the *subordination* of communications, denoting a continuum from a highly passive role on the part of the

Marketing Executive, through to a more active one on the part of those respondents recording high negative scores upon it.

None of the six components depicted in Table 6.10 encompass either particular aspects of content or particular types of respondent. Indeed, customer interaction as such is best described with respect to four separate components, the interpretation of which is made more difficult by the negative direction of the loadings associated with the variable denoting percentage of customer contacts. It is easiest, therefore, to interpret customer contact patterns by contrasting them directly with:

(1) more diversified and wider ranging communications (Component I):
(2) patterns of market communication mediated by some form of organisational infrastructure (Component II);
(3) those communications fields in which contacts with regulatory institutions are an important element (Component IV); and
(4) managerial contact patterns more concerned with corporate and competitor relationships (Component V).

Moreover, the two components in which the percentage of contact taking place with customers does not contribute to interpretation are revealing with respect to the role of market information in firm management. Thus, Component III implies that a heavy involvement in orientation activities will act against close or direct monitoring of the segment of the environment comprising customers or potential customers, while Component VI indicates that in technologically less sophisticated or independent firms the tasks of monitoring the market and technical environments become indistinguishable.

Conclusion   In Part I of this volume, linkages and information flows were identified as the avenues whereby an organisation interacts with its environment, and they were thought to have the potential to improve the calibration and specification of the notion of the task environment, developed in organisation theory. The present chapter has, therefore, examined these forms of interaction in the context of the UK electronics industry in order to describe their configuration in general and their geographical configuration in particular. An attempt has also been made to develop summary indices of these different types of interaction according to a uniform and improved methodology which would allow the incorporation of these key sets of variables into the testing of the previously developed *a priori* model of organisation–environment interaction.

The descriptive facet of the chapter tended to reinforce the conclusions of previous linkage and information flow studies. For patterns of material linkage – both inputs and outputs – it was shown that distance, location, parochialism (local dependence) and an urban hierarchy, map effect were the principal determinants of the spatial form of organisations' interaction fields. The configuration of these fields was also shown to be modified by a range of contextual variables including technology, internal organisational structure, sectoral and corporate affiliations and the existence of contractual agreements between organisations, especially for the supply of material inputs.

In contrast with material linkages, the spatial characteristics of information flows have received considerably less attention in the literature. Nevertheless, from an analysis of communications data collected in contact diaries it can be concluded that the same factors of distance, parochialism, location and an urban hierarchy, map effect also determine the general form of organisations' information and communications fields. However, it was also shown that while day-to-day external communication was spatially quite widespread, the communications and information flows associated with less routine functions were spatially more constrained. In other words, as they relate to organisations' task environments the information flows associated with less routine and presumably unprogrammed decision-making suggest that parochialism is likely to strongly influence strategic decision-making.

Given this confirmation and extension of previous linkage and information flow studies, an attempt was made to develop a uniform and consistent methodology for the measurement of both of these forms of interaction between an enterprise and its task environment in order to calibrate subsequently the modes of organisation–environment interaction proposed in Chapter 3. A multivariate methodology was adopted which enabled composite, descriptive indices to be created to act as summary variables for the empirical regularities which had been described in detail for both interaction fields and communication fields. The principal characteristics of organisations' interaction fields defined by their material linkages were:

(1) purchasing variability (the range of input lengths);
(2) purchasing orientation (levels of local dependence);
(3) sales variability (the range of output lengths); and
(4) sales orientation (level of dependence on local markets).

From a comparable analysis of electronics manufacturers' market information flows, revealed in contact diaries, two equivalent measures were developed to describe and summarise the characteristics of communications fields. The first measure depicted information orientation (dependence on local sources once again) and the second depicted the range of distances over which information contacts had been established (communications variability). However, six additional composite variables were generated to describe the nature or 'texture' of the information environment defined by these flows. These descriptive variables referred to the following:

(1) diversity of communications;
(2) obliquity or indirectness of market communications;
(3) orientation activity;
(4) communication with institutions, especially regulatory institutions;
(5) routine and intracorporate communication;
(6) subordination within the communication network.

It remains, however, to integrate these characteristics of organisations' interaction and information fields with the internal structural and performance characteristics of the same enterprises which were described and calibrated in Chapter 5. In so doing it should be possible to draw on and test the propositions and directions of causality which were made explicit in the earlier *a priori* model of organisation–environment interaction and the operation of business enterprises within an explicitly spatial context. This is the task of Chapter 7.

7   Towards a spatial model of organisation — environment interaction

Chapter 4 described the societal environment and environmental domain within which the United Kingdom electronics industry operates. The sources and rate of technological change, the nature of various market sectors, the role of government and the major institutions which dominate these environments were all considered. Chapter 5 focused attention upon the internal structure of a sample of the enterprises in this industry, and measures of internal development and rates of change or effectiveness in the external environment. Chapter 6 described the interface between these enterprises and their environments in terms of both interaction fields and communications fields. These fields define an organisation's task environments in geographical terms, encompassing the information and opportunities upon which its survival, development, and future structure depend. It was shown that, despite their membership of an industry marked by the international nature of its technology, electronics enterprises' interaction fields are highly localised. It was also shown that the individual task environments, to which most organisations respond through their internal structuring, vary according to the locations at which they operate. It remains, however, to establish more formally the network of connections between an organisation's domain, its more specific task environment, internal structure, and performance, and to establish directions of causality within this framework. This is the aim of the present chapter, in which the empirical measures developed in preceding chapters are drawn together.

From the survey information collected from the sample of British electronics enterprises, parameters can be estimated by which the strength and direction of the connections between environment, structure and performance can be measured. While it cannot be assumed that these parameters will hold good in other empirical situations, the directions and relative strengths of causality that they indicate will provide an indication of the empirical validity of the model of organisation–environment interaction which was advanced in Chapter 3. The analysis should also provide further insight into the structure of the model and into the nature and interaction of a range of complex variables which have only been considered in abstract or very simple terms in the past.

The impact of the environmental domain

In the preceding chapters considerable attention was devoted to the compilation of variables measuring aspects of environment and interac-

166

tion at the individual enterprise level. This section examines the general relationships between broad variations in environmental domains, or the 'external' elements of the model proposed in Chapter 3, and the enterprise-based variables. Attention is directed towards the technology, regional location and corporate contexts within which subgroups of respondent organisations operate.

Major variations in the environmental domains of UK electronics manufacturers can be measured by differentiating between organisations based in London, the Outer Metropolitan Area (OMA) and Scotland; between those involved in different sectors of the electronics industry; and between independent enterprises and members of wider corporate groups. In this way three nominal dimensions of organisations' domains can be expressed as a series of point dichotomous variables. Direct relationships between these nominal variables and the various measures of organisation and interaction could be estimated through analysis of variance. However, this procedure assumes the existence of a direct causal relationship between the nominal variables describing environmental domains and the continuous variables measuring organisations' structures or spatial behaviour. This is at odds with the model advanced in Chapter 3 in which individual enterprises could influence their own development through the exercising of 'choice'. Furthermore, analysis of variance becomes cumbersome when there are a number of continuous variables to be considered.

Therefore, discriminant analysis has been used as the basis of the following discussion. Discriminant analysis can be used to identify the variables which best differentiate between organisations according to the categories describing each of the dimensions of the domain within which they operate, and to determine, at the same time, which of these variables is most closely associated with their internal structure and spatial behaviour.

Discriminant analysis describes the differences between subgroups or samples drawn from the same population but located at different points in multivariate space (Cooley and Lohnes, 1971; Kerlinger and Pedhazur, 1973; Klecka, 1975; Tatsouka, 1971). The method establishes the differences between categories by minimising within-group and maximising between-group variation. It involves derivation of the regression equation(s) (discriminant function(s)) which maximises 'explanation' of a nominal variable by a number of interval variables. The effectiveness of the discriminating functions can be measured through the canonical correlation between them and the individual point dichotomous categories (in this study location, sector, or corporate affiliation). Discriminant functions are derived sequentially, in terms of discriminatory power, and relatively few may be necessary for meaningful discrimination. Furthermore, the scores of individual variables on these functions indicate their contribution to discrimination, and they can be interpreted in much the same way as factor loadings or standardised regression coefficients.

For the purposes of the present analysis, three categories were defined for each of the variables defining dimensions of the environmental domain. In the case of *location* this is consistent with the differentiation of respondent organisations according to whether they were located in Scotland, London or the OMA. Three classes were also used to define *sectoral affiliations*. All manufacturers of domestic and capital equipment were allocated to one category and a distinction was drawn between instrument and computer peripheral manufacturers, on the one hand, and component producers on the other. Finally, three categories of ownership were distinguished: organisations which were themselves Head Offices or were located in the same region as their Head Office; organisations owned or controlled from elsewhere within the United Kingdom; and organisations owned and controlled by overseas multinationals.

The interval variables used to establish the discriminant functions were the measures of organisational structure and spatial interaction, derived in Chapters 5 and 6. These composite and often complex indicators of organisational performance, structure and spatial behaviour are summarised in Table 7.1. The distribution of responses through the sample is such that complete sets of data are available for only 27 electronics enterprises. However, when the purchasing interaction variables, which are peripheral to the analysis, given emphasis upon market boundary functions, are omitted the number of data sets increases to 33. When the components denoting firm size and growth are discarded it rises yet further to 44 sets. The discriminant analyses described below, therefore, have been undertaken using data for these 44 enterprises.

To derive the most efficient discriminant functions a stepwise procedure has been used which maximises a generalised measure of intergroup distances – Rao's V (Heyck and Klecka, 1973; Klecka, 1975). Through the stepwise process the variable leading to the greatest overall separation of categories, taking into account variables previously entered into the function, is added at each step. In the present study when the partial F ratio pertaining to a variable falls below 1.0, indicating that residual between-group variance is less than residual within-group variance and that the statistical probability of meaningful discrimination is 0.50, the variable is excluded from the function altogether. In practice this is a very liberal criterion for entry, allowing any variable which contributes at all to discrimination to enter the functions.

The results of the three separate discriminant analyses are presented in Table 7.2. The capacity of the variables to discriminate between groups of organisations is obviously greatest with respect to location and least with respect to ownership. A total of nine variables contribute to the relatively high value obtained for Rao's V in the case of location. Seven variables were drawn upon to discriminate on the basis of sectoral affiliation and only three were meaningfully associated with ownership. In the case of location the incremental contribution made by each variable at the step at which it entered was statistically significant at the 10 per cent probability level. However, the contribution of management delegation to discrimination was effectively offset by subsequent variables in the stepwise procedure, leading to its exclusion from the

Table 7.1 *Variables measuring performance, organisation and the spatial behaviour of organisations*

Label	Description	Source	Cases
(1) *Performance*			
Size	Component of size incorporating employment, turnover, etc.	Table 5.2	64
Growth	Component of short term change, independent of size, based upon one-year shifts in employment, turnover. Incorporates age and is related to five-year growth records.	Table 5.2	64
Development	Density of topologically ordered attributes denoting increasing levels of organisation.	Table 5.3	121
(2) *Structure*			
Differentiation	Structuring of task environment; component of specialisation and differentiation based upon level of involvement with most and least frequent attributes.	Table 5.1	121
Delegation	Delegation of task responsibility and associated configuration.	Table 5.4	121
Integration	Integration of external and internal tasks based upon level of corporate influence in their performance.	Table 5.4	121
Production flexibility	Number of product lines and evidence of recent change.	Table 5.4	121
Production complexity	Complexity of manufacturing process.	Table 5.4	121
Marketing	Level of development and role of marketing function.	Table 5.4	121
(3) *Interaction fields*			
Purchasing variability	Variability or range of input linkage lengths; indicative of distance decay.	Table 6.5	78
Purchasing orientation	Level of localisation of input linkages; high scores indicate dependence upon non-local sources.	Table 6.5	78
Sales variability	Variability or range of distances over which sales linkages established; high scores indicate widespread interaction.	Table 6.5	89
Sales orientation	Level of localisation of sales linkages; measure of spatial market monopoly and local customer dependence; high scores indicate dependence upon non-local outlets.	Table 6.5	89

Table 7.1 *Variables measuring performance, organisation and the spatial behaviour of organisations*—(contd)

Label	Description	Source	Cases
(4) *Information fields*			
Orientation	Dependence upon local sources of information; high score indicates considerable non-local bias in information contacts.	Table 6.9	52
Variability	Variability in range of distances over which information contacts are established.	Table 6.9	52
(5) *Communications activity*			
Diversity	Based upon variety of roles in communication networks. Importance of non-market contact functions. High scores act against market and customer contact.	Table 6.10	52
Obliquity	Existence of organisational infrastructure intervening between marketing executive and customers. Extent to which market information filtered by agencies.	Table 6.10	52
Complexity	Importance of complex, orientation contacts involving discussion, negotiation, etc.	Table 6.10	52
Institutional	Contact with institutions other than sales support and customers, suggesting involvement in longer-term, periodic contact functions.	Table 6.10	52
Management	Emphasis upon management and associate contacts. Implies monitoring and general information exchange within corporate context.	Table 6.10	52
Subordination	Relative activity, contribution or responsiveness of respondent in contact network. High score implies passive contacts aimed at satisfying external demands.	Table 6.10	52

final equations. The additional contributions made by two variables in the analysis for sectoral affiliation and by one in the analysis for ownership were not statistically significant.

In the first two analyses, both functions extracted made some contribution to discrimination as indicated by their respective eigenvalues and canonical correlations. However, for ownership only the first function served to discriminate among respondents. The general conclusion

Table 7.2 *Differentiating amongst organisations by location, sector and ownership; discriminant analyses*

Step variable[1]	Discriminant coefficients		F	Rao's V	Significance of change in V
	I	II			
Analysis 1, Location					
(1) Information variability	0.391	0.134	10.552	22.552	0.000
(2) Delegation			5.406	33.420	0.002
(3) Sales variability	0.451	−0.075	3.270	44.666	0.004
(4) Information orientation	0.424	−0.225	4.656	60.560	0.000
(5) Production complexity	−0.271	−0.133	4.053	79.783	0.000
(6) Marketing	0.324	0.083	3.086	98.230	0.000
(7) Diversity	0.012	−0.402	3.651	109.799	0.000
(8) Development	−0.323	0.613	1.666	117.636	0.020
(9) Delegation		Removed	0.4005	115.794	1.000
(10) Production flexibility	0.188	−0.329	2.334	129.708	0.001
(11) Integration	0.044	−0.274	1.294	135.385	0.059
Eigenvalue	2.473	0.829			
% Common Variance	74.89	25.11			
Canonical correlation	0.844	0.673			
Analysis 2, Sector					
(1) Production complexity	−0.380	−0.13	4.798	9.595	0.008
(2) Marketing	0.517	−0.154	4.417	20.766	0.004
(3) Information variability	0.379	−0.108	4.420	34.713	0.001
(4) Sales orientation	−0.203	−0.081	2.977	46.382	0.003
(5) Complexity (information)	−0.141	−0.224	1.359	62.976	0.065
(6) Delegation	−0.062	0.562	1.493	66.623	0.162
(7) Obliquity	0.075	−0.283	1.137	70.205	0.167
Eigenvalue	1.518	0.194			
% Common Variance	88.64	11.36			
Canonical correlation	0.776	0.406			
Analysis 3, Ownership					
(1) Information variability	−0.782	0.682	5.344	10.688	0.005
(2) Complexity (information)	0.723	−0.363	2.592	17.384	0.035
(3) Integration	0.582	0.084	1.537	21.884	0.105
Eigenvalue	0.529	0.005			
% Common variance	99.10	0.90			
Canonical correlation	0.588	0.069			

Note: [1] For description of variables, see Table 7.1

to be drawn from Table 7.2 is that the variables considered tend to be much more closely associated with the location of organisations than with their sectoral affiliations or with the location of their ownership and control. Although this may reflect, in part, a particular research emphasis, it does confirm the importance of the impact of regional variations in the organisational domain upon the development and interaction of individual enterprises. It suggests that this regional effect is greater than that of either ownership or technology insofar as these various aspects of domain have been defined for the present study. This is a clear indication of the mutual benefit to be gained from the integration of concepts from industrial geography and organisation theory and, in particular, emphasises the significance of space as an important aspect of organisations' environments.

Interpretation of the discriminant functions is impeded, however, by the fact that they are composite variables, the initial interpretation of which has been neither fully objective nor conclusive. Nevertheless, it is possible to interpret broadly the clusters of variables which discriminate amongst electronics organisations according to contrasts in their environmental domains. Thus, the location of an enterprise is distinguished primarily by its spatial interaction patterns. The level of variability in the distance over which sales and information contacts are established, together with the localisation of information flows, act to discriminate between enterprises operating at different locations (Table 7.2). The development of the marketing function and a tendency towards greater technical flexibility are positively associated while there is evidence of contrasting involvement with the complexity of production and the level of development. The first location function contrasts technically based, functionally structured organisations characterised by relatively constrained spheres of activity, with enterprises in which the marketing function is more important and interaction takes place over a wider area. Although accounting for only one-third as much variance as the first function, the second location function can still be given a substantive interpretation as it contrasts higher levels of organisational development with undeveloped organisations in which there is heavy dependence upon the local area for information, little integration of marketing and production functions, little production flexibility, and dependence upon market intelligence gleaned through a communications network incorporating a diversity of non-market information.

Scores can be estimated for each of the 44 respondent organisations on the basis of these two functions which allows them to be positioned in two-dimensional multivariate space. For clarity, only group centroids have been plotted in this way in Figure 7.1. For the first *location* function, a strong contrast emerges between London and Scotland, with the OMA falling between them. This implies that more highly developed marketing and spatially more variable market behaviour characterises the London respondents. The negative score for Scotland is consistent with Burns and Stalker's (1961) findings on organisations in the same region over 20 years ago; the relative failure of firms to become viable electronics manufacturers results from the management legacy associated with the longer-established, more stable and traditional engineering environment. This has led to a separation of technological and market functions within individual organisations and the emergence of only poorly developed information monitoring and processing functions. The intermediate position of the centroid for the OMA, on the other hand, suggests the achievement by electronics

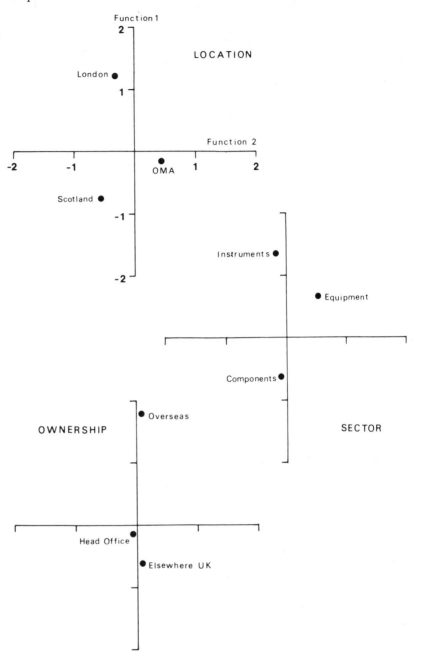

Figure 7.1 Separation of
subgroup centroids by
discriminant functions

manufacturers in that location of a form of organisation which brings
internal technological tasks and externally oriented market functions
into a reasonable balance.

Although the second discriminant function in the analysis of location
does not force the subgroup centroids as far apart, the ordering is
consistent with the interpretation advanced above. OMA organisations
emerge as the most advanced in terms of general levels of development,
while their London and Scottish-based counterparts stand in contrast.

However, the difference between the London and Scottish groups of organisations on this more general developmental function is minimal, despite the contrasts in structure and interaction indicated by the first function.

The first function derived from the analysis of the *sectoral* affiliations of electronics manufacturers (Table 7.2, Analysis 2) is similar to that of the main location function, contrasting an emphasis upon production complexity with marketing development and a relatively high level of variability in the communication fields of organisations. Production complexity is associated with a high degree of local field variability. Also, production complexity is associated with a high level of local market dependence. The second sectoral discriminant function from this analysis, although of limited importance, is almost entirely dependent upon the delegation of authority, which contrasts with the subordination and complexity of communications by the Chief Marketing Executive. It can be concluded once more that the centralisation of authority within an organisation or enterprise acts against the establishment of effective market communications.

Table 7.2 indicates that, for the first sectoral function, relative emphasis upon the marketing task is associated with instrument manufacture and, to a lesser extent, with the production of electronic equipment. A narrower sales interaction field and a greater level of production complexity, as defined by the second function, are far more characteristic of components manufacturers than the remainder. As no manufacturers of active components fell within the subset of 44 respondents upon which the analysis is based, this contrast is consistent with the dependence of the passive components sector upon the technical and market requirements of the customers which it serves within the wider environmental domain (Chapter 4).

Although, for clarity and comparability of presentation, the centroids of subgroups on the two discriminant functions from the analysis by *ownership* are plotted in Figure 7.1, only the first of these functions merits interpretation (Table 7.2). Indeed, it is less comprehensive and generalised than its counterparts in the first two analyses. It is based upon only three variables, and is positively associated with a relatively high level of localised information contacts, considerable organisational integration, and complexity in the nature of communications conducted by the Chief Marketing Executive. Not surprisingly, it reflects a marked contrast between overseas owned and controlled and UK owned and controlled organisations (Figure 7.1), although the ability of the function to discriminate between local and non-local ownership and control within the UK is limited. The function suggests that the organisational impact of differences in the location of parent organisations lies in the integration of marketing and technical tasks associated with overseas ownership and the channelling effect this has on market information flows.

The discriminant functions in Table 7.2 have been used to allocate cases to their 'most probable' classes as a means of further investigating the nature of the variables depicting environmental domains (see

Table 7.3 *Sources of error in the discriminant analyses*

Subgroups	Number of cases	Classified to Subgroups			In Error	
		1	2	3	No.	%
Analysis 1, Location	44				6	15.91
(1) London	10	9	0	1	1	11.11
(2) OMA	22	1	19	2	3	15.78
(3) Scotland	12	1	1	10	2	16.67
Analysis 2, Sector	44				7	15.91
(1) Capital Goods	4	3	1	0	1	25.00
(2) Instruments	10	1	9	0	1	11.11
(3) Components	30	3	2	25	5	16.67
Analysis 3, Ownership	52				29	63.46
(1) Head Office	28	9	14	5	19	67.86
(2) Elsewhere UK	16	6	9	1	7	43.75
(3) Overseas	8	2	1	5	3	37.50

Cooley and Lohnes, 1971, Chapter 10). Comparison of observed group membership and the distributions derived from the discriminant analyses (Table 7.3) enables identification of the major sources of error and assessment of the validity of the categories employed. For both location and sector, 44 organisations could be included but, for the ownership variable this number could be increased to 52 owing to the absence of any sales interaction variables in the discriminant functions. In general, Table 7.3 confirms and reinforces earlier conclusions. The smallest classification error is recorded with respect to location, a marginally greater one with respect to sector, and a considerably greater one for the location of ownership aspect of environmental domains. Indeed, the inability of the functions to discriminate between local ownership and ownership elsewhere within the UK is particularly pronounced.

No London firms were allocated by the discriminant functions to the OMA (Table 7.3). One, however, a small component manufacturer managed by, and dependent for technological development upon, a single entrepreneur–owner, was classified to the predominantly Scottish group, an outcome which is also consistent with this particular organisation's dependence upon a few, major, long-standing customers. Minimal effort was put into selling or marketing a product compared with continuous endeavours to meet the technical demands of those few, local customers – a pattern of dependence observed for a considerable proportion of the surveyed Scottish electronics producers. Two OMA respondents of a similar nature, both involved in subcontract component manufacture or subassembly, were also allocated to the Scottish group. In turn, one of the more successful and dynamic Scottish enterprises, a diversified, independent manufacturer of instruments, was allocated to the predominantly OMA group, while a very small, specialised and static organisation manufacturing medical instruments near Glasgow was allocated to the London group.

No firm was allocated by the discriminant procedure to the components sector unless it was a member of that sector. However, five component firms were classified to other sectors. This suggests that a product-based industrial classification might be inappropriate for the differentiation of organisations and enterprises within the electronics industry from the point of view of the environmental domain. Similarly, the difficulty of distinguishing instrument from capital equipment manufacturers may account for the misclassification of two enterprises between these categories, rather than any exceptional behaviour on their part in terms of the norms established by other enterprises in their sector.

It can be concluded, therefore, that location and technology, as measured here, are meaningful and important dimensions of the environmental domains of electronics manufacturers in the United Kingdom. The functions suggest that they influence modes of internal organisation, particularly with respect to the development of marketing, but also production complexity and flexibility. They also appear to impinge upon the spatial behaviour of organisations. In this context, the impact of variations in ownership appears less important, although the role of corporate integration does differentiate effectively between UK and overseas-owned enterprises. These results confirm that any extension of the structural contingency model, as has been proposed in this volume, must make location a central and explicit consideration. Indeed, the present analyses suggest that, given an inadequate industrial classification upon which to base the technological differentiation of organisations, their regional locations may be a more meaningful and significant element of environmental domains. Failure to include location explicitly in comparative analyses of organisational structure and behaviour introduces the risk of dealing with location-specific relationships only, or of obscuring relationships which apply only to organisations in particular regional environments.

Specifying the model   Drawing upon the insights and variables developed in the preceding chapters, it is appropriate to complete the empirical study by attempting to draw together those variables which appear likely to contribute to the conceptual model advanced in Chapter 3. This section is concerned with selection of the appropriate interval variables drawing upon those described in Table 7.1 prior to two attempts to estimate parameters for the model described in the following two sections. It also seeks to place an essentially dynamic process (Figure 3.2) within a static, cross-sectional empirical framework (Figure 7.2).

Statistical specification of the model is undertaken through the technique of path analysis. Given a set of causal propositions and appropriate measurements, path analysis can be used to identify the internal parameters of a model (Duncan, 1966; Land, 1969). The logic underlying the present model (Chapter 3) can be summarised in the causal proposition that, through its impact upon information availability

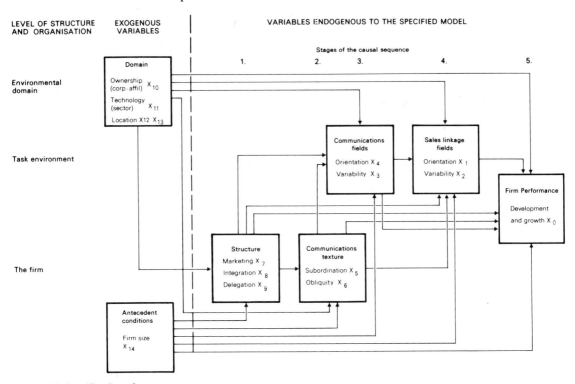

LEVEL OF STRUCTURE AND ORGANISATION

EXOGENOUS VARIABLES

VARIABLES ENDOGENOUS TO THE SPECIFIED MODEL

Stages of the causal sequence

1.   2.   3.   4.   5.

Environmental domain

Domain

Ownership (corp. affil) X_{10}

Technology (sector) X_{11}

Location X12 X_{13}

Task environment

Communications fields

Orientation X_4

Variability X_3

Sales linkage fields

Orientation X_1

Variability X_2

Firm Performance

Development and growth X_0

The firm

Structure

Marketing X_7

Integration X_8

Delegation X_9

Communications texture

Subordination X_5

Obliquity X_6

Antecedent conditions

Firm size X_{14}

Figure 7.2 Specification of the conceptual model of firm–environment interrelationships and firm structure within a spatial framework (Figure 3.2)

and the accessibility of market opportunities, the environmental domain of an enterprise (particularly as determined by location) interacts with aspects of its internal structure to define the task environment. This in turn influences the organisational performance as measured by the rate and nature of enterprise growth and development.

Figure 7.2 brings together the major elements of the model in these terms, although only selected variables are included. Causal influence is indicated by arrows or causal 'paths' moving from left to right through the diagram. Within the path analytical framework both the task environment and antecedent conditions are taken as given at the time of the survey and are therefore treated as exogenous variables. All remaining variables are to some extent 'dependent' (or endogenous) in that some of their variation can be attributed to shifts or differences in preceding variables. In all but the simplest of such systems, a number of endogenous forces will act upon the dependent variable both directly and indirectly through lower order endogenous variables. Thus, the exogenous variables, size, location, ownership and technology, can be expected to influence structure, following the flow of increasing environmental intrusion within the model (Figure 7.2). They will then influence, indirectly, the configuration and nature of spatial linkage patterns. Structure itself, following the direction of the feedback arrow in Figure 3.2 will also influence linkages which, by defining the task environment of particular organisations, will bear directly upon its performance.

Figure 7.2 can be conceived, then, as representing a multivariate, multistage model through which the empirical measurements made in the course of the study can be placed in a causal framework compatible with the deductive model developed in Chapter 3. The stages represent the causal sequence which is implicit rather than explicit in a cross-sectional representation. Thus, in the present example antecedent conditions and the major dimensions of the environmental domain are treated as causally prior to the nature of the internal structure of an organisation (Stage 1). In turn, the dimensions of internal structure are assumed to be causally prior to the texture of communications (Stage 2) which then influence the form of organisations' communication field (Stage 3) and, subsequently, the form of their sales linkage fields (Stage 4). Within this framework the last affected variable is firm performance (Stage 5).

Specification of the environmental domain is straightforward following the preceding analysis. The discriminant analysis made use of a widely used procedure for the treatment of nominal variables within a regression framework, based upon conversion to a series of dichotomous, or dummy, variables. The use of dummy variables in path analysis has been described by Boyle (1970) who demonstrated that there was no loss of information in the transfer from an ordinal to a point dichotomous system of measurement. As a result, the inclusion and interpretation of dummy variables will not detract from identification and evaluation of the framework outlined in Figure 7.2.

Following the contrasts and major sources of discrimination revealed in the preceding analysis, four dummy variables can be used to depict major variations in the environmental domains within which electronics manufacturers operate. These are:

(1) whether or not an organisation is owned *overseas*;
(2) whether or not an organisation manufactures *components*;
(3) whether or not an organisation is located in *Scotland*;
(4) whether or not an organisation is located in *London*.

The first two variables isolate the single subgroups of enterprises which stood apart in terms of structure and interaction as a result of ownership and sectoral affiliations. Rather than define a simple dichotomy and risk losing the depth of information implicit in the three-way location-based contrasts apparent in Figure 7.2, two dummy variables are used to capture the extremes in this respect, namely location in Scotland or in London.

In addition to ownership, production and location, the fourth exogenous variable incorporated into the model is organisational size, measured as the number of full-time employees to ensure widest coverage and comparability within the sample. Insofar as the cross-section of surveyed organisations together with their structural and operational characteristics can be considered as a representation of relationships at a single point in time, their earlier development can be considered to have given rise to variations in their employment size. Organisation size can therefore be treated as having been determined outside the causal system under consideration in the present analysis.

The remaining variables selected for inclusion in the model reflect a wider emphasis inherited from the structural contingency literature (Chapter 2) on market-related behaviour. They have been selected according to the clarity of their interpretation, their particular substantive connotations and their relevance in terms of the *a priori* model (Chapter 3). Three indicators of organisational *structure* have been selected: (1) the *delegation* of responsibility, increases in which suggest closer alignment of particular internal tasks with specific segments of the external environmental domain; (2) the *integration* of marketing and technology activities within a wider corporate context, which implies the removal of constraints to the movement of information between subsystems both within the enterprise and within a wider corporate environment; and (3) the development of *marketing* as a specialised boundary function. Two dimensions of communications activity have been built into the model. The first, *obliquity*, represents the degree of formalised or specialist contacts intervening between an organisation's Chief Marketing Executive and the market itself. A reasonable level of indirect communications may be necessary for the expansion of the area from which market information can be drawn. The second communications dimension is the degree of *subordination* of the Chief Marketing Executive within the external communications network. This should be related inversely to the dimensions of the information field, with a high level of subordination implying spatially constrained market search behaviour.

The context within which the enterprise operates, the nature of its internal organisation, and the texture of communications activities might all be expected to influence its *communications field* which, in the context of the present model, can be measured and specified by the components of *orientation* and *variability*. In turn, these dimensions of communications in space can be expected to influence the areas over which the enterprise establishes *sales linkages*. The latter are calibrated in the model in terms of the *orientation* and *variability* dimensions of the interaction fields. Finally, these two components of sales interaction can be considered to represent the spatial aspect of market behaviour most likely to influence directly the *performance* of an organisation. Two measures of performance have been incorporated, with the component of short-term change denoting the effectiveness of an enterprise in coping with its external environment, and the development component measuring the internal or structural 'efficiency' of an enterprise.

Fourteen indicators have thus been identified as possible causal elements within the framework outlined in Figure 7.2. Before investigating their integration within a multivariate system, it is useful to consider their direct interrelationships and to investigate, also, the impact of size upon each. Not only does the inclusion of organisation size promise to accommodate the circularity implicit in the model, but it may act also to reduce spurious relationships or to strengthen relationships which might otherwise be obscured by its overriding impact.

The role of organisation size

The study has now examined and measured, in some detail, a number of elements contained in the model of organisational structure and environmental interaction developed in Chapter 3. Drawing upon these various concepts and their operationalisation, the interaction of different elements of the model along the paths depicted in Figure 7.2 can be considered. However, the original model (Figure 3.2) is implicitly dynamic in nature, especially given the feedback loop it contains, through which organisations modify their response to environmental change, and, indeed, may also modify the environment within which they operate. The nature of the present study and the technique available has meant, however, that specification of the model must be based upon static observations.

Within the present study, it is assumed that each element in the model is in a constant state of change and this change has to be coped with through adjustments within the focal organisation – adjustments facilitated not only by management competence or inspiration, but also by earlier success at coping. The notion of organisational performance or development is, therefore, critical both to the interpretation and to the specification of the model. The appropriateness or otherwise of an organisation's structure and its ability to exert some control within its task environment through linkage behaviour, will be reflected in its immediate past performance. This, in turn, will influence its future success. Within a causal framework, performance becomes a logical dependent variable, with the other elements of the model interacting sequentially as independent variables. At the same time, it is necessary to make allowance for previous performance and for this reason organisational size is introduced as a surrogate and rather arbitrary indicator of previous performance (or initial advantage). Organisational size may act directly on performance or it may act through the structure and linkage characteristics of the enterprise (Figure 7.2). Investigation of these relationships is necessary in the face of evidence that size is in fact associated with dimensions of organisational structure, although it may not be a determinant of those dimensions (Blau and Schoenherr, 1971, pp. 302–05). Indeed, it has been claimed that the effects of size are ubiquitous and that any relationships between size and organisation development are 'unidirectional', with other parameters having minimal effects on size (Meyer, 1972).

Table 7.4 presents the zero order correlation coefficients between the various independent variables selected for the path analysis, other than the dummy variables denoting different environmental domains, together with the first order correlation coefficients with the impact of size held constant. It is revealing that when the impact of size differences between respondents is controlled (Table 7.4b), the statistical independence imposed upon the three indicators of structure derived from factor analysis (Table 5.4) disappears to some extent. Bearing in mind the original directions of variation of these components, it is

Table 7.4 *Structure, interaction and organisation size; correlation analysis*

(a) *Zero order correlation coefficient*

	(1)	(2)	(3)	(4)	(5)	(6)	(7)	(8)	(9)
(1) Delegation	1.000								
(2) Integration	0.091	1.000							
(3) Marketing	0.155	0.013	1.000						
(4) Communications obliquity	0.525	0.331	0.150	1.000					
(5) Subordination	−0.116	0.028	−0.182	0.400	1.000				
(6) Communications orientation	0.647	0.109	0.314	0.568	−0.501	1.000			
(7) Communications variability	0.103	−0.373	−0.039	−0.116	−0.042	0.000	1.000		
(8) Sales orientation	−0.218	−0.059	−0.098	0.221	−0.067	0.454	0.008	1.000	
(9) Sales variability	−0.004	−0.362	−0.058	−0.217	0.299	−0.316	0.385	0.000	1.000
(10) Size	0.636	0.430	0.039	0.507	−0.025	0.415	−0.180	0.087	−0.046

(b) *First order correlation coefficients, size constant*

	(1)	(2)	(3)	(4)	(5)	(6)	(7)	(8)
(1) Delegation	1.000							
(2) Integration	−0.263	1.000						
(3) Marketing	0.299	−0.004	1.000					
(4) Communications obliquity	0.305	0.146	0.152	1.000				
(5) Subordination	−0.129	0.043	−0.181	0.456	1.000			
(6) Communications orientation	0.287	−0.333	−0.033	−0.029	−0.539	1.000		
(7) Communications variability	−0.104	0.235	0.077	0.000	−0.048	0.084	1.000	
(8) Sales orientation	0.211	−0.107	−0.102	0.206	−0.065	0.461	0.024	1.000
(9) Sales variability	0.032	−0.379	−0.056	−0.225	0.299	−0.327	0.384	0.004

demonstrated that the increased delegation of management responsibility within an enterprise is associated with improved integration of corporate subsystems and with the emergence of a full marketing subsystem.

The zero order correlation coefficients show that size is moderately associated with the first of these two structural dimensions, particularly, though not surprisingly, with delegation. It is also associated with the obliquity or indirectness of marketing communications and the orientation of the communication field. The larger the organisation, the more indirect the contact between the Chief Marketing Executive and customers appears to become, and the wider the field from which marketing information is drawn. There is, however, no evidence of a direct relationship between enterprise size and the spatial dimensions of the interaction fields through which these enterprises sell their output.

The zero order linear correlations among the selected variables are not generally strong, although if a threshold concept of organisational development is accepted, non-linear associations could be strong (Table 4.9). However, directing attention towards the first order correlation coefficients, with size having been held constant, delegation is only weakly associated with communication and linkage orientation. These relationships may result from a more highly structured information network (communications obliquity) in organisations in which market responsibility has been delegated to appropriate subsystems. Similarly the integration dimension of structure is weakly related to the measures describing spatial interaction fields although not, in this case, through its impact upon the nature of the market communications network. Perhaps even more surprising is the fact that the marketing dimension of structure is apparently unrelated to the various measures of interaction, although this may be a function of the weakness of the measure, on the one hand, and of the relatively undeveloped nature of the marketing function throughout the sample, on the other.

When the impact of organisation size is controlled for statistically (Table 7.4b), a strong relationship emerges between the two dimensions of organisations' communications network, obliquity and subordination (variables 4 and 5). Bearing in mind the directions of variation in the original components (Table 6.10) this suggests that the more market contacts are oblique the more likely is the Chief Marketing Executive to take a more active or less subordinate role within his communications network. The obliquity of communications (variable 4) is associated to some degree with the orientation and variability of the sales interaction field (variables 8 and 9). However, once differences associated with organisation size are taken into account, the obliquity of communications bears no linear relation with variables 6 and 7, measuring the dimensions of the communications fields. Subordination (variable 5), on the other hand, has a strong negative relationship with the orientation of communications (variable 6), but only very limited association with the form of the interaction field as defined by variables 8 and 9.

In these simple, non-causal terms it can be seen that some of the relationships which might be expected from the structural contingency model do exist within the sample, but are only relatively weak. This weakness may reflect the measurement and interpretive difficulties implicit in the multivariate approach used to derive the variables or it may be indicative of non-linear relationships. Size certainly emerges as an important variable, although it by no means dominates other relationships. It does account for some relationships, however, such as those between delegation and communication orientation, although it obscures others, especially those between the structural dimensions.

Bearing these caveats in mind, the remainder of this chapter seeks to establish and measure the causal directions which the *a priori* model imparts upon the simple relationships depicted in Table 7.4, dealing firstly with their association with the notion of internal organisational development as measured in the topological analysis (Chapter 4), and secondly with short term performance as measured by organisation growth.

The organisation in space: Model I, the development component

The multivariate approach which has characterised the study has been concerned with the measurement of a number of abstract dimensions through the extraction of components underlying the covariance of groups of more concrete variables. Within this framework the primary role of the model developed in Chapter 3 has been to focus attention upon the subset òf particular variables described above. These variables include location, sector, and corporate affiliation, as major dimensions of the environmental domain; delegation, integration and marketing as indicators of organisational structure; the obliquity and subordination of market information in the context of information fields; and the spatial form of both communications fields and market linkage fields. They might all be expected to interact and to act upon organisational performance. This and the following section seek to specify and identify the model using this subset of variables, making use of a path analytic regression framework.

Obviously, the analyses have limitations and shortcomings. In the first place the survey data are cross-sectional although the model they are used to test is explicitly dynamic. Furthermore, there are relatively few cases available for analysis and the composite nature of the indices that have been derived in the study might be expected to deflate parameter estimates (Romsa *et al.*, 1969). The highly structured nature of the study also acts against generalisations of the findings of path analysis, notwithstanding methodological problems such as the relative advantages of using standardised or non-standardised regression coefficients. All these caveats suggest that generalisations from this test of the model developed in Chapter 3 should not be extended too far beyond the data that have been employed and the industry which has been examined.

Path analysis itself involves a series of conventions and a number of assumptions which enable the parameters representing a causal system to be estimated through a series of 'staged' multiple regression equations. The technique generates considerably more information than regression analysis alone, enabling causal paths to be traced through intervening variables. The relative contribution of a causal variable can be broken down into its indirect, direct and non-causal association with the dependent variable. Apart from the usual assumptions of multiple regression analysis, which, in the present study are largely satisfied by the use of component scores, it is necessary to assume that the error terms in the separate regressions equations are uncorrelated (Duncan, 1966).

One of the major sources of disagreement in the application of path analysis lies in the choice between standardised and non-standardised path coefficients (Tukey, 1954; Wright, 1960; Blalock, 1967). The former are represented by unstandardised regression coefficients, the latter by standardised regression coefficients. Because the concern in the present study is with interpretation of the structural contingency model within the constraints imposed by research design and data, and not with statistical inference and the identification of general causal processes or laws, standardised coefficients are used (Kim and Kohout, 1975, p. 397). These path coefficients can be interpreted as denoting the proportion of the standard score by which the dependent variable would shift in response to a change of one standard deviation unit in the independent variable, in the absence of change in any other variable in the system. The full extent of induced change in the dependent variable can be estimated as the product of all the paths by which it is linked with the original causal variable.

The total impact of the five exogenous and nine endogenous variables upon the dependent variables, growth and development, can be estimated from a set of ten recursive equations representing the five-stage model previously described (Figure 7.2). These equations are listed below, observing the conventions of path analysis. Thus, P_{ij} represents the path coefficient measuring the impact of variable j on variable i. The equations are grouped according to causal stages, moving from the impact of environmental domain upon organisational environments in the first stage through to the impact of interaction fields (task environments) upon performance stage. As variables are introduced at each stage, so they are maintained at succeeding stages to capture indirect and subsequent direct effects upon lower order variables. The equations become correspondingly more complex at successive stages. In the estimation of equations, variables are measured as deviations from their respective means. The term 'e' represents residual variation unrelated to the causal structure defined by the model.

Given:

X_{14} employment size (Model I), or the size component (Model II);
X_{13} location in London;
X_{12} location in Scotland;
X_{11} component manufacture;
X_{10} overseas ownership;
X_9 delegation of authority;
X_8 corporate integration;
X_7 marketing development;
X_6 obliquity of marketing communications;
X_5 subordination of marketing communications;
X_4 orientation of the information field;
X_3 variability of the information field;
X_2 variability of the sales interaction field;
X_1 orientation of the sales interaction field;
X_0 development component (Model I), or growth component (Model II).

Then we have:

Stage 1 (the impact of environmental domain upon structure)
$$X_9 = P_{9\,10}X_{10} + P_{9\,11}X_{11} + P_{9\,12}X_{12} + P_{9\,13}X_{13} + P_{9\,14}X_{14} + e_9$$
$$X_8 = P_{8\,10}X_{10} + P_{8\,11}X_{11} + \ldots + e_8$$
$$X_7 = P_{7\,10}X_{10} + P_{7\,11}X_{11} + \ldots + e_7$$

Stage 2 (the impact of structure upon communications activity)
$$X_6 = P_{6\,10}X_{10} + P_{6\,11}X_{11} + P_{6\,12}X_{12} + P_{6\,13}X_{13} + P_{6\,14}X_{14} + P_{67}X_7 + P_{68}X_8 + P_{69}X_9 + e_6$$
$$X_5 = P_{5\,10}X_{10} + P_{5\,11}X_{11} + \ldots + P_{59}X_9 + e_5$$

Stage 3 (the impact of communications activity upon information fields)

$$X_4 = P_{4\,10}X_{10} + P_{4\,11}X_{11} + P_{4\,12}X_{12} + P_{4\,13}X_{13} + P_{4\,14}X_{14} + P_{4\,7}X_7 + P_{4\,8}X_8 +$$
$$P_{4\,9}X_9 + P_{4\,5}X_5 + P_{4\,6}X_6 + e_4$$
$$X_3 = P_{3\,10}X_{10} + P_{3\,11}X_{11} + \ldots P_{3\,6}X_6 + e_3$$

Stage 4 (the impact of information fields upon interaction fields)

$$X_2 = P_{2\,10}X_{10} + P_{2\,11}X_{11} + P_{2\,12}X_{12} + P_{2\,13}X_{13} + P_{2\,14}X_{14} + P_{2\,7}X_7 +$$
$$P_{2\,8}X_8 + P_{2\,9}X_9 + P_{2\,5}X_5 + P_{2\,6}X_6 + P_{2\,3}X_3 + P_{2\,4}X_4 + e_2$$
$$X_1 = P_{1\,10}X_{10} + P_{1\,11}X_{11} + \ldots P_{1\,4}X_4 + e_1$$

Stage 5 (the impact of interaction fields upon organisational performance)

$$X_0 = P_{0\,10}X_{10} + P_{0\,11}X_{11} + P_{0\,13}X_{13} + P_{0\,14}X_{14} + P_{0\,7}X_7 + P_{0\,8}X_8 +$$
$$P_{0\,9}X_9 + P_{0\,5}X_5 + P_{0\,6}X_6 + P_{0\,3}X_3 + P_{0\,4}X_4 + P_{0\,1}X_1 +$$
$$P_{0\,2}X_2 + e_0$$

And,

$$e_j = \sqrt{1 - R^2},$$

where R is the multiple coefficient of determination based upon the set of all causal variables with paths leading to $j = 0$. Thus e_j, the residual path coefficient, 'represents the proportion of the standard deviation, and its square represents the proportion of the variance, of the endogenous variable that is caused by all (unmeasured) variables outside the set under consideration' (Land, 1969, p. 12). The value of e_j for exogenous variables is, however, unity, since all variance in these variables is assumed to be determined outside the causal system.

Two separate analyses have been undertaken. The first, Model I, incorporates the general development component as the independent variable and is based upon the 44 respondent organisations who provided both sales linkage data and contact diaries. The second analysis, Model II, directed more towards an analysis of the external effectiveness of organisations, is based upon the smaller subset of these respondents who also provided data on changes in turnover and employment.

The path coefficients derived from solution of the full set of recursive equations in each analysis can be presented as 'path diagrams' (see Figures 7.3 and 7.4). However, to simplify the diagrams all paths with coefficients of less than 0.1 are indicated by broken lines. Paths with coefficients exceeding 0.2 are depicted as solid lines and paths exceeding 0.3 as heavy lines. Decimal points have been omitted from the coefficients, while residual paths are not depicted in the diagrams at all.

Despite the complexity of the present models, the path diagram for Model I (Figure 7.3) permits some interpretation of the major relationships within the extended structural contingency framework. In the first place, two variables are omitted from the diagram completely (although not from the estimates of paths, Table 7.5), because of their very weak impact upon organisational development. These are the spatial orientation of sales interaction fields (X_1) and the spatial variability of market communications fields (X_3). In addition, the orientation of information contacts (X_4) assumes importance only indirectly through its impact upon the variability of interaction fields (X_2). Even then the total indirect impact, the product of the two paths $(P_{24}P_{02} = -0.052)$, is minimal. Other variables which have minimal direct impact upon organisational development include the subordination of market communication (X_5) and, amongst exogenous variables, overseas ownership (X_{10}) and membership of the components sector (X_{11}). The strongest direct independent effects are recorded for organisational size (X_{14}), location in London (X_{13}) and the extent of task delegation (X_9). The importance of the latter is consistent with the suggestion that the failure by management to delegate responsibility for both market and technical tasks acted as a major impediment to organisational development (Chapter 5). Not unexpectedly, organisational size is positively associated with development, implying that the larger business organisations within the sample possess an advantage in their movement along an organisational development continuum, an interpretation which is consistent with the earlier observations on obstructions to structural development based upon the topological analysis (Chapter 5).

Location in either Scotland or London, as opposed to location in the OMA, appears to act against development. Respondent organisations in London tend to be more retarded in their general level of development than those located elsewhere, partly because they represent 'remnant' industry in an area which has been subjected to considerable outmigration of firms and enterprises (Keeble, 1976; 1977). Although there is only limited evidence of decline in electronics manufacturing employment in London during the early 1970s, employment there is concentrated into a relatively small number of large organisations. In their inability or unwillingness to move from London, these few large organisations and the far greater number of small, static firms can be considered less adaptive and dynamic than their migrant counterparts (McDermott, 1978). Even the very large enterprises may be organisationally underdeveloped as they constitute the substantial, long-standing consumer and capital equipment subsidiaries of UK groups. Their continued presence in London may be attributable to industrial inertia as much as to specific locational factors. Conversely, the small firms and business organisations usually occupy restricted, although perhaps specialised, niches as manufacturers of instruments and components and also suffer from a form of organisational inertia. In contrast, growth enterprises within London (the active adaptors) are unlikely to remain there as their market performance improves and as they develop in organisational structure, size and complexity.

Electronics is a relatively more recent and dynamic activity in Scotland, yet there are a number of factors which appear to act against the development of organisations in the region. These have been covered in detail elsewhere and include the dependence of indigenous enterprise upon external capital and ownership, and the level of

correlation between each one in turn and the development component. This effect is measured in each case by summing the products of all indirect paths occurring between the remaining exogenous variables and their correlation coefficients with the variables under consideration. Given the total causal impact of organisational size upon development, the relationship of each exogenous variable with size is the major source of non-causal correlation within the model structure. Thus, the fact that London respondents in the subset of 44 organisations tended to be smaller than their counterparts elsewhere increases the negative association between a London location and development. The advantages of larger than average size meant that the total level of negative association between location in Scotland and organisational development diminished. The tendency for overseas firms to be larger than their UK counterparts increased their correlation with development and, because component firms tended to be smaller than average, the weak positive relationship between component manufacturing and development was eliminated completely. However, only a minor part of the covariation between organisational size and development was attributable to non-causal influences.

The main determinant of the development process suggested by this analysis is, therefore, an organisation's antecedent conditions – its *previous* level of development. This can be thought of as having a lagged effect through the influence of organisational size and the position of an enterprise on the dimension of task delegation. The impact of spatial behaviour as measured by interaction and information fields is far less pronounced. Location plays a role through its effect upon the modes of organisation which characterise enterprises in different areas and through its effect upon variability in sales linkage fields. More important, however, is the direct association between location and development which implies in the present context that the attributes of the regional environments (environmental domains) influence organisational development to a greater extent than do more particularised task environments defined by established linkages and information flows. From Model I it might be concluded that the major impact of task environments in shaping organisational development, as hypothesised in the structural contingency model, has been overemphasised in comparison with the significance of organisational domains. It appears that the internal characteristics of a firm or organisation, its previous growth and prior organisation, are central to an understanding of its continuing structural development, with the regional environmental domain playing a secondary and rather general role which is only marginally dependent upon the influence of spatial interaction fields. However, this qualified conclusion may be a function of the specification and identification techniques used, rather than a result of an inappropriate conceptualisation of organisational development.

The organisation in space: Model II, the growth component

Before rejecting, or at least qualifying, the structural contingency framework on the basis of the analysis and discussion in the previous section, it should also be observed that the level of *development*, as

Table 7.6 *Residual path coefficients*

Variable	x_j	Model I[1] e_j	Model II[2] e_j	Difference
Employment (log)	x_{14}	0.837		
Size component	x_{14}		0.910	
London	x_{13}	0.721	0.810	−0.089
Scotland	x_{12}	0.915	0.902	0.013
Component manufacture	x_{11}	0.839	0.954	−0.115
Overseas ownership	x_{10}	0.922	0.910	0.012
Delegation	x_9	0.711	0.748	−0.037
Integration	x_8	0.732	0.776	−0.044
Marketing	x_7	0.927	0.927	0.000
Obliquity	x_6	0.773	0.762	0.011
Passivity	x_5	0.931	0.951	−0.020
Information orientation	x_4	0.507	0.498	0.009
Information variability	x_3	0.694	0.721	−0.027
Sales Variability	x_2	0.731	0.756	−0.025
Sales Orientation	x_1	0.739	0.605	0.187
Development	x_0	0.516		
Growth component	x_0		0.681	

Notes: [1] Based upon 44 cases.
       [2] Based upon 33 cases.

measured in the topological analysis, was only one of the possible dependent variables which could have been considered. In particular, it reflected the ordering of tasks within enterprises. The present section, therefore, considers the relevance of this framework to the explanation of a second dependent variable, short-term differences in the *growth* of enterprises and business organisations, a measure which relates more directly to their success or otherwise in the external environment. However, since this second analysis (Model II) is based on data from a reduced number of respondents (only 33 enterprises) it is important to consider the residual coefficients from both Model I and Model II to determine what the effects of this smaller data base might be.

To this end, Table 7.6 indicates that less covariation between sector and the dependent variable is attributable to non-causal paths in Model II than in Model I. On the other hand, location in London is more closely associated with the remaining exogenous variables. Of particular importance, however, is the fact that amongst the endogenous variables the shift in the residual path coefficient from Model I to Model II exceeded 0.04 only in the case of sales orientation, a variable which played a negligible role in Model I and is of only marginally greater importance in Model II. Its position at the penultimate stage of the causal sequence means that any instability associated with sample bias is not transmitted through the model. It can be concluded from Table 7.6 that there is considerable stability amongst residual coefficients, certainly sufficient to ensure the comparability of the two models and to eliminate any possibility that results are dependent upon sample configuration.

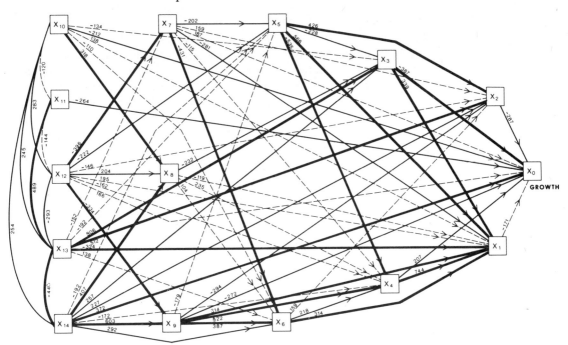

Figure 7.4 Causal paths
and firm growth: Model II

Although based upon shifts in employment and turnover for a single year only, it was observed in Chapter 5 that the dependent variable for Model II, the component of short-term growth, was closely related to longer-term trends. Nevertheless, it is to be expected that any modelling of causes of growth will reflect particular conditions prevailing within the electronics industry prior to 1974. It is possible that these conditions favoured certain forms of organisational behaviour, which may be less conducive to favourable growth rates in other periods. Despite this additional constraint to interpretation, organisational growth or decline may be considered a more relevant dependent variable in the structural contingency framework than the measure of development used in Model I, in that it is a direct and recognisable measure of performance.

While no less static in nature, comprising simply a single observation for a particular period in time, a measure of relative growth emphasises the more practical implications of the model and the study. To what extent might location in one region impede the growth of firms and organisations compared with the performance that might be achieved by the same or similar enterprises in other regions? To what extent is the ability of organisations to take advantage of expansionary conditions, such as prevailed in the electronics industry in the period immediately preceding the survey, constrained or modified by the regional domains within which they operate?

The path coefficients derived for the orientation of sales linkages (X_1) and the variability of the information field (X_3) exceeded 0.1 in Model II and so are included in the path diagram (Figure 7.4). Owing to their relationships with a number of preceding variables in the causal chain the overall result is a considerable increase in the visual complexity of the model compared with Model I. However, it is still possible to trace the main direct and indirect causal paths. The strongest direct influence upon change, holding all other elements constant, was the general component of size (X_{14}). Again the resources accumulated from previous growth apparently enhance performance. Delegation (X_9), which acted to bring about further organisational development in Model I, had a negative effect upon organisational growth over the short time period covered. Other differences are apparent with respect to direct relationships with the two dependent variables, while the variability of interaction fields (X_2) had more pronounced effects upon growth than development. In the case of Model II this impact is negative so that more spatially *constrained* sets of linkages were associated with higher levels of growth whereas spatially *diverse* fields were associated with higher levels of development. Similarly, it appears that more highly localised interaction fields (X_1) favoured growth. Non-localised (X_4) but relatively concentrated information fields (X_3) also fostered growth. Again in contrast to Model I, component manufacture (X_{11}) and overseas ownership (X_{10}) had direct and relatively important effects upon the dependent variable. In the first instance this suggests that passive component manufacturers may not have shared in the general expansion in the electronics industry during the early 1970s, perhaps as a result of market erosion through increasing large-scale product integration by active component manufacturers. While overseas ownership apparently acted against enterprise growth in the period immediately preceding 1974, it did carry with it counteractive indirect benefits, especially in terms of integration of the marketing production function (X_8) and through constraining the variability of the information fields (X_3).

While the direct impact of location in London upon growth was negligible (Figure 7.4), Table 7.7 suggests a considerable indirect impact. In particular, the variability of sales linkages and information fields (X_2 and X_3) and the relative lack of marketing development (X_7) have acted against growth by London enterprises. In contrast, the indirect effects of location in Scotland, although limited, have reinforced the direct advantages. It is tempting to interpret this last finding in terms of the role of policy dependent employment creation in the industry, and through reference to the expansion of overseas capital and organisations within the UK in the early 1970s. Further, the relative simplicity of the electronics industry's environment within Scotland may enhance the growth prospects of individual enterprises in that location at a time of general expansion, although whether such an advantage can be maintained at a time of contraction is open to question. The results outlined in Table 7.7 for Scotland and London suggest that in terms of both indirect and direct effects, OMA-based organisations would fall between these two extremes, although total indirect benefits may exceed this in Scotland, a result consistent with the fact that OMA-based organisations maintained growth rates intermediate to those recorded by their counterparts in the other two regions.

Table 7.7 *Decomposing the influence of differences in environmental domains upon organisational growth, Model II*

Effects	Size	London	Scotland	Component manufacture	Overseas ownership
(1) *Direct causal*	0.372	0.038	0.166	−0.264	−0.212
(2) *Indirect causal*					
Via:					
Sales orientation	−0.004	0.056	−0.033	0.007	−0.024
Sales variability	−0.065	−0.149	0.042	0.021	0.009
Information variability	−0.108	−0.212	0.038	−0.020	0.056
Information orientation	−0.016	0.003	−0.015	0.008	0.003
Passivity	−0.009	0.014	0.017	−0.005	0.003
Obliquity	0.036	0.017	0.002	−0.009	−0.013
Marketing	0.001	−0.025	−0.062	0.009	0.010
Integration	0.066	0.008	0.033	−0.013	0.052
Delegation	−0.076	0.009	0.042	0.009	0.008
Total indirect	−0.175	−0.282	0.062	0.007	0.104
Total causal	0.197	−0.240	0.228	−0.257	−0.108
(3) *Non-causal*					
Via:					
Size		−0.154	0.006	−0.001	0.089
London	0.106		0.071	−0.118	0.059
Scotland	0.004	−0.067		−0.033	0.065
Component manufacture	0.001	−0.126	0.037		0.031
Overseas ownership	−0.027	0.026	−0.031	0.013	
Total non-causal	0.083	−0.320	0.083	−0.139	0.243
Total path correlation	0.280	−0.561	0.311	−0.396	0.135
Simple *r*	0.287	−0.511	0.312	−0.404	0.100

Table 7.7 also demonstrates a number of conflicting tendencies concerning the indirect effects of organisation size. Its association with spatial behaviour acted against growth over the period, as did the influence of size upon delegation. The result is a considerable reduction in the causal influence of size upon growth, so that the impact of organisation size falls below that of both location and sectoral affiliation. Membership of the component sector has negligible indirect advantages to offset the substantial and negative direct impact it had upon growth. Non-causal covariation between growth and the exogenous variables reinforce the causal association in each case except overseas ownership. Relatively fewer overseas-owned organisations in the sample were component manufacturers, more were located in Scotland than elsewhere, and they tended to be larger than their UK counterparts. Consequently, they recorded only a weak positive relationship with growth. Although positively associated with organisational growth as a result of a variety of intervening relationships, overseas ownership *per se* acted against favourable growth rates in the period covered by the study and amongst the organisations that were surveyed.

Within Model II, emphasising external performance, organisations' spatial interactions play a considerably greater role than they did in Model I, which emphasised internal structure. In Model II, sectoral affiliation is also more important, presumably reflecting wider sectoral-based disparities in growth. In effect, the second model offers substantially more support for the structural contingency framework. Whereas the general development component is associated primarily with previous performance, both directly through the size variable and indirectly through the structural dimensions, organisations' short-term growth is closely associated with the spatial character of their external linkages, both for the exchange of information and the sale of goods. In the first model location had a direct, independent effect upon development and only a minor impact through its association with organisational structure or spatial behaviour. In the second model the direct effects of location were less pronounced, with influence being transmitted primarily through the interaction variables. Model II therefore offers strong support for the general proposition that through its impact upon both information availability and the relative accessibility of market opportunities, the location at which an enterprise is based influences its *rate* of subsequent development.

In comparing the two models, it is of note that development tends to accompany increased complexity, both of organisation and interaction. Growth, on the other hand, was enhanced by a simpler organisational environment and more constrained patterns of communications and sales interaction *amongst* the organisations and within the period under consideration. This contrast suggests that in the short-term, or perhaps during periods of industrial expansion, location and spatial behaviour may provide the key to understanding variations in performance. However, as organisational development is more of an on-going process, the long-term survival of firms and business organisations, their levels of organisational complexity and the definition of appropriate, flexible internal structures may be far less dependent upon location and spatial behaviour. The ability of an organisation to exploit market success, manifest in *short-term* growth rates, by developing a favourable internal structure, may make the difference between an enterprise for which the opportunities and environment of the local region are critical for *long-term* survival and one which can operate independently of regional constraints or local economic fluctuations.

Conclusion   The models of organisation–environment interaction explored in this chapter demonstrate clearly that the fusion of ideas from organisation theory and industrial geography greatly enhances any explanation of the operation of firms and business organisations in a spatial context. From organisation theory in general, and the structural contingency model in particular, the improved conceptualisation and specification of the internal structure of business organisations has been shown to greatly enhance explanation in this more broadly based geography of organisations. A similar improvement has resulted from the introduction of spatial dimensions into the organisation theory notions of task environment and environmental domain. On the one hand, the spatial dimensions of task environments calibrated in terms of interaction fields and communications fields defined by material linkages and information flows, have been shown to be strongly related to short-term growth. On the other hand, the spatial characteristics of environmental domains were shown to be more strongly related to a longer-term internal development sequence which organisations might be expected to follow.

The results of the analyses for the UK electronics industry have given general support to the basic tenet of the structural contingency model that enterprises must be appropriately structured to confront their relevant environments. Nevertheless, short-term growth was seen to be possible, in this industry at least, without commensurate organisational change. This failure to restructure internally was, however, also seen to increase the susceptibility and vulnerability of these enterprises to general shifts in the supply and demand relationships within their broader environmental domains. Several reasons can be advanced for the failure of some organisations to develop on the basis of short-term market success including, in particular, the failure to delegate critical technical and boundary spanning tasks – a phenomenon observed amongst Scottish and, to a lesser extent, London respondents. In more general terms, a simplified structuring of tasks might prevent an organisation or enterprise from developing the organisational complexity necessary or sufficient to allow it to become independent of either its regional, sectoral or corporate domain.

It would appear that greater internal complexity and advanced structural development may have acted against the achievement of particularly high rates of short-term growth amongst OMA-based electronics manufacturers. This is in direct contrast with the higher rates of short-term growth recorded by Scottish organisations. It might be concluded, therefore, that increased organisational complexity might serve to reduce the importance of organisations' regional environments and the spatial dimensions of environmental domains for their continued survival and development. Complexity of organisational structure might, at the same time, constrain the extent to which an organisation can take advantage of short-term fluctuations in external market conditions. It will, nevertheless, ensure that the impact of any local shifts in the environmental domain will not be critical, and that more general reversals in economic conditions are likely to have a less adverse effect than will be the case for their less internally differentiated counterparts.

8 Summary and conclusions

The introduction to this study argued that an understanding of the structure of organisations is important to an understanding of the geographic distribution of economic activity. The spatial dimension of organisational structure should be recognised as being intimately associated with regional economic trends and disparities, especially with respect to investment for production and employment. In addition, however, the study demonstrated the critical role of the dimensions of space and place in organisations' environments.

The conceptual studies contributing to the contingency explanation of organisational design and performance were reviewed in Chapter 2 in an attempt to derive some insights into the relationship between organisational structures and various dimensions of their operational environments. Chapter 3 reviewed studies in industrial geography which have also addressed this theme to elaborate the spatial dimension of the relationship between organisational structure and form and the external linkages which define task environments. This review material was then integrated within the framework of a single, comprehensive model of organisation–environment interaction with the individual organisation as its focus.

For purposes of emphasis and continuity a somewhat critical tone was adopted in the literature review upon which the model was based, revolving around the weak empirical foundations of the structural contingency paradigm, on the one hand, and the limited conceptual depth of linkage and information flow studies in industrial geography on the other. As a result, the model of organisation development was advanced at a general level with more precise specification being reserved for the empirical part of the study. The model suggested that the geographical configuration of linkages (the impact of *space*) defines the task environment within which an enterprise or organisation operates, encompassing the opportunities for, and conditions of, exchange upon which its survival and growth depend.

The degree of spatial conformity between communication and material linkage fields was held to indicate the level of uncertainty which might confront an organisation. The extension of linkage fields and the reduction of long-term uncertainty (although not necessarily short-term risk) were seen to depend upon the way in which an enterprise organised internal tasks to cope with information received concerning the condition of the external environment. It was suggested that the operation of dynamic feedback processes could obscure this rela-

196

tionship, as previous interaction fields influence both present communication fields and internal structures. The organisation was assumed to structure tasks in such a way, however, as to optimise within these information constraints and given conditions of inertia either internal efficiency or external effectiveness in the environment, or both. Various factors were held to define the environmental domains within which organisations sought to be effective, especially *location, technology* and *corporate affiliations*. The model avoided the deterministic overtones associated with the structural contingency approach, however, by including structure itself as a causal force, and by recognising that as an organisation's task environment expands and contracts so its relationship with its external domain will also change.

Clearly, such a wide-ranging model could not be rigorously tested within the scope of a single study. Part Two of the book was, therefore, selective in approach. It explored in separate chapters elements of the model proposed in Chapter 3 within the context of the electronics industry in the UK. Emphasis was placed upon the geographical component of each major element within the model and, to a lesser extent, upon the temporal forces underlying the observed variability. Chapter 4, following the approach adopted by Hirsch (1975), highlighted the historical basis of the environmental domain for the electronics industry. While the importance of internationally founded technology and capital (firm ownership) in the electronics industry was demonstrated, the discussion was limited to those conditions of environmental domains most likely to impinge upon firms located within the United Kingdom. By and large, these conditions revolved around the coalition of technological advantage and commercial strength in particular dominant organisations. The emergence of distinctive interorganisational structures and product–market relations within the domain for this industrial sector during the 1960s was also indicated.

Chapter 5 explored measures of organisational performance, with effectiveness in the environment measured by means of composite factors measuring enterprise scale and growth, and the dimensions of internal efficiency being considered through q-analysis of enterprise development. Principal components analysis revealed several dimensions of internal structure which, in structural contingency terms, might have been expected to underlie differences in organisational performance.

Chapter 6 addressed the question of defining organisations' task environments by developing a set of descriptive indices which enabled task environments to be mapped in such a way as to quantify the importance of *space* as a constraint upon organisational structure. In Chapter 7, the impact of *place* was emphasised through both discriminant and path analyses. The various threads of the original model, as they had been developed in preceding chapters, were brought together in analyses which emphasised the interaction of place and space. These analyses indicated the very different foundations of internal efficiency in comparison with external effectiveness. They also confirmed not only the existence of distinctive spatio – temporal relationships between organisations and their environments, but also the essential complexity of these relationships.

Organisations and space   In the past, geography has sought to explain the spatial distribution of industrial activity as the outcome of explicitly locational processes. Particular emphasis has been placed upon plant formation and movement in response to sets of locational forces or factors. Since the 1960s, however, much work in industrial geography has been less intransigent in the assumptions that have been made about investment behaviour, but it too has concentrated upon the processes of location decision-making and the internal and external circumstances accompanying various types of location decision.

The present book represents a markedly different conceptual approach through the emphasis it places upon spatial variations in the nature and character of organisations and enterprises. Traditional location processes (such as branch plant establishment) are only incidental to the wider concern for organisational structure and development. Although empirical analysis has been confined to British electronics enterprises, the main contribution of the study to geography lies not in its empirical emphasis, but in the adoption of an *organisation-centred* rather than an *environment-centred* approach. Furthermore, by recognising the contribution which organisations make to the wider environments of which they are part, the approach is intrinsically dynamic, emphasising organisations as the vehicles of change.

It follows from the analyses described in the book that shifts in patterns of industrial activity will reflect not only the nature of *locations*, and the factors peculiar to them, but also consistent variations from place to place in the nature of *organisations*. The spatial differentiation of organisations and the way in which internal subsystems are mobilised to effect production and exchange, reflect three sets of forces:

(1) factors specific to individual locations and places, which may influence firm movement or firm adaptation (spatial sorting);
(2) the imperfect diffusion of information between organisations, particularly information on management practices; and
(3) the cumulative impact of different management practices over time.

Geographic variations in the nature of enterprises can be expected to have consequences for subsequent economic activity and development between regions similar to those associated traditionally with differences between industrial sectors or product mixes.

While evidence on the role of variations in organisation upon subsequent industrial development patterns is inconclusive, the present study lends support to the significance of location as a factor influencing firms' growth. Extending the approach used by Fisher (1962) to demonstrate the impact of location in Scotland upon firm performance within particular industries, Ingham (1976) also demonstrated that three factors – location, sector, and ownership – had significant and largely independent effects upon measures of profitability and performance in the mechanical engineering industry in Britain. From his analysis,

Ingham suggested that 'agglomeration economies, external to the firm, but internal to the industry, do not enhance company performance' (p. 146). The implication is that variations in organisation more than factors specific to locations *per se*, will influence performance.

Following from the analyses, the approach developed in the present study does not support to any degree the types of policy which have been directed traditionally towards reducing regional disparities in economic activity in the United Kingdom. If the spatial mix of enterprises differentiated according to organisational structure varies from place to place, regional growth prospects will vary in ways not accommodated by policies directed simply towards spatial variations in production costs or product mix. Indeed, macro-policies may have unfavourable consequences if emphasis upon particular elements of the environment distorts the organisation of enterprise. They may encourage organisational structures to develop which are inappropriate for a firm's particular domain or task environment, or they may foster the undesirable simplification of organisational structures in those areas most in need of policy assistance. Capital subsidies, for example, while increasing employment opportunities in peripheral areas, may also encourage the establishment of undifferentiated branch plants. Assistance is thereby directed towards organisationally inflexible units incapable of dealing either through linkage change or internal structural adjustments with adverse shifts in their task environments. As a result the employment opportunities generated by this type of policy will be vulnerable, and at best temporary.

The 'carrot-and-stick' policies which have used Industrial Development Certificates to constrain enterprise expansion in the metropolitan areas of South East England and the Midlands, and subsidies on capital and, to a lesser extent, labour to make peripheral areas most attractive to industry, may well have encouraged and accelerated the emergence of a dualistic economy in the UK (Averitt, 1968; Taylor and Thrift, 1980). The components of such a dualistic economy, large corporations and smaller firms, can be considered to vary in relative importance from place to place, although they may well be connected by linkages between centres. Thus, very large and very small, often static, firms with the smaller ones marked by deficiencies of internal structure, may predominate in the traditional industrial hearth areas of London and Birmingham, for example. More complex, actively adapting and potentially more mobile and resilient firms may be concentrated in suburban and small town locations in the south of England, while large, undifferentiated and dependent production units dominate the labour markets of peripheral areas.

As part of this dualistic framework the spatial pattern of organisational control will parallel the distribution of the urban hierarchy within the space economy. Through spatial stratification, information-based control and orientation functions within multilocational firms (those functions dealing with external information and with technology as external knowledge) are postulated as being concentrated in the traditionally dominant upper levels of the urban hierarchy, while production-based functions which operate on internalised information handled by routine procedures are located in peripheral regions at lower levels in the urban hierarchy. By reinforcing this tendency within an urban hierarchy spatial investment policies may have acted to prejudice the promotion of more equitable, diversified, flexible, spontaneous and possibly more resilient employment growth in traditionally slow growing regions.

If the approach advanced in this book and the insights gained in the course of the study are to have any relevance in applied fields it will be in the area of regional development studies, policy formation, and impact evaluation. In this arena the study presents a case for placing emphasis upon the structural evolution of organisations as a process with distinctive spatial (and therefore distinctive social) ramifications. In particular, the process of the spatial evolution of organisations may provide connections, at the aggregate level, with the evolution of urban systems, given that particular functions within separate organisations tend to be concentrated at similar locations, and that multilocational organisations tend to accommodate in their spatial structure the demands and opportunities they encounter in the external environment.

In the specification of the contingency model, it was indicated that environmental influence was transmitted less directly but more obviously into patterns of short-term organisational growth or decline (external effectiveness; Model II, Chapter 7) than into structural development (internal efficiency; Model I, Chapter 7). Thus, the structural response of the organisation to environmental forces, in the form of differentiation of internal functional subsystems and the establishment of interrelationships between them, depends upon previous success or failure in coping with external forces. Success in coping may be conceived in terms of the open systems concept of entropy, or more concretely in terms of accumulated resources, such as capital, skills, equipment or information, the integration of which will give rise to structural change. It will also determine whether the organisations in a particular area become dominated by complexly structured 'leaders' or undifferentiated, dependent enterprises.

Perhaps the most important result of the present study in relation to the structural contingency paradigm was the demonstration of the importance of location in defining the environmental domain of individual organisations and, consequently, in moulding their task environments. For the great majority of its constituent enterprises, the electronics industry is one in which technology largely comprises information from the external environment. Consequently, the majority of these enterprises, in numerical terms, may be thought of as dependent upon a minority which exercise control through its core technology. A principal task of any organisation in its dealings with the environment is to assemble that set of information appropriate to its particular domain and task environment and compatible with its own performance objectives. In some organisations the collection of this information has been simplified by formalising their dependence upon the controllers of technology. In others, the responsibility for the collection of this information is placed on that level in the organisational structure at which customer relationships are established. In the present study of the electronics industry, location rather than corporate affiliations, technology or market variations (insofar as these were measured) played the principal role in influencing organisational growth and development. This outcome is possibly the result of two factors: the level of distance decay to which linkages were shown to be subject in the aggregate, and the predominance of dependent organisations in the sample on which the empirical analyses were based.

This finding raises the possibility that spatial monopoly is an important mechanism which is used by all types of organisation to achieve external effectiveness and internal efficiency in relation to a physically constrained and therefore more certain external environment. The tendency towards divisionalisation by geographic area as organisations develop and expand is clearly explicable in these terms. Incremental growth through the extension or replication of spatial monopoly situations would mean that parallel mechanisms and structures to reduce environmental uncertainty could be adopted by all types of organisation at all stages of development.

However, it can be inferred from the study's results that subdividing respondent organisations according to location would reveal for each group different specific relationships between structure, interaction and, indeed, performance. An important contribution to organisation theory has been the demonstration of the critical importance of regional location for the interpretation and evaluation of these relationships.

Towards a theory of organisations in space

The study has highlighted explicitly the role of *space* and *place* in shaping organisational structures and interorganisational relationships. Implicitly, the role of time has been recognised through the treatment of long-term development and short-term growth as indices of internally measured 'efficiency' and 'effectiveness' in external environments. As such, the study emphasises and elevates to central status the spatio – temporal dimensions which Giddens (1979) considers fundamental to explanation and understanding in all subjects and subsets of the social sciences in general. There appears to be, in fact, a synergic quality to the blending of propositions from organisation theory and empirically derived generalisations from industrial geography which has emerged in the course of the study.

Industrial geography has done more than contribute notions of place and space to an understanding of organisation – environment interrelationships. It has also shown, through its linkage emphasis, that environments of organisations can be conceived as particularised aggregates of identifiable counterparts. To a major extent this illustrates Karpik's (1978) ideas that the definition of environments in organisation theory – societal, domain or task environments – is neither possible nor necessary since the network of interconnections which it establishes with counterparts encompasses these interrelationships which will bear upon its structure and therefore provides an effective definition of its environment.

However, the conceptualisation of this network of interconnections has been far from complete in industrial geography. Valuable emphasis has been put on place and space, to some extent to counteract the deterministic qualities associated with the costs involved in interorganisational transactions which have tended to constrain and limit the vision of the neoclassical approach to the location question. To emphasise place and space, however has tended to emasculate linkage and information flow networks as constraints upon organisational structures and forms. What have been neglected are the *control* and *power* relationships that are integral to these networks (Benson, 1975, 1978). To some extent the present study took these power relationships into account through its concern for the quality of organisational autonomy and through its recognition of the two-way interaction between an organisation and its environment. However, the study did not explore the character or form of power networks in any depth.

Such dependencies of power have recently been recognised in organisation theory as basic to the understanding of organisational form and the development of any theory of 'structuration' in relation to organisations and enterprises (Ranson, Hinings and Greenwood, 1980). The significance of these relationships was recognised first in organisation theory by Benson (1975) who pointed out that

> . . . interaction [between organisations] . . . may include extensive reciprocal exchanges of resources, at one extreme, or intense hostility at the other . . . Some networks may consist of a series of organisations linked together by multiple direct ties to each other. Others may be characterised by a clustering or centring of linkages around one or a few mediating or controlling organisations. (Benson, 1978, p. 71)

It was his contention that:

> The features of specific organisations . . . are determined to some degree by the tendencies of the networks. Intra-organisational features become outcroppings of multi-organisation networks or sets. (Benson, 1977, p. 10)

Other organisation theorists have built on or added to this approach, including Pfeffer (1972*a*, 1972*b*) and Pfeffer and Salancik (1978).

Couched in these terms, the present study has been rather partial in its approach. However, it would be wrong to maintain that power relationships within systems of organisations had not been recognised in industrial geography. They were implicit, for example, in Keeble's (1968) treatment of subcontracting, Raby's (1978) analysis of reverse multipliers and contraction poles, Marshall's (1979) attempt to measure autonomy and McDermott's (1976, 1979) exploration of the interactions between indigenous and externally owned enterprises in the Scottish electronics industry. Nevertheless, in none of these studies have power networks and their associated interdependencies been made central to the specification, analysis and description of organisational interrelationships. In the present study, which focused on space, these networks were, in the first instance, given no special significance. Their importance, however, has become increasingly obvious in the course of the analysis. Indeed, it would appear that space is more than a variable simply influencing power networks. Rather it is an intrinsic ingredient of all such networks – the stage on which all power relationships are played out.

At its very simplest, power networks can be considered to divide organisations into two broad groups – those that are constrained by the linkage networks that prescribe their environments and those that are able to exercise a degree of control over those networks (Clegg and Dunkerley, 1980). By and large, organisation theory has been concerned only with organisations constrained by their environments and this has been especially true of the structural contingency approach (Taylor and Thrift, 1979). In large measure this distinction between the controllers and the controlled divides the small single-plant firm, at one extreme, from the diversified multinational conglomerate at the other. It does not imply that these two sets of organisations are functionally discrete. The reverse is, in fact, the case for it is the interdependence of these groups that is of prime importance.

It may, however, be wrong to speak of a simple dichotomisation of organisations creating a dualistic economy (Averitt, 1968; Taylor and Thrift, 1980). Organisations may possess varying degrees of control within their relevant power networks. In the present study it has nevertheless been shown that a development sequence for electronics organisations is by no means a continuous and smooth progression involving the steady accretion and acquisition of new functions (Chapter 5). More typically in the electronics industry a stepped development progression occurs, a finding which confirms the conclusions of earlier studies (e.g. Moore, 1959; Starbuck, 1971; Taylor, 1975). Those steps and thresholds in development sequences may well represent, at least in some circumstances, insurmountable barriers to development. This has been the proposition advanced by Taylor and Thrift (1980) in developing a dualistic interpretation of interorganisational relationships. It is their contention that access to capital creates the deepest rift between organisations, a rift which has grown progressively wider since the late 19th century, first with the development of the joint stock company, reinforced in the interwar years with the emergence of finance gaps (the MacMillan Gap denying small firms access to equity finance, and the venture capital gap) and intensified in more recent years by the operations of a wide spectrum of financial institutions, including merchant banks, insurance companies and pension funds. This rift has had the effect of intensifying interdependence between a corporate sector, on the one hand, and a smaller firms sector on the other.

Interdependence between organisations, which is more properly called small firm dependence, can take many forms, from licensing, franchising and subcontracting at one extreme to take-over and merger at the other. Dependence might also be manifest in less formalised relations. Small firms may simply become increasingly dependent upon larger counterparts after relying on the purchases of only one or two such corporate customers, as has been demonstrated in the present study. Furthermore, 'control' may be exercised simply through the control of technology so that increasingly the small firm economy depends upon, but is marginal to, the prevailing production technologies contained within an ever diminishing number of corporate leader organisations. Finally, the subordination of smaller firms is also increased by the ability of the corporate sector to obtain the assistance or simply to co-opt the power of the state in an effort to achieve goals it has established (Renners, 1969; McMillan, 1973).

It must be concluded that the structural contingency approach to organisation – environment interaction has proved fruitful in its application in the present study. However, to appreciate fully both the structuring of organisations and their impact upon the communities within which they operate, and to come to grips with the clearly critical feedback processes embedded within the model's framework, attention in the future may need to be directed more towards the network of interacting organisations than towards individual organisational structures. Linkages, then, should be treated as points of intersection between organisations through which power relations are established or played out. The study itself has shown that space is intrinsic to these relationships and can not be isolated as some form of independent variable. At the same time, interorganisational relationships can not be considered independently of space. By focusing upon the organisation in this study and its ability to establish and maintain linkages in space, the importance of the much wider relationships existing within the political economy have been highlighted as the basis for future work, both in economic geography and in the study of organisations.

References

Alchian, A. A. (1950) Uncertainty, evolution and economic theory. *J. Polit. Econ.*, **43**, 211–21.

Aldrich, H. E. (1972) Technology and organizational structure: a re-examination of the findings of the Aston Group. *Admin. Sci. Q.*, **17**, 26–43.

Allen, G. C. (1970) *The Structure of Industry in Britain*, 3rd edition. Longmans, London.

Allen, T. J. (1977) *Managing the Flow of Technology*. M.I.T. Press.

Allen, T. J. and Cohen, S. I. (1969) Information flow in research and development laboratories. *Admin. Sci. Q.*, **14**(1), 12–19.

Ansoff, H. I. (1965) *Corporate Strategy*. McGraw-Hill, New York.

Atkin, R. H. (1974*a*) *Mathematical Structure in Human Affairs*. Heinemann, London.

Atkin, R. H. (1974*b*) An approach to structure in architectural and urban design, 1. *Environ. Plann. B.*, **1**, 51–67.

Atkin, R. H. (1974*c*) An approach to structure in architectural and urban design, 2. *Environ. Plann. B.*, **1**, 173–91.

Atkin, R. H. (1976) Soft and hard science, (mimeo). Paper presented to Joint Conference of Inst. Br. Geogr. Quantitative Methods Study Group and Reg. Sci. Ass., University College, London.

Averitt, R. T. (1968) *The dual economy: the dynamics of American Industry*. Norton, New York.

Barlow, M. (1940) *Royal Commission on the Distribution of Industrial Employment*. Cmnd 6153, HMSO, London.

Bater, J. H. and Walker, D. F. (1970) Further comments on industrial location and linkage. *Area*, **2**, 59–63.

Beacham, A. and Osborne, W. (1970) The movement of manufacturing industry. *Reg. Stud.*, **4**, 41–7.

Bell, D. (1974) *The Coming of Post Industrial Society*. Heinemann, London.

Benson, J. K. (1975) The interorganisational network as a political economy. *Admin. Sci. Q.*, **20**, 229–48.

Benson, J. K. (1977) Innovation and crisis in organisational analysis. *Sociol. Q.*, **18**, 3–16.

Benson, J. K. (1978) The interorganisational network as a political economy, in Karpik, I. (ed) *Organisation and environment: theory, issues and reality*, 69–102. Sage, London.

Berle, A. A. and Means, G. C. (1932) *The modern corporation and private property*. Macmillan, New York.

Bertalanffy, L. von (1968) *General Systems Theory: foundations, development, application*. G. Braziller, New York.

Black, W. R. (1971) The utility of the gravity model and estimates of its parameters in commodity flow studies. *Proc. Ass. Am. Geogr.*, **3**, 28–32.

Blackbourn, A. (1974) The spatial behaviour of American firms in Western Europe, in F. E. I. Hamilton (ed.) *Spatial Perspectives on Industrial Organisation and Decision-making*, 245–64. Wiley, London.

205

Blalock, H. M. (1967) Path coefficients versus regression coefficients. *Am. J. Sociol.*, **72,** 675–6.

Blalock, H. M. (1971) *Causal Models in the Social Sciences.* Macmillan, London.

Blau, P. M. (1970) A formal theory of differentiation in organisations. *Am. Sociol. Rev.*, April 1970, 201–18.

Blau, P. M., McHugh Falbe, C., McKinley, W. and Phelps, K. T. (1976) Technology and organization in manufacturing. *Admin. Sci. Q.*, March 1976, 20–40.

Blau, P. M. and Schoenherr, R. A. (1971) *The Structure of Organizations.* Basic Books, New York.

Booz, Allen and Hamilton (1979) *The Electronics Industry in Scotland.* Report to The Scottish Development Agency, Glasgow.

Boyle, R. P. (1970) Path analysis and ordinal data. *Am. J. Sociol.*, **75,** 461–80.

Britton, J. N. H. (1969) A geographical approach to the examination of industrial linkages. *Can. Geogr.*, **13,** 185–98.

Britton, J. N. H. (1974) Environmental adaptation of industrial plants: service linkages, locational environment and organization, in F. E. I. Hamilton (ed.) *Spatial Perspectives on Industrial Organization and Decision-making,* 363–92. Wiley, London.

Britton, J. N. H. (1976) The influence of corporate organization and ownership on the linkages of industrial plants: a Canadian enquiry. *Econ. Geogr.,* **52,** 311–24.

Brown, A. J. (1972) *The Framework of Regional Economics in the United Kingdom.* National Institute of Social and Economic Research, Cambridge University Press, Cambridge.

Buck, T. W. and Atkins, M. H. (1976) Capital subsidies and unemployed labour, a regional production function approach. *Reg. Stud.*, **10,** 215–22.

Burns, T. (1954) The directions of activity and communications in a departmental executive group. *Hum. Relat.*, **7,** 73–97.

Burns, T. and Stalker, G. M. (1961) *The Management of Innovation.* Tavistock, London.

Cameron, G. C. (1971) Economic analysis for a declining urban economy, *Scott. J. Polit. Econ.*, **18,** 315–45.

Cameron, G. C. (1974) Regional economic policy in the United Kingdom, in M. Sant (ed.) *Regional Policy and Planning for Europe,* 1–41. Saxon House, Farnborough.

Cameron, G. C. and Clark, B. D. (1966) Industrial movement and the regional problem, *Occasional Paper,* 5, Department of Social and Economic Studies, University of Glasgow.

Cameron, G. C. and Reid, G. L. (1966) Scottish economic planning and the attraction of industry, *Occasional Paper,* 6, Department of Social and Economic Studies. University of Glasgow.

Carrier, R. E. and Schriver, W. R. (1968) Location theory: an empirical model and selected findings. *Land Econ.*, **64,** 450–60.

Carroll, J. B. (1961) The nature of data, or how to choose a correlation coefficient. *Psychometrika,* **26,** 347–72.

Chamberlain, N. W. (1968) *Enterprise and Environment: the Firm in Time and Place.* McGraw-Hill, New York.

Chandler, A. D. (1966) *Strategy and Structure.* Anchor Books, New York.

Channon, D. F. (1973) *The Strategy and Structure of British Enterprise.* Macmillan, London.

Child, J. and Mansfield, R. (1972) Technology, size and organization structure. *Sociology,* **6,** 369–93.

Chinitz, B. (1961) Contrasts in agglomeration: New York and Pittsburgh. *Am. Econ. Rev.*, **51,** 279–89.

Chisholm, M. (1971*a*) In search of a basis for location theory: micro-economics or welfare economics? *Prog. Geogr.*, **3**, 111–33.

Chisholm, M. (1971*b*) Freight transport costs, industrial location and regional development, in M. Chisholm and G. Manners (eds) *Spatial Policy Problems of the British Economy*, 213–44. Cambridge University Press, Cambridge.

Chisholm, M. (1974) Regional policies for the 1970s, *Geogr. J.*, **140**, 215–44.

Chisholm, M. (1975) *Human Geography: Evolution or Revolution*. Penguin, London.

Chisholm, M. (1976) Regional policies in an era of slow population growth and higher unemployment, *Reg. Stud.*, **10**, 201–13.

Chisholm, M. and Oeppen, J. (1973) *The Changing Pattern of Employment: Regional Specialisation and Industrial Localisation in Britain*. Croom Helm, London.

Cigno, A. (1971) Economies of scale and industrial location, *Reg. Stud.*, **5**, 295–301.

Clark, W. A. V. (1969) Information flows and intra-urban migration: and empirical analysis. *Proc. Ass. Am. Geogr.*, **1**, 38–42.

Clegg, S. and Dunkerley, D. (1980) *Organisation, Class and Control*. Routledge and Kegan Paul, London.

Colberg, M. R. and Greenhut, M. L. (1962) *Factors in the Location of Florida Industry*. Florida State University, Tallahassee.

Collins, H. (1972) The telecommunications impact model; Stages I and II. *Communications Studies Group Paper* P/72356/CL, London.

Connell, S. and Pye, R. (1973) Survey methods in applied telecommunications research. *Communications Studies Group Paper* W/73319/CN.

Cooley, W. W. and Lohnes, P. R. (1971) *Multivariate Data Analysis*. Wiley, New York.

Cooper, M. J. M. (1976) The industrial location decision-making process, *Occasional Paper*, *34*, Centre for Urban and Regional Studies. University of Birmingham.

Cureton, E. E. (1959) A note on phi max. *Psychometrika*, **24**, 89–91.

Cyert, R. M. and March, J. G. (1963) *A Behavioural Theory of the Firm*. Prentice-Hall, New Jersey.

Czamanski, S. (1971) Some empirical evidence of the strength of linkages between groups of related industries in urban-regional complexes. *Pap. Reg. Sci. Ass.*, **27**, 137–60.

Czamanski, S. (1974) *Study of Clustering of Industries*. Institute of Public Affairs, Dalhousie University.

Czamanski, S. (1976) *Study of Spatial Industrial Complexes*. Institute of Public Affairs, Dalhousie University.

Dale, E. (1952) Planning and developing the company organization structure. *American Management Association*, 28–49, New York.

Daniels, P. W. (1969) Office decentralisation from London – policy and practice. *Reg. Stud.*, **3**(2), 171–8.

Daniels, P. W. (1976) *Office Location: An Urban and Regional Study*. Bell, London.

Diamond, D. (1974) The long-term aim of regional policy, In M. Sant (ed.) *Regional Policy and Planning for Europe*, 217–23. Saxon House, Farnborough.

Dicken, P. (1971) Some aspects of the decision-making behaviour of business organizations. *Econ. Geogr.*, **47**, 426–37.

Dicken, P. and Lloyd, P. (1976) Geographical perspectives on United States investment in the United Kingdom. *Environ. Plann.*, **A8**, 685–705.

Dill, W. R. (1958) Environment as an influence on managerial autonomy. *Admin. Sci. Q.*, **2**, 409–43.

Donnison, D. (1974) Regional policies and regional government, in M. Sant (ed.) *Regional Policy and Planning for Europe*, 189–99. Saxon House, Farnborough.

Douglass, M. E. (1976) Organisation–environment interaction patterns and firm performance. *Mgmt. Int. Rev.*, **16**, 79–87.

Duncan, O .D. (1966) Path analysis: Sociological examples. *Am. J. Sociol.*, **72**, 1–16.

Duncan, O. D. (1975) *Introduction to Structural Equation Models*. Academic Press, New York.

Duncan, R. B. (1972) Characteristics of organizational environments and perceived environmental uncertainty. *Admin. Sci. Q.*, **17**, 312–27.

Duncan, R. B. (1973) Multiple decision-making structures in adapting to environmental uncertainty. *Hum. Relat.*, **36**(3), 273–91.

Duncan, W. J. (1978) *Organizational Behaviour*. Houghton Mifflin, Boston.

EIA (1968) *Electronic Industries Yearbook*. Electronic Industries Association, Washington.

Emery, F. E. and Trist, E. L. (1965) The causal texture of organizational environments. *Hum. Relat.*, **18**, 21–31.

Estall, R. C. and Buchanan, R. O. (1966) *Industrial Activity and Economic Geography*. Hutchinson, London.

Eurolec (1974) *Electronic Manufacturers: Alphabetical Listing*. David Rayner, Chelmsford.

Evan, W. M. (1966) The organisation-set: towards a theory of interorganisational relations, in J. D. Thompson (ed.) *Approaches to Organisational Design*. University of Pittsburgh Press, Pittsburgh.

Evans, A. W. (1973) The location of the headquarters of industrial companies. *Urban Stud.*, **10**, 387–95.

Ference, T. P. (1970) Organizational communication systems and the decision process, *Mgmt. Sci.*, **B**, 83–96.

Financial Analysis Group (1973) *Company Financial Performance in the Electronics Industry, 1968/69–1971/72*. Electronics Economic Development Committee, National Economic Development Office, London.

Firn, J. R. (1974) Indigenous growth and regional development: the experience and prospects for West Central Scotland. *Urban and Regional Discussion Papers*, **11**, University of Glasgow.

Firn, J. R. (1975) External control and regional development: the case of West Central Scotland, *Environ. Plann.*, **A7**, 393–414.

Fisher, G. (1962) Further calculations on regional differences in profitability and growth, *Scott. J. Polit. Econ.*, **9**, 147–58.

Flemming, D. K. and Krumme, G. (1969) The 'Royal-Hoesch Union': case analysis of the adjustment patterns in the European steel industry. *Tijdschr. Econ. Soc. Geogr.*, **59**, 177–99.

Florence, P. S. (1948) *Investment, Location and Size of Plant*. Cambridge University Press, Cambridge.

Forer, P. (1978) A place for plastic space? *Prog. Hum. Geogr.*, **2**(2), 230–67.

Forsyth, D. J. C. (1972) *United States Investment in Scotland*. Praeger, New York.

Freeman, J. H. (1973) Environment, technology and the administrative intensity of manufacturing organizations, *Am. Soc. Rev.*, **38**, 750–63.

Friedlander, F. and Pickle, H. (1968) Components of effectiveness in small organizations. *Admin. Sci. Q.*, **13**, 289–304.

Friedrich, C. J. (1929) *Alfred Weber's Theory of the Location of Industries*. Chicago University Press, Chicago.

Friend, W. N. and Jessop, J. K. (1969) *Local Government and Strategic Choice*. Tavistock, London.

Fuguitt, G. V. and Lieberson, S. (1974) Correlation of ratios having common terms. *Sociol. Meth.*, 1973–1974, 128–44.

Gabarro, J. J. (1973) Organisational adaptation to environmental change, in Baker, F. (ed.) *Organisational Systems: General Systems Approaches to Complex Organisations*, 196–215. Richard Irwin Inc., Homewood, Illinois.

GEC (1974) *Reports and Accounts*. The General Electric Company, London.

Gibson, W. A. (1961) Three multivariate models: factor analysis, latent structure analysis and latent profile analysis. *Psychometrika*, **24**, 229–52.

Giddens, A. (1979) *Central Problems in Social Theory*. Cambridge, Cambridge University Press.

Gilmour, J. M. (1974) External economies of scale, inter-industrial linkages and decision-making in manufacturing, in F. E. I. Hamilton (ed.) *Spatial Perspectives on Industrial Organization and Decision-making*, 335–62, Wiley, London.

Goddard, J. B. (1971) Office communications and office location; a review of current research. *Reg. Stud.*, **5**(4), 263–80.

Goddard, J. B. (1973) *Office Linkages and Location*. Progress in Planning, 1. Pergamon, Oxford.

Goddard, J. B. (1975) Organizational information flows and the urban system. *Economie Appliquée*, **28**, 125–64.

Goddard, J. B. and Morris, D. M. (1976) The communications factor in office decentralisation. *Progress in Planning*, 6. Pergamon, Oxford.

Goddard, J. B. and Pye, R. (1977) Telecommunications and office location. *Reg. Stud.*, **11**, 19–30.

Goddard, J. B. and Smith, I. J. (1978) Changes in corporate control in the British urban system, 1972–1977, *Environment and Planning*, A, **10**, 1073–84.

Golding, A. M. (1971) *The Semiconductor Industry in Britain and the United States: a Case Study in Innovation, Growth and the Diffusion of Technology*. D.Phil. Thesis, University of Sussex.

Golledge, R. G. and Brown, L. (1967) Search, learning, and the market decision process. *Geografiska Annaler*, **49B**, 116–24.

Goodman, R. A. (1973) Environmental knowledge and organizational time horizon: some functions and dysfunctions. *Hum. Relat.*, **26**(2), 215–26.

Gould, P. R. (1970) Tanzania 1920–1962: the spatial impress of the modernization process. *World Politics*, **22**, 149–70.

Graves, D. (1972) Reported communications ratios and informal status in managerial work groups. *Hum. Relat.*, **25**, 159–70.

Green, D. H. (1974) *Information Perception and Decision-making in the Industrial Relocation Decision*. Ph.D. Dissertation, University of Reading.

Green, D. H. (1977) Industrialists information levels and regional incentives, *Reg. Stud.*, **11**, 7–18.

Greenhut, M. L. (1956) *Plant Location in Theory and Practice*. University of North Carolina Press, Chapel Hill.

Grinyer, P. H. and Norburn, D. (1975) Planning for existing markets; perceptions of executives and financial performance, *J.R. Statist. Soc. A.*, **138**, 70–97.

Guilford, J. P. (1965) *Fundamental Statistics in Psychology and Education*. McGraw-Hill, New York.

Gysberts, A. P. (1974) *Contact Patterns of Auckland Plastics Manufacturers*. M.A. Thesis, University of Auckland.

Haas, J. E. and Drabeck, T. E. (1973) *Complex Organisations: A Sociological Perspective*. Macmillan, New York.

Hage, J. and Aiken, M. (1969) Routine technology, social structure and organizational goals, *Am. Sci. Q.*, **14**, 366–79.

Hägerstrand, T. (1967) *Innovation Diffusion as a Spatial Process* (Translation and Postscript A. Pred). University of Chicago Press, Illinois.

Haire, M. (1962) What is organized in an organization?, in M. Haire (ed.) *Organization Theory in Industrial Practice*. Wiley, New York.

Hall, P. G. (1962) *The Industries of London Since 1861*. Hutchinson, London.

Hall, R. H. (1962) Intraorganisational structure variation, *Am. Sci. Q.*, **7**, 295–308.

Hallett, G. (1973) British regional problems and policies, in G. Hallett, P. Randall and E. G. West, *Regional Policy for Ever?*, 77–101. Institute of Economic Affairs, London.

Hamann, U. (1961) Merkmalbestand und Verwandstshaftsbezeihungen der Farinosae, *Willdenowia*, **2**, 639–68.

Hamilton, F. E. I. (ed.) (1974) *Spatial Perspectives on Industrial Organization and Decision-making*. Wiley, London.

Hamilton, F. E. I. (1976) Multinational enterprise and the European Economic Community. *Tijdschr. Econ. Soc. Geogr.*, **67**, 258–78.

Harrison, E. F. (1978) *Management and Organizations*. Houghton Mifflin, Boston.

Hart, P. E., Utton, M. A. and Walshe, G. (1973) *Mergers and Concentration in British Industry*. National Institute of Economic and Social Research. Cambridge University Press, Cambridge.

Harvey, E. (1968) Technology and the structure of organizations. *Am. Sociol. Rev.*, **33**, 247–59.

Hesseling, P. (1970) Communications and organization structure in a large multi-national company, G. Heald (ed.) *Approaches to the Study of Organizational Behaviour*, 40–70. Tavistock, London.

Heyck, T. W. and Klecka, W. (1973) British radical M.P.s, 1874–1895: new evidence from discriminant analysis, *J. Interdisciplinary Hist.*, **4**, 161–84.

Hickson, D. J. (1966) A convergence in organization theory, *Admin. Sci. Q.*, **11**, 225–37.

Hickson, D. J., Pugh, D. S. and Pheysey, D. (1969) Operations technology and organization structure: an empirical reappraisal. *Admin. Sci. Q.*, **14**, 378–97.

Hill, W. (1974) Typology and environment, in McGuire, J. W. (ed.) *Contemporary Management: Issues and Viewpoints*, 293–4. Prentice-Hall, Englewood Cliffs.

Hinings, C. R., Pugh, D. S., Hickson, D. J. and Turner, C. (1967) An approach to the study of bureaucracy, *Sociology*, **1**, 62–72.

Hirsch, P. M. (1975) Organisational effectiveness and the institutional environment, *Admin. Sci. Q.*, September 1975, 327–44.

Hirschi, T. and Selvin, H. C. (1967) *Delinquency Research: an Appraisal of Analytical Methods*. Free Press, New York.

HMSO (1968) *Standard Industrial Classification*. Central Statistical Office, London.

HMSO (1971) Directory of Business: Instrument Engineering, Electrical. *Report on the Census of Production 1968*, 164. Business Statistics Office, London.

HMSO (1971*a*) Telegraph and telephone apparatus and equipment. *Report on the Census of Production 1968*, 73. Business Statistics Office, London.

HMSO (1971*b*) Radio and electronic components. *Report on the Census of Production 1968*, 74. Business Statistics Office, London.

HMSO (1971*c*) Broadcast receiving and sound reproducing equipment. *Report on the Census of Production 1968*, 75. Business Statistics Office, London.

HMSO (1971*d*) Electronic computers. *Report on the Census of Production 1968*, 76. Business Statistics Office, London.

HMSO (1971*e*) Radio, radar and electronic capital goods. *Report on the Census of Production 1968*, 77. Business Statistics Office, London.

HMSO (1972) *Industrial and Regional Development*. Secretary of State for Trade and Industry, Cmnd 4942, London.

HMSO (1973) *Input-Output Tables for the United Kingdom 1968*. Central Statistical Office, London.

HMSO (1974*a*) Telegraph and telephone apparatus and equipment. *Report on the Census of Production 1971*, PA363. Business Statistics Office, London.

HMSO (1974*b*) Radio and electronic components. *Report on the Census of Production 1971*, PA364. Business Statistics Office, London.

HMSO (1974*c*) Broadcast receiving and sound reproducing equipment. *Report on the Census of Production 1971*, PA365. Business Statistics Office, London.

HMSO (1974*d*) Electronic computers. *Report on the Census of Production 1971*, PA366. Business Statistics Office, London.

HMSO (1974*e*) Radio, radar and electronic capital goods. *Report on the Census of Production 1971*, PA367. Business Statistics Office, London.

HMSO (1974*f*) Input–output tables for the United Kingdom 1970. *Business Monitor* PA1004. Business Statistics Office, London.

HMSO (1974*g*) Summary tables: area analyses. *Report on the Census of Production 1968*, 157. Business Statistics Office, London.

HMSO (1975*a*) Telephone and telegraph apparatus and equipment. *Business Monitor* PQ363. Business Statistics Office, Newport.

HMSO (1975*b*) Radio and electronic components. *Business Monitor* PQ364. Business Statistics Office, Newport.

HMSO (1975*c*) Broadcast receiving and sound reproducing equipment. *Business Monitor* PQ365. Business Statistics Office, Newport.

HMSO (1975*d*) Electronic computers. *Business Monitor* PQ366. Business Statistics Office, Newport.

HMSO (1975*e*) Radio, radar and electronic capital goods. *Business Monitor*. Business Statistics Office, Newport.

Hoare, A. G. (1975) Linkage flows, locational evaluation, and industrial geography: a case study of Greater London. *Environ. Plann.*, **7**, 41–58.

Hoare, A. G. (1978) Industrial linkages and the dual economy: the case of Northern Ireland. *Reg. Stud.*, **12**, 167–80.

Hoare, A. G. (1978) Three problems for industrial linkage studies. *Area*, **10**(3), 217–21.

Hoover, E. M. (1937) *Location Theory and the Shoe and Leather Industries*. Harvard University Press.

Hoover, E. M. (1948) *The Location of Economic Activity*. McGraw-Hill, New York.

Hoover, E. M. (1971) *An Introduction to Regional Economics*. Knopf, New York.

Horst, P. (1965) *Factor Analysis of Data Matrices*. Holt, Rinehart and Winston, New York.

Howard, R. S. (1968) *The Movement of Manufacturing Industry in the United Kingdom*. Board of Trade, HMSO, London.

Hower, R. M. and Lorsch, J. W. (1967) Organisational inputs, in Seiler, J. A. (ed.) *Systems Analysis in Organizational Behaviour*, 157–76. R. D. Irwin and Dorsey Press, Homewood, Illinois.

Huff, D. L. (1960) A topographical model of consumer space preferences, *Pap. Proc. Reg. Sci. Ass.*, **6**, 159–73.

Ingham, K. D. P. (1976) Foreign ownership and the regional problem; company performance in the mechanical engineering industry. *Oxf. Econ. Pap.* (New Series) **28**, 133–48.

Isard, W. (1956) *Location and the Space Economy*. M.I.T. Press.

Jantsch, E. (1967) *Technological Forecasting in Perspective*. Organization for Economic Cooperation and Development, Paris.

Jones, R. and Marriott, O. (1972) *Anatomy of a Merger*. Pan, London.

Jurkovich, R. (1974) A core typology of organisational environments. *Admin. Sci. Q.*, **19**, 380–94.

Karaska, G. J. (1969) Manufacturing linkages in the Philadelphia economy: some evidence of external agglomeration forces, *Geogr. Analysis*, **1**, 354–69.

Karpik, L. (1978) Organisations, institutions and history, in Karpik, L. (ed.) *Organisation and environment: theory, issues and reality*, 15–68. Sage, London.

Kast, F. E. and Rozenzweig, J. C. (1974) *Organization and Management: A Systems Approach*. McGraw-Hill, Kogakusha, Tokyo.

Katona, G. and Morgan, J. N. (1952) The quantitative study of factors determining business decisions. *Q. J. Econ.*, **66**(1), 67–90.

Katz, D. and Kahn, R. L. (1966) *The Social Psychology of Organizations*. Wiley, New York.

Keeble, D. E. (1968) Industrial decentralisation and the metropolis: the North West London case. *Trans. Br. Geogr.*, **44**, 1–54.

Keeble, D. E. (1969) Local industrial linkage and manufacturing growth in Outer London. *Town Plann. Rev.*, **15**, 163–88.

Keeble, D. E. (1971) Employment mobility in Britain, in M. Chisholm and G. Manners (eds) *Spatial Policy Problems of the British Economy*, 24–68. Cambridge University Press, Cambridge.

Keeble, D. E. (1972*a*) Regional policy after Davies. *Area*, **4**, 132–6.

Keeble, D. E. (1972*b*) The South East and East Anglia, in G. Manners, D. Keeble, B. Rodgers and K. Warren, *Regional Development in Britain*, 71–152. Wiley, London.

Keeble, D. E. (1974) Industrial migration in the United Kingdom in the 1960s (mimeo). Paper presented to the International Geographical Union Working Group on Industrial Geography Conference, London School of Economics.

Keeble, D. E. (1976) *Industrial Location and Planning in the United Kingdom*. Methuen, London.

Keeble, D. E. (1977*a*) Spatial policy in Britain: regional or urban? *Area*, **9**, 3–8.

Keeble, D. E. (1977*b*) Recent developments in industrial geography, *Prog. Hum. Geogr.*, **1**(2), 304–12.

Keeble, D. E. and McDermott, P. J. (1978) Organisation and industrial location in the United Kingdom. *Reg. Stud.*, **12**(2), 139–41.

Kerlinger, F. N. and Pedhazur, E. J. (1973) *Multiple Regression in Behavioural Research*. Holt, Rinehart and Winston, New York.

Khandwalla, P. N. (1974) Mass output orientation of operations, technology and organizational structure. *Admin. Sci. Q.*, **19**, 74–97.

Kim, J. and Kohout, F. J. (1975) Special topics in general linear models, in N. H. Nie *et al. Statistical Package for the Social Sciences*, 368–97. McGraw-Hill, New York.

Klecka, W. R. (1975) Discriminant analysis, in N. H. Nie *et al. Statistical Packages for the Social Sciences*, 434–67. McGraw-Hill, New York.

Krumme, G. (1969) Towards a geography of enterprise. *Econ. Geogr.*, **45**, 30–40.

Krumme, G. (1970) The interregional corporation and the region. A case study of Siemens growth characteristics. *Tijdschr. Econ. Soc. Geogr.*, **61**, 318–33.

Kruskal, J. B. (1964*a*) Multidimensional scaling by optimizing goodness of fit to a non-metric hypothesis. *Psychometrika*, **29**, 1–24.

Kruskal, J. B. (1964*b*) Nonmetric multidimensional scaling; a numerical method. *Psychometrika*, **29**, 115–29.

Lamberton, D. M. (1971) *Economics of Information and Knowledge*. Penguin, London.

Land, K. C. (1969) Principles of path analysis. *Sociol. Meth.*, 1969, 3–37.

Larner, R. J. (1966) Ownership and control in the 200 largest non-financial corporations, 1929 and 1963, *Am. Econ. Rev.*, **56**, 777–87.

Lasuen, J. R. (1969) On growth poles, *Urban Stud.*, **6**(2), 137–61.

Lasuen, J. R. (1971) Multi-regional economic development: an open system approach, in Hägerstrand, T. and Kuklinski, A. R. (eds) *Information Systems for Regional Development – A Seminar*, 169–211. *Lund Studies in Geography, Series B*, **37**.

Lawrence, P. R. and Lorsch, J. W. (1967*a*) *Organization and Environment: Managing Differentiation and Integration*. Graduate School of Business Administration, Harvard.

Lawrence, P. R. and Lorsch, J. W. (1967*b*) Differentiation and integration in complex organizations, *Admin. Sci. Q.*, **12**, 1–47.

Lazarsfeld, P. F. and Henry, N. W. (1967) *Latent Structure Analysis*. Houghton Mifflin, Boston.

Le Heron, R. B. (1976) *Manufacturing in North Taranaki: An Introductory Study*. Department of Geography, Massey University, Palmerston North.

Le Heron, R. B. and Schmidt, C. G. (1976) An exploratory analysis of linkage change within two regional industries, *Reg. Stud.*, **10**, 465–78.

Leigh, R. and North, D. J. (1976) The spatial consequences of takeovers in some British industries and their implications for regional development. Paper presented to International Geographical Union Working Group on Industry Conference, Bochum.

Leigh, R. and North, D. J. (1978) Regional aspects of acquisition activity in British manufacturing industry. *Reg. Stud.*, **12**, 227–46.

Lever, W. F. (1972) Industrial movement, spatial association and functional linkages, *Reg. Stud.*, **6**, 371–84.

Lever, W. F. (1974*a*) Regional multipliers and demand leakages at establishment level, *Scott. J. Polit. Econ.*, **21**, 111–22.

Lever, W. F. (1974*b*) Manufacturing linkages and the search for suppliers and markets, in F. E. I. Hamilton (ed.) *Spatial Perspectives on Industrial Organization and Decision-making*, 309–34. Wiley, London.

Lever, W. F. (1974*c*) Changes in local income multipliers over time. *J. Econ. Stud.*, (New Series) **1**, 98–112.

Lever, W. F. (1975) Mobile industry and levels of integration in subregional economic structures, *Reg. Stud.*, **9**, 265–78.

Lösch, A. (1954) *The Economics of Location* (Translated W. H. Woglom). Yale University Press, New Haven, Conn.

Luttrell, W. F. (1962) *Factory Location and Industrial Movement*. National Institute of Economic and Social Research. Cambridge University Press, Cambridge.

Lutz, V. C. (1962) *Italy: a study in economic development*. Oxford University Press, London.

Malik, R. (1975) *And Tomorrow the World: Inside I.B.M.* Millington, London.

Manners, G. (1972) National perspectives, in G. Manners, D. Keeble, B. Rodgers and K. Warren, *Regional Development in Britain*, 1–69. Wiley, London.

Marples, D. L. (1967) Studies of managers; a fresh start, *J. Mgmt. Stud.*, **10**, 282–99.

Marris, R. (1964) *The Economic Theory of 'Managerial' Capitalism*. Macmillan, London.

Marshall, J. N. (1979) Ownership, organisation and industrial linkage: a case study in the Northern Region of England, *Reg. Stud.*, **13**, 531–57.

Martin, J. E. (1966) *Greater London: an Industrial Geography*. Bell, London.

214   *Industrial organisation and location*

Martin, J. E. (1969) Size of plant and location of industry in Greater London, *Tijdschr. Econ. Soc. Geogr.*, **60**, 369–74.
Massey, D. (1974) Towards a critique of industrial location theory. *Research Paper*, *5*, Centre for Environmental Studies, London.
Massey, D. and Meegan, R. A. (1976) The inner city and the international competitiveness of British industry. *Working Note*, *437*, Centre for Environmental Studies, London.
Meyer, M. W. (1972) Size and structure of organizations. *Am. Sociol. Rev.*, **37**, 434–41.
Mohr, L. B. (1971) Organizational technology and organizational structure, *Admin. Sci. Q.*, December, 444.
Moore, B. and Rhodes, J. (1976) A quantitative analysis of the effects of the Regional Employment Premium and other regional policy instruments, in A. Whiting (ed.) *The Economics of Industrial Subsidies*, 191–219. HMSO, London.
Moore, C. W. (1972) Industrial linkage development paths in growth poles: a research methodology. *Environment and Planning*, *A*, **4**, 253–71.
Moore, C. W. (1973) Industrial linkage development paths: a case study of the developments of two industrial complexes in the Puget Sound region. *Tijd. Econ. Soc. Geog.*, **64**, 93–107.
Moore, D. G. (1959) Managerial strategies in W. L. Warner and N. H. Martin (eds) *Industrial Man*. Harper and Row, London.
Morrill, R. L. and Pitts, F. R. (1967) Marriage, migration and the mean information field: a study in uniqueness and generality, *Ann. Ass. Am. Geogr.*, **57**, 401–22.
Moseley, M. J. and Townroe, P. M. (1973) Linkage adjustment following industrial movement. *Tijd. Econ. Soc. Geog.*, **64**(3), 137–44.
Moses, L. N. (1958) Location and the theory of production, *Q. J. Econ.*, **73**, 259–72.
Mulligan, R. M. (1974) *The United Kingdom Electronics Industry*. M.Sc. Thesis, University of Bradford.
McCrone, G. (1968) *Regional Policy in Britain*. Allen & Unwin, London.
McCrone, G. (1972) The location of economic activity in the United Kingdom. *Urban Stud.*, **9**, 369–75.
McDermott, P. J. (1972) *Industrial Location Theory and the Distribution of Manufacturing in New Zealand*. M.A. Thesis, University of Auckland.
McDermott, P. J. (1974) Market linkage and spatial monopoly in New Zealand manufacturing. *N.Z. Geogr.*, **30**, 1–17.
McDermott, P. J. (1976) Organization, ownership and regional dependence in the Scottish electronics industry, *Reg. Stud.*, **10**, 319–35.
McDermott, P. J. (1977a) Overseas investment and the industrial geography of the United Kingdom. *Area*, **9**, 200–7.
McDermott, P. J. (1977b) Regional variations in enterprise: electronics firms in Scotland, London and the Outer Metropolitan Area. Unpublished Ph.D. Thesis, University of Cambridge.
McDermott, P. J. (1979) Multinational manufacturing firms and regional development: external control in the Scottish electronics industry. *Scott. J. Polit. Econ.*, **26**, 183–202.
McDermott, P. J. and Taylor, M. J. (1976) Attitudes, images and location: the subjective context of decision-making in New Zealand manufacturing, *Econ. Geogr.*, **52**, 325–47.
McMillan, C. J. (1973) Corporations without citizenship: the emergence of multinational enterprise, in G. Salaman and K. Thompson (eds) *People and organisations*, 25–44. Longman, London.
McNee, R. B. (1958) Functional geography of the firm, with an illustrative case history from the petroleum industry. *Econ. Geogr.*, **34**, 321–37.

McNee, R. B. (1974) A systems approach to understanding the geographic behaviour of organizations, especially large corporations, in F. E. I. Hamilton (ed.) *Spatial Perspectives on Industrial Organization and Decision-making*, 47–57. Wiley, London.

NEDO (1973) See Financial Analysis Group (1973).

NEDO (1974) *Annual Statistical Survey of the Electronics Industry 1972*. Electronics Economic Development Committee, National Economic Development Office, London.

Negandhi, A. R. and Reimann, B. C. (1973) Task environment, decentralisation and organisational effectiveness. *Hum. Rel.*, **26**(2), 203–14.

Newby, P. (1971) Attitudes to a business environment, in K. J. Gregory and W. Ravehill (eds) *Exeter Essays in Geography*, 185–97. Exeter University Press, Exeter.

Newman, W. H., Summer, C. E. and Warren, E. K. (1972) *The Process of Management* (3rd edition). Prentice-Hall, Englewood Cliffs, N.J.

North, D. J. (1974) The process of locational change in different manufacturing organizations, in F. E. I. Hamilton (ed.) *Spatial Perspectives on Industrial Organization and Decision-making*, 213–44. Wiley, London.

Nourse, H. O. (1967) *The Electronics Industry and Economic Growth in Illinois*. Department of Business and Economic Development, State of Illinois.

Parsons, G. F. (1972*a*) The giant manufacturing corporations and balanced regional growth in Britain. *Area*, **4**, 99–103.

Parsons, G. F. (1972*b*) *Spatial Productivity Differentials in British Manufacturing Industry*. Ph.D. Dissertation, University College, London.

Parsons, T. (1960) *Structure and Process in Modern Societies*. Free Press of Glencoe, New York.

Penning, J. M. (1975) The relevance of the structural contingency model for organizational effectiveness. *Admin. Sci. Q.*, **20**, 393–407.

Penrose, E. T. (1959) *The Theory of the Growth of the Firm*. Blackwell, Oxford.

Peregrinus (1974) Electrical and Electronic Trades Directory (92nd edition). Peter Peregrinus Ltd., London.

Perrow, C. (1967) A framework for the comparative analysis of complex organizations. *Am. Sociol. Rev.*, **32**, 194–208.

Petit, T. A. (1967) A behavioural theory of management, *J. Acad. Mgmt.*, 341–50.

Pfeffer, J. (1972*a*) Size and composition of corporate boards of directors: the organization and its environment. *Admin. Sci. Q.*, **17**, 218–28.

Pfeffer, J. (1972*b*) Merger as a response to organizational interdependence, *Admin. Sci. Q.*, **17**, 382–94.

Pfeffer, J. and Salancik, G. (1978) *The external control of organisations: a resource perspective*. Harper and Row, New York.

Picton, G. (1953) Notes on the establishment of branch factories, *H. Indust. Econ.*, **1**, 126–31.

Plessey (1973) *Report and Accounts 1972/1973*. The Plessey Company Ltd., London.

Pred, A. (1966) *The Spatial Dynamics of US Urban-Industrial Growth, 1800–1914*. Cambridge, Mass: M.I.T. Press.

Pred, A. R. (1967) Behavior and location: foundations for a geographic and dynamic location theory, Part 1. *Lund Studies in Geography*, B 27.

Pred, A. R. (1969) Behavior and location: foundations for a geographic and dynamic location theory, Part 2. *Lund Studies in Geography*, B 28.

Pred, A. R. (1973) The growth and development of systems of cities in advanced economies, in Pred, A. R. and Törnqvist, G E. *Systems of Cities and Information Flows: Two Essays*, 1–82. *Lund Studies in Geography*, B 38.

Pred, A. R. (1974) Industry, information and city-system interdependencies, in

F. E. I. Hamilton (ed.) *Spatial Perspectives on Industrial Organization and Decision-making*, 105–39. Wiley, London.

Pred, A. R. (1976) The interurban transmission of growth in advanced economies: empirical findings versus regional planning assumptions, *Reg. Stud.*, **10**, 151–71.

Pugh, D. S., Hickson, D. J., Hinings, C. R., MacDonald, K. M., Turner, C. and Lupton, T. (1963) A conceptual scheme for organizational analysis. *Admin. Sci. Q.*, **8**, 289–315.

Pugh, D. S., Hickson, D. J., Hinings, C. R. and Turner, C. (1968) Dimensions of organization structures. *Admin. Sci. Q.*, **13**, 65–105.

Pugh, D. S., Hickson, D. J., Hinings, C. R. and Turner, C. (1969) The context of organization structures. *Admin. Sci. Q.*, **14**, 91–114.

Pye, R. (1972) The telecommunications impact model: Stage II. *Communications Studies Group Paper* P/72319/PY, London.

Pye, R. (1973) The description and classification of meetings. *Communications Studies Group Paper* P/71360/PY, London.

Raby, G. F. (1978) Industrial linkage and communication flows: an organisational communication approach to the geography of enterprise, University of Newcastle upon Tyne, Centre for Urban and Regional Development Studies, Discussion Paper No. 5.

Ranson, S., Hinings, R. and Greenwood, R. (1980) The structuring of organisational structures. *Admin. Sci. Q.*, **25**, 1–17.

RECMF (1974) *Directory and Products Guide*. Radio and Electronic Component Manufacturers Federation, London.

Rees, A. (1966) Information networks in labour markets, *Am. Econ. Rev.*, **56**, 559–66.

Rees, J. (1972) The industrial corporation and location decision analysis. *Area*, **4**, 199–205.

Rees, J. (1974) Decision-making, the growth of the firm and the business environment, in F. E. I. Hamilton (ed.) *Spatial Perspectives on Industrial Organization and Decision-making*, 189–211. Wiley, New York.

Renners, K. (1969) The development of capitalist property and the legal institutions complementary to the property norm, in V. Aubert (ed.) *The Sociology of Law*, 33–45. Penguin, Harmondsworth.

Reynolds, P. (1974) *Guglielmo Marconi*. The Marconi Company Ltd., Chelmsford.

Rhenman, E. (1969) *Företaget och dess Omvärld* (English summary). Bonnier, Stockholm.

Rice, A. K. (1963) *The Enterprise and its Environment*. Tavistock, London.

Richter, C. E. (1969) The impact of industrial linkages on geographic association. *J. Reg. Sci.*, **9**, 19–28.

Roepke, H., Adams, D. and Wiseman, R. (1974) A new approach to the identification of Industrial Complexes using input–output data. *J. Reg. Sci.*, **14**(1), 15–29.

Romsa, G. H., Hoffman, W. L., Gladin, S. T. and Brunn, S. D. (1969) An example of the factor analytic regression model in geographic research. *Prof. Geogr.*, **21**, 344–6.

Rosenberg, N. (1969) The direction of technological change: inducement mechanisms and focusing devices. *Economic Development and Cultural Change*, **18**, 1–24.

Rummel, R. J. (1970) *Applied Factor Analysis*. Northwestern University Press, Evanston.

Sant, M. (1967) Unemployment and industrial structure in the United Kingdom. *Reg. Stud.*, **1**, 83–91.

Sant, M. (ed.) (1974) *Regional Policy and Planning for Europe*. Saxon House, Farnborough.

Schmidt, C. G. (1973) *Spatial Structure of Industrial Linkages and Regional Economic Growth: an Analysis of Linkage Changes Among Pacific Northwest Steel Firms*. Ph.D. Dissertation, University of Washington.

Schmidt, C. G. (1975) Firm linkage structure and structural change: a graph theoretical analysis. *Econ. Geog.*, **51**(1), 27–36.

Schon, D. A. (1973) *Beyond the Stable State*. Penguin, London.

Sciberras, E. (1975) Multinational Electronics Companies and National Economic Policies. Unpublished D.Phil. Thesis, University of Sussex.

Scottish Council (1973) *Electronics and Allied Industries in Scotland*. Scottish Council (Development and Industry), Edinburgh.

Short, J., Williams, E. and Christie, B. (1976) *The Social Psychology of Telecommunications*. Wiley, London.

Shubik, M. (1967) Information, rationality and free choice in a future democratic society. *Daedalus*, **96**, 771–8.

Simmons, J. W. (1970) *Patterns of Interaction within Ontario and Quebec*. University of Toronto Centre for Urban and Community Studies, Research Paper No. 41.

Simon, H. A. (1957) *Models of Man*. Wiley, New York.

Simon, H. A. (1960) *The New Science of Management Decisions*. Macmillan, New York.

Smith, D. M. (1966) A theoretical framework for geographical studies of industrial location. *Econ. Geogr.*, **42**, 95–113.

Smith, D. M. (1970) On throwing out Weber with the bathwater: a note on industrial location and linkage. *Area*, **2**, 15–18.

Smith, D. M. (1971) *Industrial Location: an Economic Geographical Analysis*. Wiley, New York.

Sneath, P. H. A. and Sokal, R. R. (1973) *Numerical Taxonomy*. Freeman, San Francisco.

Stafford, H. A. (1972) The geography of manufacturers. *Prog. Geogr.*, **4**, 183–213.

Stafford, H. A. (1973) Industrial location decision-making in Appalachian Ohio, in State of Ohio, Department of Economic and Community Development, Economic Development Division. *Appalachian Selective Development Program: Final Report*.

Stafford, H. A. (1974) The anatomy of the location decision: content analysis of case studies, in F. E. I. Hamilton (ed.) *Spatial Perspectives on Industrial Organization and Decision-making*, 169–87. Wiley, London.

Stanfield, G. G. (1976) Technology and organisation structure as theoretical categories. *Admin. Sci. Q.*, **21**, 489–93.

Starbuck, W. H. (1965) Organizational growth and development, in J. G. March (ed.) *Handbook of Organizations*, 451–522. Rand McNally, New York. Reprinted in W. H. Starbuck (1971) *Organizational Growth and Development*, 11–141. Penguin, London.

Starbuck, W. H. (ed.) (1971) *Organizational Growth and Development*. Penguin, Harmondsworth.

Steed, G. P. F. (1968) The changing milieu of the firm. *Ann. Ass. Am. Geogr.*, **58**, 506–25.

Steed, G. P. F. (1971) Changing processes of corporate environment relations. *Area*, **3**, 207–11.

Steele, F. I. (1972) Organisational overlearning. *J. Mgmt. Stud.*, **9**, 303–13.

Stewart, J. A. (1974) Objectives for regional policy: the view from industry, in M. Sant (ed.) *Regional Policy and Planning for Europe*, 225–34. Saxon House, Farnborough.

Stewart, J. C. (1976) Linkages and foreign direct investment. *Reg. Stud.*, **10**(2), 245–58.

Stewart, R. (1965) The use of diaries to study managers jobs. *J. Mgmt. Stud.*, **2**, 228–35.

Stigler, G. J. (1958) The economies of scale. *J. Law Econ.*, **1**, 54–71.

Stigler, G. J. (1961) The economics of information. *J. Polit. Econ.*, **69**, 213–25.

Stinchcombe, A. L. (1965) Social structure and organisations, in J. G. March (ed.) *Handbook on Organisations*, 150.

Stollsteimer, J. F. (1963) A working model for plant numbers and locations. *J. Farm Econ.*, **45**, 631–45.

Stopford, J. M. and Wells, L. T. Jnr. (1972) *Managing the Multinational Enterprise*. Basic Books, New York.

Streit, M. E. (1969) Spatial associations and economic linkages between industries. *J. Reg. Sci.*, **9**, 177–89.

Tatsouka, M. M. (1971) *Multivariate Statistics*. Wiley, New York.

Taylor, F. (1942) *Scientific Management*. Harper and Row, New York.

Taylor, M. J. (1969) Industrial linkage, seed-bed growth and the location of firms. *Occasional Paper*, *3*, Department of Geography, University College, London.

Taylor, M. J. (1970) Location decisions of small firms. *Area*, **2**, 51–4.

Taylor, M. J. (1971) *Spatial Linkage and the West Midlands Ironfoundry Industry*. Ph.D. Dissertation, University College, London.

Taylor, M. J. (1973) Local linkage, external economies and the ironfoundry industry of the West Midlands and East Lancashire conurbations. *Reg. Studies*, **7**, 387–400.

Taylor, M. J. (1974) The industrial linkages of Auckland manufacturers, *Proc. Int. Geogr. Union Conf. and Eighth N.Z. Geogr. Conf.*, 203–17. Massey University, Palmerston North.

Taylor, M. J. (1975) Organizational growth, spatial interaction and location decision-making. *Reg. Stud.*, **9**, 313–23.

Taylor, M. J. (1977) Spatial dimensions of inventiveness in New Zealand. *Tijd. Econ. Soc. Geog.*, **68**, 330–40.

Taylor, M. J. (1978) Linkage change and organisational growth: the case of the West Midlands ironfoundary industry. *Econ. Geogr.*, **54**(4), 314–36.

Taylor, M. J. and Hosking, P. L. (1979) Spatial monopoly and functional economic regions: the impact of manufacturers' limited spatial knowledge in the New Zealand space economy. *N.Z. Geogr.*, **35**(1), 3–15.

Taylor, M. J. and McDermott, P. J. (1977) Perception of the economic environment by New Zealand manufacturers. *N.Z. Geogr.*, **33**, forthcoming.

Taylor, M. J. and Thrift, N. J. (1979) Guest editorial. *Environ. Plann. A.*, **11**, 973–975.

Taylor, M. J. and Thrift, N. J. (1980) Finance and Organisations: towards a dualistic interpretation of the geography of enterprise. Paper presented to 76th Annual Meeting of the Association of American Geographers, Louisville, Kentucky, April 1980.

Taylor, M. J. and Wood, P. A. (1973) Industrial linkage and local agglomeration in the West Midlands metal industries. *Trans. Inst. Br. Geogr.*, **59**, 129–54.

Technical Indexes (1974) *Electronics Engineering Index*. Technical Indexes Ltd., Bracknell.

Terreberry, S. (1968) The evolution of organizational environments. *Admin. Sci. Q.*, **12**, 590–613.

Thomas, M. D. and Le Heron, R. B. (1976) Perspectives on technological change and the process of diffusion in the manufacturing sector. *Econ. Geogr.*, **51**, 231–51.

Thompson, J. D. (1967) *Organizations in Action*. McGraw-Hill, New York.

Thompson, J. D. (1973) Organisations and output transactions, in Baker, F.

(ed.) *Organisational Systems: General Systems Approaches to Complex Organizations*, 216–35. Richard D. Irwin, Homewood, Illinois.

Thompson, J. D. and McEwen, W. J. (1958) Organizational goals and environment: goal setting as an interaction process. *Am. Sociol. Rev.*, **23**, 23–31.

Thorn (1973) *Thorn Electrical Industries, Profile*. Thorn Electrical Industries Ltd., London.

Thorngren, B. (1970) How do contact systems affect regional development. *Environ. Plann.*, **2**, 409–27.

Thorngren, B. and Goddard, J. B. (1973) Groupings of government agencies through an analysis of contact flows. Economic Research Institute, Stockholm School of Economics, Stockholm.

Thrift, N. (1979) Unemployment in the inner city: urban problems or structural imperative? A review of the British experience, in Herbert, D. T. and Johnston, R. J. (eds) *Geography and the Urban Environment*, **2**, 125–226. John Wiley, Chichester.

Tiebout, C. (1957) Location theory, empirical evidence and economic evolution. *Pap. Proc. Reg. Sci. Ass.*, **3**, 74–86.

Tinkler, K. J. (1971) A coefficient of association for binary data. *Area*, **3**, 31–35.

Todd, D. (1978) *Polarization and the Regional Problem: Manufacturing in Nova Scotia 1960–1973*. Manitoba Geographical Studies, 6, Department of Geography, University of Manitoba, Winnipeg.

Tolosa, H. and Reiner, T. A. (1970) The economic programming of a system of planned poles. *Econ. Geogr.*, **46**, 449–58.

Toothill, J. N. (1961) *Report of the Committee of Inquiry into the Scottish Economy*. Scottish Council (Development and Industry), Edinburgh.

Törnqvist, G. (1968) Flows of information and the location of economic activities. *Geogr. Annlr.*, **50B**, 99–107.

Törnqvist, G. (1970) Contact systems and regional development. *Lund Studies in Geography*, B 35.

Törnqvist, G. (1973) Contact requirements and travel facilities: contact models of Sweden and regional development alternatives in the future. *Lund Studies in Geography, B 38*, 83–121.

Townroe, P. M. (1969) Locational choice and the individual firm. *Reg. Stud.*, **3**, 15–24.

Townroe, P. M. (1970) Industrial linkage, agglomeration and external economies. *J. Town Plann. Inst.*, **56**, 18–20.

Townroe, P. M. (1971) Industrial location decisions: a study in management behaviour. *Occasional Paper, 15*, Centre for Urban and Regional Studies, University of Birmingham.

Townroe, P. M. (1972) Some behavioural considerations in the industrial location decision. *Reg. Stud.*, **6**, 261–72.

Townroe, P. M. (1974) Post-move stability and the location decision, in F. E. I. Hamilton (ed.) *Spatial Perspectives on Industrial Organization and Decision-making*, 287–307. Wiley, London.

Townroe, P. M. (1975) Branch plants and regional development. *Town Plann. Rev.*, **46**, 47–62.

Tugendhat, C. (1973) *The Multinationals*. Penguin, London.

Tukey, J. W. (1954) Causation, regression and path analysis, in O. Kempthorne (ed.) *Statistics and Mathematics in Biology*, 35–66. Iowa State College Press, Ames.

Turner, R. G. (1971) Empirical studies of plant location: a survey. *Area Indust. Dev. J.*, **6**, 13–30.

Vernon, R. (1957) Production and distribution in the large metropolis. *Ann. Am. Acad. Polit. Soc. Sci.*, **314**, 15–29.

Walker, S. R. (1977) Linkage structures in an urban economy. *Reg. Stud.*, **11**, 263–73.

Wallace, I. (1974) The relationship between freight transport, organization and industrial linkage in Britain. *Trans. Inst. Br. Geogr.*, **62**, 25–43.

Warren, K. (1972) Yorkshire and Humberside and the North East, in G. Munroe, D. Keeble, B. Rodgers and K. Warren, *Regional Development in Britain*, 327–86. Wiley, London.

Watts, H. D. (1972) Further observations on regional growth and large corporations. *Area*, **4**, 269–73.

Weber, M. (1947) *The Theory of Social and Economic Organisations* (Translated and edited by A. M. Henderson and T. Parsons). Free Press, New York.

Weinshall, T. D. (1966) The communicogram: a method for describing the pattern, frequency and accuracy of organization and communication, in R. Lawrence *Operational Research and the Social Sciences*, 619–33. Tavistock, London.

West Midlands Group (1948) *Conurbation: A Survey of Birmingham and The Black Country*. Architectural Press, London.

Westaway, J. (1974a) Contact potential and the occupational structure of the British urban system 1961–1966; an empirical study. *Reg. Stud.*, **8**, 57–73.

Westaway, J. (1974b) The spatial hierarchy of business organization and its implications for the British urban system. *Reg. Stud.*, **8**, 145–55.

Wood, P. A. (1966) Industry in the towns of the West Midlands. Unpublished Ph.D. Thesis, University of Birmingham.

Wood, P. A. (1969) Industrial location and linkage. *Area*, **2**, 32–9.

Wood, P. A. (1978) Industrial organisation, location and planning. *Reg. Stud.*, **12**(2), 143–52.

Woodward, J. (1965) *Industrial Organization: Theory and Practice*. Oxford University Press, London.

Woolmington, E. (1975) Information distortion and ritual behaviour. *Occasional Paper, No. 7*. University of New South Wales, Faculty of Military Studies, Duntroon.

Wray, M., Markham, R. and Watts, D. R. (1974) *Location of Industry in Hertfordshire: Planning and Industry in the Post-war Period*. Hatfield Polytechnic, Hertfordshire.

Wright, S. (1960) Path coefficients and path regressions: alternative or complementary concepts? *Biometrics*, **16**, 189–202.

Young, S. and Lowe, A. V. (1974) *Intervention in a Mixed Economy*. Croom Helm, London.

Zwerman, W. L. (1970) *New Perspectives on Organization Theory*. Greenwood Publishing Corp., Westport, Conn.

Author index

221

Subject index